THEY DON'T PLAY HOCKEY IN HEAVEN

A Dream, a Team, and My Comeback Season

KEN BAKER

THE LYONS PRESS
Guilford, Connecticut
An imprint of The Globe Pequot Press

The Lyons Press is an imprint of The Globe Pequot Press.

10 9 8 7 6 5 4 3 2 1

Printed in the United States of America

ISBN 1-59228-605-4 (paperback)

The Library of Congress has previously cataloged a hard cover edition as follows:

Baker, Ken, 1970-
  They don't play hockey in heaven : a dream, a team, and my comeback season / by Ken Baker.
     p. cm.
  ISBN 1-59228-149-4 (hard : alk. paper)
  1. Hockey–United States. 2. Baker, Ken, 1970- 3. Hockey goalkeepers–United States. I. Title.
  GV848.4.U6B34 2003
  796.962'092–dc22

                              2003016729

Permission to use lyrics from "Turn the Page," written by Bob Seger, © 1973 (renewed) by Gear Publishing Co.

Photo credits:
• Cover: photo by Michael Duffy
• Page 3 (top): photo by John Hubbard
• Page 3 (bottom): uncredited
• Page 79 (top and bottom): photos by Pam Sears
• Page 209 (top and bottom): photos by Chuck Barton/Quad City Mallards
• Page 265 (top): photo by Michael Duffy
• Page 265 (bottom): photo by Susan Sears
• Page 278: photo by Elizabeth Roberts and Lesley Langs
• Page 279: photo by Michael Duffy

For Brooke, Jackson, and Chloe
and
Everyone who believed

The proper function of man is to live, not to exist.
I shall not waste my days
in trying to prolong them.
I shall use my time.

–Jack London (1876–1916)

A Note from the Goalie

As someone who has made his share of mistakes—among them one that nearly killed me were it not for a skilled brain surgeon—I am familiar with the collective errors of our human ways:

> We lie to others and to ourselves.
> We let love slip away.
> We sacrifice long-term health for short-term happiness.
> We don't say what we mean.
> We practice selfishness even though selflessness feels better.
> We don't listen to our bodies.
> We recognize greatness in others but not ourselves.
> We accept things as they are rather than make them what they could be.
> We allow fear to keep us from embarking on journeys.
> We let dreams die on our pillows.

The lucky and the blessed among us sometimes get a second chance to chase those repressed dreams. As an "old" man I returned to the sport that had inspired infinite childhood fantasies. As hard as it was to drop all the adult things I had been doing for the last ten years, I'm glad I did. By risking everything in my life, I ended up saving it.

Pro hockey taught me nearly everything I will ever need to know about the game of life. I hope it will do the same for you.

WARM-UP

December 8, 1999

Dream

I'm peering through the metal bars of my mask, the only thing keeping the hard-rubber puck from turning my face into hamburger. Adrenaline courses through my body as he whacks the puck with all his might, aiming straight for the top right corner of the net. The challenge is clear: stop this shot, and my team will win. I will be the hero, the man! But if I don't stop it, I will be the guy who is blamed, because I am the goalie, my team's last line of defense, the one who let those bastards from Harvard score.

But I'm not thinking about the pressure, or about anything really, as this hard disc the size of a biscuit but the weight of a brick soars toward the net behind me. I hear no noise—no blaring pep-band trumpets, no howling college kids, no yelling coaches. I'm in The Zone. And, despite the moment's enormous physical and mental demands, I'm at peace. All that matters is this streaking black blur speeding my way at almost 100 mph.

Along with most every other player on this sheet of ice, I have aspirations to move on to the next level, to impress the well-dressed NHL scouts and slimy agents who come to see who among us has the potential to make it to The Show. We're also playing for our college, for our teammates, for our friends and family, for that cute girl in the front row in the sweater and tight jeans. The arena is electric, and, as the home-team goalie, I am the crowd's lightning rod.

Athletic challenges like this are beautiful in their simplicity. Rarely in "real life" is the line separating success from failure so easily discernible. These moments are the drug to which athletes grow addicted, the narcotic that makes old guys come back for more, because they know that athletic intoxication beats anything you can drink, snort or smoke.

With a Zen-like focus I've spent all but seven of my twenty years per-fecting, my eyes slow the film of this split-second moment of athletic truth. Then, without even having to tell it to do so, as if the almighty hand of God Himself were orchestrating this balletic feat, I stretch out my arm and the mesh of my catching glove snags the puck, inspiring thousands of Colgate University fans to stand and chant, "Baker! Baker! Baker!"

Heal

It all seemed so real, so vivid and so beautiful. Was I really playing hockey? When my morning eyes flutter open, however, the reality sets in: It was only a dream.

But I haven't had such a powerful dream—let alone one about *hockey*—since I quit playing eight years ago. Back when athletic feats like the one in my dream were my everyday reality, I was too young to appreciate the miracle that is having a healthy body, too young to realize that I will never again feel so alive as when I am playing hockey.

Somewhere along the way from boyhood to manhood I stopped dreaming about the joy of making a glorious glove save in the final moments of a game. Adults do that. No one tells us to, but there are things we stop dreaming about. Maybe we think it's childish, or maybe we think the fantasy world is passé in a contemporary world of reality TV, twenty-four-hour global news and Web cams capturing real-life fantasy and drama. Or maybe it's just easier not to dream than to deal with the pain of having let our hopes and dreams die.

I never stopped having the everyday dreams, the neurotic dreams, the disturbing sexual ones, the nightmares that jolt you awake in a cold sweat. But it has been a long time, possibly the first in my life, since I've had a dream so powerful that it could send the direction of my life into a U-turn, a dream forcing me to confront the seemingly impossible goals set by my heart, not my head. Until now, I have only been dreaming of the way things are, rather than the way things could be.

* * *

I can't fall back asleep, no matter how badly I want to recapture the beautiful dream. Brooke, the woman I am to marry in seven months, lies asleep, her blond hair resting princess-like on her pillow. Though Brooke knows me better than anyone else, even she has no idea how profoundly I have changed overnight. Then again, neither do I.

It would be easy to dismiss the dream as just plain silly. I did quit hockey back in 1992 for some very good reasons, after all. I was tired of the mental exhaustion that resulted from not meeting the high expectations that my coach, my fans, my teammates, and my father had for me, tired of spending most of my free time hanging out with a bunch of guys with enough testosterone to start World War III, tired of trying to force my body to do something–stop pucks–that it was no longer wired to do well.

Hockey wasn't always hell. In fact, hockey had been heaven. As a teenager, I was an Olympic prospect, an NHL star-in-the-making. Professional scouts flocked to see me play. But by my senior year of college I had fallen out of love with the sport. I wanted nothing more than to forget the pain of my failure. I moved on, earned a master's degree in journalism from Columbia University, became a journalist. I decided to focus on pursuits of the mind rather than the body. I buried the broken childhood dreams and hoped the mourning wouldn't last for long . . . though it did.

In 1996 I moved to California in an effort to reinvent myself, and I'm quite happy with my invention. So what if I haven't won a Pulitzer Prize? At least I get paid to write–from the comfort of my living room, no less. Why bother dreaming about stupid pro hockey when I'm living a different dream as a pro writer?

In just four months, though, I will turn thirty. Thirty. It's an age at which a man is no longer young, yet he's not yet middle age, a time in an athlete's life when his increasingly injury-prone body forces him to let go of his youth. A few months ago, gray hairs began sprouting from my thatch of brown. I no longer can go for a long run without knee pain. I'm fast becoming an old fart, and, at last check, old farts don't play pro hockey.

Now this dream has happened. And for the first time since my premature hockey retirement eight years ago, I'm considering the possibility that I actually might not be washed up. In the dream, at least, I felt as young as I did the day I quit. If perception is what frames reality, my once moribund Pollock is now a brilliant Picasso.

As I stare at the bedroom ceiling, the mere thought of getting up, pouring coffee, and then dutifully shuffling over to my living room desk to write about celebrities for the next eight hours depresses me. I don't want to write about other people–especially rich-and-gorgeous movie stars who are living their dreams while I repress mine. It's early, not quite six o'clock. For the first time since I fled my past for California I am feeling reinvented yet again . . . as my former self.

My fiancée, Brooke, whom I met last year in Los Angeles, moved here with me a few months ago to carve a new existence in this emerald land ten miles north of San Francisco. We got engaged, and, lately, Brooke, who is a year older than I am and very ready to start a family, has been talking a lot about having a baby. We've even picked names: Jackson if it's a boy, Cadence if it's a girl. The umbilical cord connecting me to my athletic past has been thinning by the day.

My morning eyes strain over our blanketed bodies and I see Arthur, our black Labrador Retriever. He's snoring away on the floor, probably dreaming about swimming in the Sausalito marsh or chasing squirrels across the creek. If only my dreams were that simple.

"Brooke," I say softly.

She groans.

"Brooke." I tap her shoulder. "I just had the coolest dream."

"Uh-huh," she says in her that's-nice-honey tone.

"It was so beautiful," I say. I finally get her attention.

"What?" she asks, now awake, if only slightly.

"It was beautiful," I say. "I was playing hockey."

* * *

It's no mystery why I've suddenly fallen back in love with the sport of my youth. Eighteen months before the event we shall herewith refer to as The Dream, I reached the physical nadir of my life when I underwent a five-hour operation to have a pituitary tumor, which had been growing undetected for the previous twelve years, removed from the base of my brain.

The operation literally saved my life. Headaches brought on by the pressure the chestnut-size tumor was placing on my skull, combined with the emotional pain of having to quit hockey, had driven me into a constant malaise.

Rather than do the logical thing and disclose my physical problems to a doctor, I did what many a lonely, confused young man whose father had just died might do: I contemplated suicide. That low point came one night in 1995 while I was working as a newspaper reporter in a Virginia fishing town. I was just dumped by a waitress who had grown frustrated with my inability to maintain an erection. Distraught over her rejection and my emasculated state, I chugged a bottle of Nyquil. I wanted out of my unathletic misery. When I woke up fifteen hours after falling asleep and realized I had not died, my only regret was that I hadn't drunk two bottles. I was that depressed.

For the next two years, I groped through my so-called life, focusing on work rather than on myself. I rose through the journalism ranks, looking up so I didn't have to look behind. I made it all the way to Los Angeles and got hired to write for *People.*

But even a good job couldn't stop the headaches. As a result, on a clear, blue-sky day in Beverly Hills in October 1997, I walked into Dr. Joshua Trabulus's office and revealed the details of my condition: the impotence, the flab, the occasional milky discharge from the nipples, the daily struggle to muster enough energy to get out of bed. The mere thought of playing competitive sports was so far out of the realm of possibility that I didn't even bother mentioning my sedentary lifestyle.

Dr. Trabulus suspected that a hormonal imbalance was to blame. A few days later, a battery of blood tests came back showing that I had 150 times the normal level of prolactin, a hormone that women secrete to produce breast milk. Then an image from an MRI confirmed it: A prolactin-secreting tumor had taken up residence a few inches behind my eyes. Trabulus explained that the more prolactin I produced, the less testosterone I produced. A normal man has a level of about ten nanograms per milliliter; a woman breast-feeding her children has a level of two hundred. My prolactin level was 1,578. In clinical terms, I had a disease called hyperprolactinemia. In lay terms, I was a bio-chemical mess. Nine months later, almost all of the tumor was surgically removed and my hormonal hell was over. But while surgery gave me back my body, it did not heal my soul.

* * *

My Northern Californian life is idyllic—in that writerly sort of way. I have the girl, the dog, good friends, a woodsy setting. I spend my mornings staring out our window watching deer eat apples in our backyard. Upon seeing the storefront-lined downtown of our city, Mill Valley, my friend John from New Hampshire called it "the Disneyland version of the perfect small town." But now I realize that comfort isn't the same as contentment.

Just a week ago, I ran a marathon in Sacramento to raise money for pituitary tumor patients. It took me almost four hours, and I ran the last few hundred yards of the twenty-six miles with my arms raised victoriously above my head. At the finish line, I collapsed to the ground and cried out, "I am alive . . . I am alive."

Look

*K*athunk.

A thud is coming from the porch.

Kathunk.

Another thud.

Then–*thwap!*–another.

Being the good boy that he is, Arthur barks–*wooo-wooo-wooo*–as though a bear is outside. I open the front door and find on the porch three brown boxes wrapped in packing tape. *Only Mom would use that much tape.*

A burly delivery guy loosens his back-support belt. "Whatever's in there sure is heavy," he exhales, handing me a plastic stylus and console with a digital screen. The high-tech gear must have replaced paper receipts some time in the last eight years, which is how long it has been since the last time I donned the equipment inside these boxes.

I've been expecting this package for the last two weeks. After waking up from The Dream, I phoned a fifty-seven-year-old woman watching *Good Morning America* in her home outside of Buffalo, New York.

"Mom," I said, "you know that bag of hockey equipment that has been sitting in the attic above the garage?"

"No," she replied. "What bag?"

"The big black one. It should have my equipment in it. Can you to send it to me?"

"I haven't been up there in a *looong* time," Mom said in her lake-effect nasal accent that reminds me of the hot chocolate and frost-bitten toes of my hockey-playing youth. " I don't know. But if you say it's there, I'll look for it."

Mom paused, perhaps struck by my request. It's a well-known fact in the Baker family that I had come to hold contempt for the sport. In fact, a few months ago my little brother, Kris, asked me why I didn't play hockey out in California. I bitterly snapped that "people in California are too busy enjoying the sun."

Now I just want to *play*. Maybe I'll play recreational hockey just for fun, maybe a few times a month, if that much. I don't want to be competitive. I might have testosterone back in my system, but I don't want to take hockey too seriously. I mean, that dream made it seem like fun, but, in reality, I might not even enjoy the sport anymore.

Mom called back. "Found it," she said. "So why do you want this old stuff?"

"I'm gonna play again," I said.

"Where?"

"Out here, in San Francisco."

"Oh . . . O.K.," she said.

People from "back East," as well as most northern states where there's almost as many ice rinks as there are pizza-and-sub shops, still have trouble believing hockey is played in warm-weather places. But Californians do play hockey. In Los Angeles, most hockey players play the roller skating version on cement rinks and beachside parking lots. Ice hockey didn't come into vogue until the late 1980s, when the great Wayne Gretzky joined the Kings and inspired hordes of kids to come into the cold.

I had read about a group of Hollywood types who played together, guys like Jason Priestley, Cuba Gooding Jr., and Kiefer Sutherland. But a half dozen rinks serving a population of more than five million is kind of paltry when you consider that the Buffalo area has about twenty-five rinks (and that's not counting the wintertime frozen lakes and ponds, which are countless).

Meanwhile, a hockey boom of sorts has been happening up in the San Francisco area ever since 1991, when the San Jose Sharks joined the NHL and ice hockey became more popular than roller hockey.

I have always liked that hockey isn't as popular out West. I didn't want it always in my face, a constant reminder of my failed dreams. If I still lived in Buffalo, I would be just another ex-jock who still wants to go pro, but whose glory days have long since faded. Back home, these kind of guys are a dime a dozen. But now that I'm eager to get back into the sport–albeit just slightly–I wish there were more rinks, if only because to play I either have to inch through traffic on the Golden Gate Bridge to a city rink or drive twenty-five miles across the bay to the Oakland Ice Center, an aging, dimly lit, two-rink facility in the sketchy downtown area.

But I will worry later about finding a place to play. Right now, I'm not even sure this crusty, old equipment will even fit me. I drag the boxes into the living room and cut through the tape with scissors, ripping open the flaps with all the eagerness of a child on Christmas morning.

One box contains my goalie pads–bulky, maroon-and-white leg pads that, when bought by my college in 1991, were cutting-edge technology but that now seem like those antiquated football helmets with the single bar across the face. My helmet is maroon (Colgate's colors) with a white-metal cage and big eye-holes. After I graduated, lightweight fiberglass masks with a cage built into them became the norm. A few goalies still wear the old-style helmet, but it's considered old school. As I pull the rest of my stinky gear (the scent: Doritos meets day-old guacamole) I put on each piece as I find it. The gear is stiff, but everything fits–except for the skates. My feet apparently have expanded, probably due to the force of gravity over the years. Old fart, indeed.

Fortunately, I'm basically the size I was when I graduated from college: about 5' 11", and, thanks to a regular running regime, just over 170 pounds. Everything else–the chest protector, arm pads, padded pants, gloves, garter belt, socks–fits me perfectly. Mom couldn't find a jersey, but my Colgate hockey jersey (which I haven't worn since the day I quit) is hanging museum-like in my living room closet. I take the musty jersey off the hanger, put it on over my equipment, and when I put on the helmet and stand in front of the living room mirror I feel I've donned Superman's cape.

Hockey always was a mirror reflecting my life. The intense challenge of performing at my peak always revealed a brutally honest portrait of my personal strengths and weaknesses. If I was lacking confidence, I would let in bad goals. When feeling self assured, I'd get shutouts. No matter how hard you can try, mirrors don't lie.

Brooke is at the gym down the street, where she's been working as a personal trainer when she's not enviously watching moms push strollers down the sidewalk outside our apartment.

When she returns and sees me standing in all the gladiator gear, Brooke is not so much struck by how "cool" I look, but by how much it smells. "Pee-yew," she says, pinching her nose. Brooke has never gotten a whiff of old hockey equipment. "What's that *smell?*"

I strike my best goalie crouch, but she's still not amused.

"Careful!" she says. "You'll cut the rug with those skates."

"Don't worry," I say. "The blades are dull as butter knives."

She finally smiles when I start performing make-believe saves. But it remains to be seen whether I will be able to save myself.

Simplify

This is strictly a reconnaissance mission. I'm in Oakland interviewing someone for a story, so I've decided to pop over to the ice rink. I enter the lobby of the Oakland Ice Center, and it conjures images of my childhood: the hot chocolate machine . . . the hum of the Zamboni . . . the fluorescent overhead lights . . . the trash cans overflowing with used tape and broken sticks. *I am home.*

Smiling as wide as Lake Erie, I push through the swinging door to the rink and hear the sounds: pucks hitting boards . . . sticks slapping ice . . . blades ripping into the ice . . . guys–and it was exclusively guys when I played–shouting: *Man on ya. . . . Got time. . . . Head's up! . . . Shoot! . . . Front! . . . I'm open!*

Being a goalie, my attention immediately turns to the two guys standing in front of the net on each end of the ice. It's hard not to notice that their equipment is nicer and newer than mine. I also see that, despite their flashy gear, they are not very good. At the beginner level, it's common for the worst skaters to be goalies, mostly due to a misconception that goalies just stand there and take up space, when, in reality, the goalies should be among the best skaters on a team, if only for the simple geometric fact that while a hockey net is six feet wide and four feet high, a puck is only four inches wide. That means you could stick a Sumo wrestler in front of the net and a shooter would still see more net than the fatso's body. Therefore, a goalie must have quick reflexes and enough athletic ability to move from one side of the net to the other, reacting quickly to a puck that flies at him in unpredictable speed and direction.

These lunchtime pickup goalies are so wobbly that a moderate gust of wind could knock them over. Then again, I should reserve judgment. I have no idea how good I am anymore.

It's the one o'clock pickup game and most of the guys circling out there are over thirty. It shows. The pace is slow, the puck sloppily sliding around the ice, most of the passes and shots missing their intended target by several feet.

Some of the guys have decent skills. One burly defenseman is a stocky guy weaving around everyone like he's Bobby Orr. Another guy skates in that smooth-strided way that suggests he played college hockey, maybe a little pro. But while a few of the guys have talent, most are the kind of ankle-bending beginners who used to make pickup games about as fun for me as a night at the opera. Yet as someone who hasn't even been to an ice rink in eight years, this level will be the perfect place to start. I'm not looking to go pro; I'm not looking to relive any glory days. I just want to enjoy my body again.

I walk back to the lobby and tell the girl at the front desk I'd like to meet the rink manager, that I want to put my name on a list of available goalies for pickup games.

She tells me the manager of the ice center is André Lacroix, a former NHL'er who, as his name suggests, is a French-Canadian. When I walk into his office, he's on the phone. André is short and round with thick glasses and puffy cheeks that make him look like a frog. I miss eccentric hockey characters. The hockey world is filled with a lot of things–brutality, violence, sexism, alcoholism, machismo, danger–but one thing it definitely isn't lacking is a cast of colorful characters. Most hockey players come from small towns, and their lives have always centered on the sport. Due to his thick French accent, André pronounces "this" like "dis" and "that" like "dat."

He hangs up the phone.

"How can I help you, my friend?" he asks, shaking my hand.

"I'm thinking of playing pickup," I say. "I'm a goalie."

"Great!" he says gleefully. "We always need goalies around here. Are you any good?"

I've decided not to reveal my background. I will keep quiet about the Olympic development years, about the NHL scouts, the college scholarship. That way, if I suck, I'm just another old guy who sucks, not a former Division One college goalie who sucks. There's a difference.

So I just say, "I'm . . . uh . . . pretty good."

"Well, it's too late to sign up for the spring adult league," André says, "but I can put you on our backup list. If a team needs a goalie, they will call you."

Evidently, André has misunderstood me.

"That's fine," I say. "But I don't want to play in a league. Just pick-up."

André insists that league play is much more fun. And since his job is to recruit as many guys as possible to play, and therefore make money for the arena, he tries selling me on joining the league.

He explains that there are five skill levels for adult players (anyone over eighteen). The divisions (from lowest to highest skill level) are Bronze, Silver, Gold B, Gold A and, for the best players, the Platinum division. That I once won a gold medal for a junior Olympic squad but now am afraid I won't be good enough for the top beer league might take time to get used to.

"How good is Platinum?" I ask.

"Oh, there are excellent players, for out here at least. A lot of former college guys, some former pros. It's a pretty elite level. You might not be ready for that yet."

* * *

Buffalo is a land of extremes—hot summers and frigid winters, ritzy old-money neighborhoods bordering African American and Latino ghettoes, a small city with big-city sports teams. Buffalo is best known for the NFL's Bills, the NHL's Sabres, and for its artery-clogging culinary specialty: deep-fried chicken wings called "Buffalo Wings."

Buffalo was a nearly perfect place to grow up in. In the summer, it was a lush land of green baseball diamonds and thick oak and poplar trees made for climbing. In the winter, it was a wonderland of igloos, snow days, and ice hockey heaven.

Due to my nomadic lifestyle as a journalist, I have since lived in Manhattan; Washington, D.C.; southern Virginia; Los Angeles; and now the San Francisco Bay area. I live in Marin County, the richest of California's fifty-eight counties and one of the five richest counties in America. But I am about as rich as I am in hockey-playing shape: not at all.

We live a relatively humble existence in our one-bedroom apartment, yet we are surrounded by affluence. The local high school parking lot is filled with Beemers and Benzes, and the local clothing shops charge fifty bucks for twenty-dollar T-shirts. There's even a gourmet food store–for dogs!

Yet I do love Marin's natural environment–the eucalyptus, redwood and cypress trees, the miles of hiking trails, the scenic coastline, the temperate year-round climate. Yet I'm ill-at-ease around most of my human neighbors, with whom I seem to share little in common but the white color of my skin.

I've only lived here for seven months and I'm already wondering if I belong. Buffalo might have its flaws, but no one would ever accuse its residents of being pretentious or overly materialistic. I don't like playing tennis at the local court because I have trouble relating to the forty-year-old bankers enjoying early, early retirement or the twenty-something trust-fund babies who have all day to tan their faces. Maybe I'm jealous– I mean, who wouldn't like to be rich enough to retire at forty?–but there's a clash that runs deeper. Perhaps I have always yearned for a simple life, and moving from hectic L.A. to the serene woods of Northern California was supposed to be a step in that direction. I want to keep things simple. But ever since The Dream, suddenly life seems *complicated.*

Even so, I have found simplistic refuge, thanks to the yoga studios that seem to be on nearly every block. Marinites were practicing yoga here decades before it became the trendy thing to do nationwide. Since I always applied an Eastern approach to hockey, it's no surprise that I have been practicing yoga. Unlike traditional Western approaches to athletics, which mostly leave attainment of the ever elusive liberated state to luck and happenstance, practitioners of yoga and the Eastern martial arts deliberately strive to unite mind and body; it's a stated, fundamental goal. Likewise, what always attracted me to goaltending was the *inner* game: mental focus meeting physical challenge. This always meant more to me than the outer game of hard pucks bruising my arms and legs and shoulders and hands and, most painfully, my face and neck. At fourteen, I read *The Inner Game of Tennis,* a guide to reaching peak athletic performance through the Zen principle of not letting the mind get in the way of the body. I must have read that book dozens of times in college, trying my best to let my body be free of my dwindling self-confidence. Of course, I didn't know that the body I was entrusting to achieve greatness was hormonally disabled.

I was in search of an athletic nirvana, the place where the pillars of performance–the mind, body, and spirit–unite for a common purpose. To get to that zone, an athlete must construct a three-legged stool out of those pillars, because without any one of the three it will collapse. As my body weakened, my three-legged stool grew weak, ultimately destabilizing my mind and spirit.

Ever since I quit, I haven't come close to finding the spiritual peace that comes with physically pushing yourself to the limits of your performance, and I have not yet found a single yoga pose that is more challenging than stopping a 100 mph slap shot. Maybe I will now.

Smile

If my return to hockey is a spiritual journey, then the Oakland Ice Center is the first stop on my pilgrimage. A week after meeting André, I drive over to the 1 P.M. Thursday pickup game.

I'm there at noon, early enough to get my new skates sharpened and to buy a new jersey and a new stick, which costs fifty dollars, as opposed to the twenty-five dollars of ten years ago. The game has changed. I also learned the other day that my alma mater, Colgate, whose team name used to be "Red Raiders," is now called the more politically correct "Raiders."

I don't know how good or bad I will be out here, or if I will hurt myself or get hurt by a puck, but I am just excited that I'm trying. I have been watching NHL games on ESPN nearly every night for the last few weeks, mostly observing the goalies, fearing that I will no longer be able to do what they do. I might have looked the part, crouched in my equipment a few weeks ago in front of the living room mirror, but will I even remember how to skate once I'm on the ice? Eighteen months ago, I lay in a Los Angeles hospital room struggling to breathe, unsure that I would even be able to sit up without my brains seeping out of my nose, let alone voluntarily stand in front of pucks speeding at my skull at don't-blink speeds.

The poorly lit arena is an unglamorous place for a comeback. And that's fine by me. By the time I'm fully dressed and ready to take the ice, only two other guys have arrived. One guy is a long-haired computer programmer from Alberta named Michael, who tells me he hasn't skated in over a year because he's recovering from knee surgery. The other player, a skinny Asian-American guy, came to shoot some pucks on his lunch hour. I don't tell them that I once had a shot at making the 1992 Olympic team until a brain tumor turned my body into an effeminate blob. I figure the less they know about me, the less pressure.

"Cool," the skinny guy says after I admit I haven't skated in eight years. "I like to score."

Hah. Thanks for the motivation, punk.

I'm the first guy on the ice. No one is in the bleachers; no one is chanting. There's no public glory in this moment. Just me and the net. Simple. Just as life would be if it weren't so damn complicated.

The Zamboni driver, a thin African-American man holding a shovel, watches me as I drop the pucks out of my glove and skate around the rink. The guy probably has never seen such old equipment. I circle near the glass so I can see my reflection. I feel unsteady on the blades, unbalanced, as you would expect of someone who hasn't skated since Bill Clinton was governor of Arkansas and Monica Lewinsky was in high school.

It will probably take time to adjust again to carrying over forty pounds of equipment on my body while trying to block shots. Balancing yourself on sharp blades a few millimeters wide isn't exactly an innate talent.

A few minutes later, Michael comes out, then Skinny Guy. I drop to my knees and start stretching, my heart racing with anticipation of facing my first shots. Neither of these two guys is good enough to have been water boys on my college team, but today they might as well be All-Americans. Aware that my body will never get loose enough to prepare my leg, back, and arm muscles (not to mention my neck, which has to hold my mask upright), I perform one last stretch of the hamstrings and skate to the front of the net.

"Go easy on me," I tell them.

Michael gathers a half dozen or so pucks about fifteen feet in front of me to fire some warm-up shots. I stand at the top of the crease and crouch down into the goalie stance: knees bent at just above ninety degrees; chest up; glove hand is held at hip's height, facing out, ready to catch; stick blade is flat on the ice in front of my toes, held tightly by my right hand, which is protected by a leather blocking glove. Except for my skates, just about every piece of equipment I'm wearing is the same as when I last played.

Michael's first shot slides along the ice slowly, maybe the speed of a bowling ball rolling down an alley. I stop it, deflecting the puck to the corner of the rink–controlling my rebound just as I was trained to do. Michael lobs the next several my way in rapid succession. None gets past me.

I've broken a sweat by the time Skinny Guy skates toward me with a puck. He is a much better skater than Michael, who is obviously amid his own comeback of sorts, with the bad knee and all. Skinny Guy fires a wrist shot to my glove and I catch it–or at least block it. My glove is too stiff to squeeze it and the puck pops out onto the ice in front of me. I used to get upset with myself for letting out a rebound like that. But that's when hockey was work; now it's play and it doesn't bother me.

For the next hour, the two guys shoot hundreds of pucks at me, but fewer than ten get by me. My save percentage–the percentage of saves I make relative to the number of shots I face–is around 98 percent, which would be the best in the NHL, not to mention the Eastern College Athletic Conference. I smile the whole time, having fun the way I never did in college.

"You're *really* good," Michael says during a break at the bench. "You seriously haven't played in eight years?"

It might not have looked like it to him, but later that night my aching groin and sore lower back are enough evidence that it has indeed been that long.

Back in the locker room, I wiggle out of my upper-body pads to find my T-shirt saturated as if I had jumped into a pool. I miss the sweat-lodge sensation of emptying my body of so much stress. Later, as I walk down the sidewalk to the car, a homeless guy across the street spots me carrying my goalie stick and leg pads.

"Yo, goalie!" he shouts across the street.

"That's me," I reply.

"You're a goalie, man! I never seen no goalie before!"

I wave goodbye, hoping he won't hit me up for money but also totally psyched that I am, once again, a *goalie.*

* * *

Every Thursday for the next few weeks, I drive over to Oakland for the pickup game, and each time I improve tenfold and gain more confidence.

I make spectacular saves; rarely does anyone score. If I see a lot of action and have to flop up and down and sideways and dive especially

far, I get dizzy and see stars, coming close to fainting. Since my surgery, I've had this problem during strenuous exercise; it's from my anti-
prolactin medication, which thins my blood, thus making me more
prone to dizzy spells. I learn to avoid passing out by not taking a pill a
day before I am playing, which is good for my orientation but perhaps
toxic over the long term. When I realize this, I anxiously start popping
my pill right after the game, fearing that the tumor will have grown during that missed-medicine day.

No one sees my performance except for the guys on the ice and, occasionally, Brooke, who sits in the chilly stands wearing mittens and a
wool hat. Sometimes I will peek out of the corner of my eye after making a save, just to see if she has noticed. Usually, she has.

On the drive home from the rink one night I finally tell Brooke the
secret I have been keeping to myself for months. I'm still sweating–as
much a statement of how out of shape I am than the intensity of the
exercise. Since Brooke is my best friend and the woman I'm supposed to
marry in three months, she should be the first to know. So on the freeway north of Oakland I just blurt it out.

"I want to play hockey," I say.

"But you *are* playing hockey," Brooke says.

"No," I say, "I mean play *professionally*. Like for a pro team."

(Cue the crickets.)

Alanis Morissette fills the silence on 97.3 FM. I turn down the music.

"I probably wouldn't make a team," I add.

Fortunately, Brooke is a jock herself, a member of the nation's top
female Ultimate Frisbee team and among the rarified group of women
who are actually willing to watch NFL games. But even women who
are jocks have their limits. I expect her to harbor the same concerns
that I do. . . . What about my job? How will I make money? Where will
I play? Will we have to move? What about that lingering piece of brain
tumor? Couldn't I get hurt and, uh, possibly die? And what about having
a baby?

Instead of giving me the third degree and telling me how immature I
am, or reminding me that I technically still have a brain tumor, she
stares ahead and says, "I think you should do it."

Join

For the first two months of my comeback, I play once or twice a week. Some games I stonewall the shooters, only allowing one or two goals. Other nights I let in ten goals. But, surprisingly, it doesn't bother me when I don't play well. I'm still having fun.

Emboldened, in March I contact an AA-level team based in Moline, Illinois. The team, the Quad City Mallards of the United Hockey League, draws nearly six thousand fans a game from the region's four cities (Moline and Rock Island in Illinois, and Bettendorf and Davenport in Iowa.) They are considered one of the most successful franchises at the AA level.

The Mallards are owned and managed by a forty-year-old upstate New York native named Howard Cornfield, who, besides having a fitting name for a team based in a city surrounded by corn fields, possesses a shrewd hockey mind and, judging by his string of consecutive league championships, is a hockey genius. Adding to Cornfield's mystique is that his cousin is Al Michaels, the ABC broadcaster whose play-by-play call of the 1980 Olympic ice hockey victory over the Soviets had inspired my own. I had read on the Mallards Web site that the team was recently back-stopped by a former Colgate goalie, Dan Brenzavich, so I thought that, by collegiate association, I might have an "in" with the team.

I phone Howard and tell him about my medical history and hockey background, about this crazy dream I had, and how I might want to try out for his team in the fall. Knowing he must get calls from wannabes and wackos all the time, I throw in that, as a writer, I would probably chronicle my experience. (Mind you, I haven't even contacted a publisher about my idea. But I need at least a little credibility).

Howard calls my idea "interesting" and we agree to talk more over the summer. But as soon as I hang up I know I have made a mistake. I'm deathly afraid that I am not nearly good enough to play pro hockey, and what I told Howard Cornfield—that I am "still good" is total bullshit. I didn't tell him I was only "good" playing against guys who would be laughed off the ice in the UHL. I didn't tell him that Brooke has never lived anywhere but in California and has already made it clear that she would rather be confined in San Quentin State Prison than in the Quad Cities. Also, I failed to inform him about my reluctance to hang out with hockey players, because the last time I did I was mocked and ridiculed for not being like them. I didn't mention that I take two powerful antiprolactin pills every week that make me dizzy and nauseated. I didn't mention the not-so-minor technicality that I still happen to have a brain tumor.

* * *

It's a brilliant June evening. The day is ending, but a new stage of my life is about to begin. I'm doing something more important than stopping a puck; I'm going to start a life with the woman I love.

More than one hundred of our closest friends and family have gathered in the backyard of Brooke's mom's house in Sonoma. My mom made it all the way from Buffalo, as did my little brother, Kris, my best man. We're getting married in the heart of the Northern California wine country, the most romantic region of the West, a land of green, rolling hills and stately wineries with undulating rows of grapevines that extend into the distance like a Monet painting. For a boy from Buffalo, this is Eden.

Brooke looks so beautiful in her white dress, her blond hair tightly pulled back from her face as she steps into the courtyard, holding a bouquet in one hand and her father's hand in the other. There's not a dry eye around. Almost two years ago to the day, I was a lonely, suicidal man struggling just to breathe in a hospital recovery room. Now look at me: surrounded by those I most love and who love me, just happy to be alive and blessed to have found true love. It doesn't get much better than this.

Following the wedding, we honeymoon at a beachside resort in Maui, where hockey never once crosses my mind. Upon our return to the mainland, I have more important things to focus on. I am soon lured away from *People* by an upstart rival magazine, *Us Weekly,* another celebrity-centric magazine that is in desperate need of experienced staff writers. *Us* substantially hikes my salary and, since the editors have no problem flying me to L.A. whenever I need to conduct in-person interviews, they let me remain based in Marin, where I can write in my undies from the comfort of my living room desk.

So the hockey dream will remain just that–a dream. I want to focus on my new job and new marriage. Now that I am a family man, it's time to nest and build a life with Brooke–not chase a stupid dream. Since the hockey season starts in just three months, I phone Howard Cornfield and tell him I won't be coming out to the Quad Cities, after all.

I figure I'll never talk to the guy again and immerse myself in magazine writing. I write stories about Demi Moore's hot new boyfriend and about Chelsea Clinton's hot new boyfriend. I pen a touching, if dark, story about an actor who killed himself at a Las Vegas casino. I fly to L.A. and interview rockers Moby and Gwen Stefani on the set of their new music-video project as braless models flirt between takes ("Can you take me to a premiere?"). I interview Cindy Crawford at a San Francisco fashion show and dine with scantily clad rapper Lil' Kim and her two giant fake breasts.

From the outside, it might look as though I have the best job in the world of entertainment journalism. Inside, though, I am miserable.

* * *

Most of my work days at home end at four thirty, which also happens to be the West Coast broadcast start time for NHL games played on the East Coast. Just as I daydreamed about hockey while in high school, I do the same in my apartment. But, still, I only make it out to play every other week–either because of business trips forcing me to miss pickup games, or due to laziness or nausea from the two Tic Tac-sized anti-prolactin pills that keep my tumor from growing.

As the fog that defines San Francisco's "summer" gives way to the crisp, sunny days of September and October, I start getting nightly phone calls from captains of various adult-league teams around the Bay Area who have heard I'm a decent goalie. Since a goalie has the power to win or lose a game, I am a valuable commodity on the local senior-league market.

The senior-league teams have odd names like "The Skateful Dead," "Roadrunners" and "Dead End." I almost always say "no thanks" to their offers and stay home and watch TV with Brooke. Whenever I do play, I feel like quitting my job and playing hockey full time. Instead of torturing myself, it's easier just to stay away from the rink—at least until I manage to get that dream out of my mind.

As a result, I've gotten less athletics-oriented since The Dream. I have stopped running and only occasionally go to the gym or a yoga class. Every morning at the coffee shop downtown I eat three bacon strips and a bagel with cream cheese smeared all over it, and sometimes a buttery blueberry muffin. Before bedtime I often eat a huge bowl of cereal. My greatest exercise is walking Arthur down to the square in the morning. I have gained almost fifteen pounds—of fat, mostly—since The Dream, and, frankly, I've enjoyed my slothfulness.

Then, in early October, I get a call that finally yanks me off the couch. It is from Al, the captain of the "Thirsty Bears," the first-place team in Oakland's Platinum division. Al is a 41-year-old guy from Minnesota who manages an apartment building in downtown San Francisco. He played pro in Austria for a few years in the late eighties, but now he only plays hockey several times a week in Oakland. "I'm a hockey nut," he says, his dream clearly still alive.

The Thirsty Bears are named after a bar in Berkeley and have a roster filled with former Division One college players. I warn him that I am not as good as I used to be, but that he could list me as the backup if he's really desperate. I mean, it's only the backup job. No pressure, no expectations.

A week later, Al calls and says he needs me to play in their next game, which is tomorrow. Their goalie is sick. I have no excuses—no interviews scheduled, no good TV shows on, no injuries being nursed—so I agree and drive over, telling myself the entire time not to take this too seriously, to have fun with it, not to be nervous.

But the minute I get to the rink I am all business. I put on my "game face" and start visualizing making saves, practicing the mental imagery that I had learned from sports psychologists when I was an Olympic prospect, not an old writer with a major-league spare tire expanding around his waist.

I play flawlessly, and we win 3–2.

"Great game, Kenny!" Al enthuses after the game.

Luke, a defenseman from Minnesota, raves in the locker room that "you should be our goalie every game. You're pretty fucking good."

As the guys shed their gear and Luke passes around cans of beer, Al stands and makes an announcement. "I think we all know who should get the game puck tonight," he tells the guys, tossing the puck at me. "Way to save our asses tonight."

When I get back home just before midnight, Brooke is sleeping. Excited, I gently wake her.

"We won," I say.

"I knew it," she says, hugging me. "You're a stud."

"Hardly." I pull down my pants and show her a blue-green bruise the size of–well, a puck–on my inner thigh. "Check this out."

"Oh, God," Brooke says. "How'd *that* happen?"

"I stopped a puck."

I head to the living room to watch Leno's monologue, but I can't laugh–and it's not because his Clinton jokes aren't funny. I'm thinking about hockey. If I play, I want to take it to the extreme and see how good I really am. I am thirty years old. *It's now or never.*

I start up my computer and type "minor league hockey" into Yahoo!. More than a 150,000 sites pop up. Showing that I have not been paying attention to the minor-league hockey business, I learn for the first time that there is AA-level league called the West Coast Hockey League, a far more geographically desirable league than the Midwest-based UHL.

When I graduated from Colgate, the WCHL didn't even exist. My last brush with minor-pro hockey was right after graduation in 1992, when I was recruited by the Nashville Knights and Raleigh Ice Caps, which then were franchises in the East Coast Hockey League, one rung below the International Hockey League and American Hockey League, the two farm leagues where NHL teams send their best players who aren't quite ready for The Show. These leagues, which players called the "I" and the "A," were equivalent to AAA teams in baseball's farm system. While many players have NHL-level skills, the minor-pro leagues play a rougher style of game and offer fans a cheap alternative to the NHL. In the minors, for ten bucks you can see a hockey game, fights, blood, scantily-clad cheerleaders, all amid a circus-like atmosphere of cheeky promotions such as "Mullet Night." Good, old, not-so-clean American fun.

At the time, the ECHL was the only legitimate minor-pro league below the elite IHL and AHL. But clicking through my search engine results I learn that minor-league hockey has undergone a rapid expansion during my eight-year hiatus. In addition to the three established leagues, there is now the United Hockey League, the Central Hockey League, the Western Professional League (covering Texas, Louisiana and Oklahoma), and the West Coast Hockey League, which, since I am living in California, I click on. The WCHL boasts a total of nine teams–from Anchorage to Colorado Springs–and includes four California clubs: the San Diego Gulls, Long Beach Ice Dogs, Fresno Falcons, and Bakersfield Condors. The WCHL has a higher average per-game attendance (over five thousand fans) than any other AA league. It's no slouch of a league. *I have to do this.*

Even so, I might as well be realistic. I will likely either try out with Fresno (three hours from home) or Bakersfield (five hours away). I choose Bakersfield simply because, having the last name Baker, I am amused at the thought of playing in the town. Bakersfield's website reports that the team is owned by Wall Street millionaire Jonathan Fleisig, and as Leno gives way to Conan I sit and write the owner an e-mail.

Mr. Fleisig,

I am a staff writer for *Us Weekly* magazine based in the San Francisco area, but the reason I am writing is that I used to be goalie in the U.S. Olympic development program and was the starting goalie on the Colgate University ice hockey team; and, as a former collegiate player who is now an author and a journalist, I would like to spend a season with the Bakersfield Condors. . . . Basically, in the very least, I would like to serve as your team's third-stringer who, if good enough, could get a shot to play–be it one minute, one game or no time at all. Being a writer, I might someday write about it.

I hope you are as excited about the possibility as I am, and I would love to discuss my idea further and would be willing to meet with you anytime.

All the best,
Ken

By the time I log on to my e-mail system the next morning, Fleisig has written back:

call me tomorrow in my office . . .
–jf

I call him at seven o'clock the next morning. Clearly not a man prone to wasting his time on idle chit-chat, Fleisig, who made his millions trading energy stocks on Wall Street, starts off by telling me what exactly he thinks of my idea. "It would be a pleasure to have you with us," he says. "I was born with birth defects in my hands and feet, so I am something of a frustrated athlete myself. I know better than anyone else that regret will eat you alive. I will live vicariously through you." Fleisig adds that he is only thirty-four years old, and, as such, I should call him "Jonathan."

"I'll be honest with you," he says. "I'm pulling for you, and I want you to play. But I am also a businessman. If you write about minor league hockey, I will love that, though it's not the only reason I am behind you. I also want you to realize your dream."

Jonathan suggests I call the team's general manager and arrange a visit and skate with the team. He adds, "If you still think you'd like to spend a year on the Condors, then let's go for it."

We don't discuss specifics: Will I get a shot at being one of the team's two goalies? Will I get paid? Will I practice with the team even if I'm not the number-one or -two goalie? Will I have to pass a physical, and could my tumor disqualify me?

When Brooke comes home late from the gym, I update her on the conversation with Fleisig.

"So what do you think?" I ask.

She plops onto the couch and says, "Selfishly, I don't want you to do this." She pauses. Unlike me, Brooke thinks before she talks. She continues, "When we first met, you asked me, 'If you could do anything for a living, what would it be?' And I said I would want to be a professional Frisbee player, and you encouraged me to go for it."

"Yeah," I say, "I remember."

The normally sunny Brooke turns serious and says, "You have to play. If you don't, you'll regret it forever."

Try

The next day I phone Bakersfield's general manager, Matt Riley, who suggests I come down the weekend before Christmas, just three weeks from now. "You can see if Bakersfield is where you want to play and we can get a chance to get to know ya," he says. Matt doesn't use the word "tryout" or wonder aloud whether I am a fat old fart, but I know what he's getting at: he wants to see if I am for real or just a freak.

"I totally agree," I reply. "But I think you'll see that I'm still pretty good in between the pipes."

This isn't totally true; my net-minding skills, thanks to weekly workouts at the Oakland Ice Center with former college guys and various other ankle-bent oldsters, may have improved substantially over the last few months, but when it comes down to it I'm still a rusty thirty-year-old goalie who hasn't faced a pro-level slap shot (90 to 100 mph) in a long, long time.

The day after my encouraging phone conversation with Matt, I fly down to Los Angeles for my company's annual Christmas party. On the shuttle bus ride to the airport, I start leafing through the *San Francisco Chronicle*'s sports section. As the bus rolls through the morning rush hour leading up to the Golden Gate Bridge, I come across this news item:

FEATHERED FRIEND

Bakersfield has a minor-league hockey team in the West Coast League, and it has a conscientious and enterprising forward in Jamie Cooke.

The Condors' right wing spent a recent weekend off living in a man-made Condors's nest, some forty feet above a busy Bakersfield intersection. When he descended two days later, he had raised $15,000 for the Juvenile Diabetes Foundation. The money was donated by a local company in exchange for people bringing in aluminum cans for recycling.

I fish the cell phone out of my backpack and call Matt Riley, wanting to find out if this is the same Jamie Cooke I had played with at Colgate. It certainly sounds like the Jamie I knew way back when.

I haven't seen Jamie since May 1991, when we were both juniors at Colgate University and teammates on the school's hockey team. But our similarities pretty much ended there.

A muscular 6' 1" right winger weighing 200 pounds, Jamie was from a suburb of Toronto. On the other hand, I was an average-sized goalie from Buffalo. Jamie was two years older than I and he already had a one-year-old son with his wife, Beth, also a Colgate student. I was neither a father, nor much of a lover. Like most of the guys on the team, Jamie and I were given nicknames. His was "Cookie"; mine was "Pear," because my barely pubescent body–narrow shoulders, wide waist–was shaped like one. Of all our differences, though, perhaps our greatest one was that while National Hockey League scouts practically drooled over the chance to sign Jamie to a contract, I could barely get playing time on our college team.

Even though we didn't have much in common, I always liked Jamie, who had what our coach called "a good head on his shoulders." Mature, serious and focused, Cookie was also polite, almost always saying "please" and "thank you" and "yes, sir" and rarely swearing (unless it was on the ice, of course, where all pretense of moral decorum evaporates). Jamie was so strait-laced that he was the only hockey player who regularly attended campus church services.

When I was a lowly freshman enduring the upperclassmen's brutal hazing rituals (shaving my pubic hair, streaking naked on the team bus, getting spanked with hockey sticks), Jamie could see that I was having a hard time and would tell me to hang in there, encouraging me to tough it out. We all knew he had a big heart, which he demonstrated publicly our sophomore year, when he learned that a twelve-year-old local boy who was a devoted Colgate hockey fan had come down with terminal cancer. Jamie organized several fund-raisers to help his parents pay for the boy's chemotherapy. There wasn't much *not* to like about Jamie Cooke.

When Jamie signed a two-year contract with the Philadelphia Flyers the summer before our senior year, in 1991, I was both happy for him and sad to see such a good guy leave the team. Over the next eight years, we blazed through our respective lives like parallel lines, each on his own path, but heading in the same, focused direction.

I'd later learn that while I bounced from city to city climbing the journalism career ladder, Jamie had been living an even more peripatetic lifestyle as a pro hockey player. From 1991 to 1993, he played for the Philadelphia Flyers' farm team, the Hershey Bears of the American Hockey League. Though he scored twenty-six goals during his two seasons with the Pennsylvania pro team one rung below The Show, the Flyers informed him that they wouldn't renew his contract.

Jamie had obtained his undergraduate degree during summer school sessions, but he was convinced the Flyers had made a mistake: He believed he could still make it to the NHL. It would be a tough road back, though. Without any offers from other AAA teams, Jamie was forced either to play in a European pro league or step down to the AA level. Or retire. With two kids by then, he ended up joining a team in Birmingham, Alabama, in the East Coast Hockey League.

Though he scored over twenty goals a season during his two years in Birmingham, Jamie's stats never improved enough to attract any AAA offers. So he became a journeyman player on the minor-league circuit, leaving Birmingham for the Flint Generals (in the UHL), followed by a two-year stint with the Memphis River Kings of the CHL, and then spending the '97–'98 season with the Idaho Steelheads of the West Coast Hockey League, the newest of the AA leagues, started in 1995. The WCHL had rapidly earned a reputation for having a disproportionately high number of older players whose careers were on the downslide, and became known for its scrappy, "Wild West" style of play featuring bareknuckle fights and beer-crazed fans.

By that point in his career, though, I had lost track of Jamie, and he of me. I was living in Los Angeles, and while I had assumed he had long ago retired and was using his Colgate degree like the rest of us in the "real world," it turns out he was playing in a minor-pro hockey league that I—who hadn't played the sport since the end of my senior season in March of 1992—didn't even know existed.

"It's the same Jamie," Matt says when I ask him about this Jamie Cooke on the roster. "He's been with us for the last three seasons, as a matter of fact. A great guy, for sure."

"So is he still with Beth?"

"Oh, yeah," Matt says. "In fact, they have five kids now."

Indeed, it has been a long, long time.

Two days later, Pittsburgh Penguins owner Mario Lemieux, a lymphatic cancer survivor and one of the greatest hockey players of all time, announces he will mount a comeback later this season. He's thirty-five years old, five years older than I am, three older than Jamie. Maybe I'm not so old, after all.

Drive

Brooke and I load Arthur and a couple of suitcases into our silver station wagon and head for Bakersfield. Tomorrow night, a Friday, the Condors are playing the Long Beach Ice Dogs.

Matt Riley has arranged with the Condors' coach, Kevin MacDonald, for me to practice with the team Saturday morning. To make Arthur more comfortable (not to mention to save Brooke from my equipment's foul odor), I tie my hockey bag and sticks to the roof. Once they are loaded, I pull our wagon out of the driveway and we leave our woodsy hamlet on a 350-mile, five-hour drive to the dusty, tabletop-flat city of Bakersfield.

It takes an hour just to inch through the molasses drip of traffic on I-580, inching through the cities of Berkeley, Oakland, Hayward, and Livermore. As we speed across the deep-green hills of Altamont Pass, the traffic eases up and we're finally cruising down I-5, heading straight through the heart of California's central valley. At the southernmost tip of the valley, where the irrigated plains meet the ring of mountains that separate the agrarian valley towns from the hyper-civilization of Los Angeles, we approach the outskirts of Bakersfield. It's ten o'clock at night and our stomachs are filled with a greasy Denny's dinner, the left-overs of which are churning inside Arthur. The city is shrouded in a blanket of thick fog, which I'll later learn often fills the Bakersfield air. (In fact, until 1996 the hockey team was called the "Fog.") Moisture isn't the only thing in the air. Second only to Los Angeles, Bakersfield is the smoggiest city in the United States.

The soupy haze hangs low above the oil fields, apricot farms, nut tree fields, beef- and chicken- processing plants, and the slaughterhouses where less fortunate creatures are meeting their maker. I know from the road map that snow-topped mountains rise to the south and east of us, but we can't even see a few hundred yards ahead.

Neither of us has ever been to Bakersfield. Like most Californians, we've driven past it on I-5 dozens of times, coming within ten miles of it while speeding across the arid flatland between San Francisco and Los Angeles, which is located just one hundred miles to the south, but socially, economically, and psychologically a world away. Without irrigation aqueducts running down from Northern California, the "fields" surrounding Bakersfield would consist mainly of a dusty, tumbleweed-strewn moonscape receiving fewer than six inches of rain a year–Las Vegas gets more rain. More than one of our friends has called it "the armpit of California."

Even so, Brooke and I have agreed to meet Bakersfield with open minds. We don't expect to encounter a dynamic cultural center, nevertheless, we have pledged not to act like a couple of latté-sipping Northern Californians, which, of course, is exactly what we are.

Probably because I grew up in Buffalo (not exactly the French Riviera), had attended college in rural upstate New York, and had recently spent two years living in southern Virginia, I am more tolerant of unglamorous places than Brooke, who, except for a few years as a kid living in a small mountain town three hours east of San Francisco, has only lived in the coastal cities of San Francisco, San Diego, and Santa Monica, at least one of which is anyone's idea of paradise.

Although Brooke supports my playing in Bakersfield, she is not ready to commit to geographically joining my crazy adventure. If she decides to move down with me for six or seven months, she will have to postpone her enrollment in an elementary teacher-credential program at Sonoma State University, a thirty-minute drive north of our Mill Valley apartment. I only want her to join me if she really, really wants to, despite the potential loneliness and strain that being apart would place on our relationship. We've only been married five months, but I figure that after the hockey season is over we will still have a lifetime to share together. So while I couldn't live with myself if I passed up the chance to play pro, I also realize I couldn't live with myself knowing I was making my wife miserable.

Even so, as we cross the Bakersfield city limits I realize I should have brought along someone from the Bakersfield Chamber of Commerce, if only to propagandize for the benefit of my wife. On our left, an oil refinery spewing noxious smoke sits right next door to a Wal-Mart. Across the street sits a dilapidated trailer park smack in the middle of an oil field. The pumps are lazily bobbing up and down like seesaws.

Just when I start wishing I had brought Brooke (who is pinching her nose) into town via a more scenic route, I attempt to put a positive spin on it, assuring her, "At least it's dark out." Her expression is the one I've seen when she's on a plane landing in a thunderstorm: horror.

We exit the freeway and loop onto Truxtun Avenue, looking for "downtown Bakersfield"–that's the term used by the lady at the Holiday Inn Select over the cell phone. The hotel, she said, sits right next door to Centennial Garden, the home of the Condors, and is in "the heart of downtown." She added, "You can't miss it."

I strain my eyes through the windshield looking for skyscrapers, busy sidewalks, anything indicating a hub of urban activity. When the Holiday Inn suddenly appears on my right, I realize that the deserted streets lined with power lines and a string of shabby storefronts is in fact downtown Bakersfield.

As I steer into a parking space next door to the hotel–taking advantage of the fact that there are only five cars in the entire lot–I begin asking myself (silently, of course, as not to alarm anyone, such as my horrified wife) the obvious question any halfway-sane man would ask: *What the hell am I doing here?*

In the room, Brooke starts getting ready for bed as I clip the leash on Arthur and take him downstairs to deposit his dinner in the bushes. Outside, I look across the foggy parking lot at Centennial Garden, a concrete box that, unless I am totally inept, chicken out, or get hurt when I try out on Saturday morning, could become my office.

* * *

Eager to start the first official day of my comeback, I wake around seven o'clock. The sun peeks through a crack in the curtains, through which I survey the landscape below our eighth-floor hotel room. Brooke is still sleeping, as is Arthur on the floor, so I quietly separate the middle crack a smidgen and poke my head out and see . . . fog. Pea soup. I nudge Brooke awake and we get dressed, keeping the curtains closed.

The plan: While I'm at the rink making a good impression and meeting everyone, Brooke will go for a ride around town, visit the mall, in order to assess the place a little to see if she could actually live here for a season.

I grab my notebook, Brooke wishes me luck, and I walk over to the rink. Matt and I have arranged to meet at the Condors office at 9:30 A.M. From there, Matt said, we'd walk down to the ice and watch the team's "pregame skate," an easygoing affair where they work on last-minute strategy and get their legs loose for the game.

"At least I can see you're not an old, fat guy," Matt jokes as we firmly shake hands in his cluttered office. He apologizes for the mess. "Game day," he explains, arching his eyebrows with a pained grimace.

Matt, who is from Iowa, has a midwestern twang he hasn't lost during his three years in California. He strokes his expertly trimmed goatee and introduces me to the young staff, who are either scurrying around the office or sitting dutifully at their cubicles. "Hey, guys, this is Ken Baker, a writer from San Francisco," Matt proudly announces to the five or six staffers who aren't on the phone. "He's thinkin' about spending a season with us." Everyone shakes my hand with the kind of folksy, damn-glad-to-meet-ya exuberance one doesn't usually get in San Francisco, but which one does see in places like, say, Buffalo or Bakersfield. I am already feeling comfortable. Most of the office guys, who are young and laid-back, have that sports-nut look: golf shirt, comfortable shoes and a red-necked golf tan. For many, this is their first job out of college, and they hope to move on to the major leagues. "It's like *Bull Durham* mosta' the time," Matt says. "We have a lot of fun 'round here."

Matt leads me back to his office and offers me a chair across from his paper-strewn desk. Condors foam fingers, souvenir pucks, bobbleheads, T-shirts, and other cheesy merchandise are stacked in sloppy piles on the floor. Surprisingly, there are no mullet wigs.

Matt explains that, as general manager, he's in charge of the day-to-day business operations–from trading players, to signing contracts, and right down to picking which local teen-ager will wear the "Colonel Claw'd" mascot outfit. "It's not your typical nine-to-five job," he says. "That's why I like it." Matt tells me the team has an operating budget of about $2.5 million, including paying players an average of $500 a week, with rookies making the minimum $325 weekly salary. "We're profitable, but not as much as we'd like to be," he says.

As I pull my pen and notebook out of my back pocket, I spot a wooden plaque stuck on the wall behind him reading, "WCHL EXECUTIVE OF THE YEAR 1999–2000." Clearly, the Condors are Matt's life.

His phone has rung about five times since we sat down, but he has ignored every one. Tonight's game is set to start in a little under nine hours. As it rings yet again, he looks at his watch and says, "Well, it's already ten o'clock. You should head down to the pregame skate and meet Mack and the guys. Have you seen Jamie yet?"

I tell him that, unfortunately, I have not.

"I know he's looking forward to seeing you. I told him about your brain tumor–showed him that letter you wrote me, and all that stuff. He had no idea you were sick."

"Neither did I for a long time," I say.

Matt says I should come back to his office after lunch, when he won't be so crazed, when we could talk more about my proposed project. He calls Deric over and asks him to show me down to the ice.

"So you really think you can play pro?" asks Deric, who looks about five years younger than I am, as we walk through the tunnel beneath the stands.

"I don't know," I say evenly. "It's been like eight years since I played in college. I guess I'll find out how good I am tomorrow, huh?"

By the smirk on his face, I sense that Deric doesn't think I'm for real. And, actually, he has no reason to think otherwise. I mean, we are about the same age, height, weight, and build. I have my own doubts that I can pull this off.

Deric opens a thick metal door and says, "This is the locker room."

It's plush and homey, with spanking-new gray carpeting and a giant TV screen stuck to the wall above the locker stalls. It's a lot nicer than my college team's dressing room. This is the pros.

I notice that, unlike in the NHL, the players' stalls don't have any permanent nameplates screwed in the locker frames; there's so much turnover in the WCHL–all but a few veterans work under weekly contracts–that they just glue plastic name tags above the stalls.

As we walk through the locker area to the hallway leading to the Condors bench, I can hear the sounds of my youth growing louder. Blades cutting into the ice. Sticks slapping pucks. Swearing. Pucks hitting the boards with a thud and striking the rigid Plexiglas with a crash. A coach barking: "I wanna see sharp passes, boys!" Coach MacDonald, himself in skates and clutching a stick, is shouting these orders like a sergeant from a patch of ice directly in front of the bench. "Put the puck on the blade!"

The players whiz by me so quickly that a cool breeze blows onto the bench and messes my hair. I can smell the frozen sheet of water, instantly conjuring a thousand memories of a time when I never envisioned doing anything else in my life but playing hockey. Here I stand, a grown man of thirty, all too aware that if I'm ever going to play pro hockey I better do it soon.

My wide-eyed gaze shoots directly to the goalie in front of the net. He looks so big and bulky in his rectangular, black leg pads, and hard plastic mask, like a gladiator. Coach MacDonald has the guys running a drill requiring them to rush at the goalie full-speed before firing a slap shot at the net. The goalie throws his body in front of the speeding rubber bullets quickly and mechanically, like a character in a video game being controlled by the jerking of a joystick. Could I ever again move that fast? I don't know. But I want to be that goalie. I don't want to be a writer standing like a dork in his street clothes; I want to be crouched in front of that goal on a Friday morning, getting paid to use the talents that my healthy body possessed before I was too old to do so. I stare at the goalie with both envy and awe.

"Mack!" my escort calls out to Coach MacDonald. Mack twists his neck around. "This is Ken Baker, the writer guy."

"Oh, yeah," he says, extending his arm for a handshake. "The goalie, right?"

I nod.

"Go get your stuff and come out," Mack says, eyeing his skaters rather than me.

"Right now?" I ask.

"Yeah." He blows his whistle and waves the guys toward the bench area. Mack, a former minor-pro player with scars etched across his chin to prove it, clearly has a personality as no-nonsense as his nickname implies. "Why the hell not?"

I look at Deric, who is as shocked as I am, and whisper, "Is he serious?"

Deric shrugs his shoulders.

First, Matt had just told me that I would skate *tomorrow*–not now. Second, I thought today I would just observe, meet the guys one-on-one, catch up with Jamie, and be on my merry way until the game tonight, then play on Saturday morning. But now I'm surrounded by twenty panting hockey players in their helmets, and they're all staring at me, obviously wondering, who's this loser?

Mack satisfies their curiosity.

"Boys, this is Ken Baker. He played with Cookie back in college, and now he's here researching a book." Embarrassed by the attention, I start studying my shoelaces.

Mack adds, "What's your book gonna be about?"

These are professional hockey players. Brutes. They get paid to make other people hurt. Except for Jamie, whom I can't even pick out of this monosartorial crowd of giant white men in black helmets, these aren't the kind of baby-stroller-pushing yuppies with whom I interact on a daily basis back at home. The last thing I'm going to say is the *Revenge of the Nerds* truth–*Uh, well, guys, I had a dream a year ago, that I was, uh, playing hockey again, and, uh, now I want to write about my comeback about playing with the Condors*–lest they laugh me out of the arena and kick my pansy ass back to San Francisco. So I say the first I'm-one-of-the-guys thing that pops into my head.

"Sex and hockey," I say, desperate to fit in.

The guys' stone-stiff faces loosen, and they start cracking up.

"Hey, hey!" one of them yelps. "You've come to the right place!"

Even Mack cracks a smile.

I have passed the first test–Am I "cool?"–of my tryout.

"O.K., let's see some two-on-ones," Mack barks before the laughter subsides. As the players dutifully skate away for the drill, Mack says to me, "So you've got your stuff with ya, right?"

"Yeah," I say, reluctantly. "Well, I mean back at the hotel, I do."

"Great. We'll be out here for another hour or so. Why don't you go ahead and get your stuff." He skates away before I can answer him.

It wasn't a question. Mack clearly wants me out there, wants to see if this guy who played in college with Jamie Cooke can still stop rubber, to determine for himself if this journalist, this apparent friend of the owner and general manager, is going to be a pain in his ass or an asset he could count on to guard his team's net if needed.

I'm not about to say no. This is my chance to shine. I have been lifting weights, running, playing in the senior league for the last few months for this opportunity.

"I'll get my gear," I tell him, pushing out my chest in the most artificial display of confidence since I told Matt a few weeks ago on the phone that I was still "pretty good."

I bid *adieu* to Deric, who is standing behind the bench area, shocked at Mack's surprise invitation, and I run back through the locker room, through the arena's back door, and straight to the Holiday Inn a few hundred yards to the east. *This is it! Maybe Mack will be so impressed with me he will ask me to join the team today, not just for next year. (Matt had said on the phone that one of their goalies had not been playing very well). Then again, maybe I am about to get pummeled like a piñata. Maybe the next time Brooke sees me it will be at some hospital, at my bedside, as she holds my hand, my jaw wired shut and a pair of adult diapers sagging around my shattered pelvis.*

Inside the lobby, I keep pressing the elevator button, as if that will make the car come quicker. At last, the doors slide open, and it delivers me to my floor. I sprint down the hallway, reaching for the card key in my pocket. Assuming that I had brought my equipment in from the car last night, so it wouldn't get stolen, I breathlessly barge in and start looking for my bag. But it's . . . not . . . there.

Shit.

I immediately realize I had left it in the car, which Brooke is driving around Bakersfield at that exact moment. I am about to make a very bad first impression on Mack. What a bummer. If I wasn't supposed to be such a tough-guy goalie, I could cry.

I run back to the rink to let Mack, possibly my future boss, know that I can't skate today. Down by the ice, I approach the coach as though he is the principal and I am the failing student. Panting, I nervously explain why I can't skate today. "That's fine," he says. "You can come out tomorrow."

Jamie then skates over to the bench. I recognize his long, flowing stride. I stand up straight and tuck my shoulders back. Like a man.

"Hey, Kenny, you doing all right?" He looks at me quizzically, as if I have just survived a plane crash or something. "I read that thing you wrote to Matt and the owner. You've been through hell, man."

"Well, yeah, sort of," I say. "But with five kids, you're probably going through your own hell."

It's always a little awkward seeing someone after so many years, like, say, at a high school reunion. I wonder if I look old to him, what he thinks about my crazy idea to come out here in the boonies for a season. But what is also strange about this reunion is that I am seeing Jamie just as I have remembered him—on the ice, a player, youthful—while my life has changed drastically since he last saw me.

Still, just like when we were college kids, we connect despite our differences.

"I bet you never thought you'd see me here, eh?" I say.

"Listen," he says, looking around the ice, "I never thought I'd see another college graduate here. Most of these guys haven't been to college. There's a few, but not many."

Mack suddenly calls the team down to the far end of the ice for a talk.

"Gotta work," Jamie says, skating away with a puck.

* * *

Deric escorts me back up to the front office to see Matt, who is less crazed than earlier in the morning. I ask him if he could give me a snapshot of what is happening with the team, which has lost two fewer games than it has won and is in last place in the Southern Division.

Matt could probably talk about the minutiae of his job all day long. He is getting riled up as he speaks about all the "issues." He calls the team's power play "the worst in the history of mankind" and complains that the team just isn't scoring goals.

"How's your goaltending?" I ask, hiding my hope that he will say it royally sucks and that they actually need me.

"Like everything lately, it hasn't been very good. I think our two guys will be the first to tell you that it hasn't been stellar."

This is good. At least I don't have to worry about some hot-shot goalie coming back next season.

Matt then offers his take on all the big issues:

- **Fighting:** "It's not something we promote, but when two guys drop the gloves, obviously the fans love that."
- **Bakersfield:** "I would describe it as a Midwest-type of city. It's sort of the best of both worlds. You have everything you need here, but you don't have the hustle and bustle of the big city."
- **The franchise:** "We're the most popular thing in town."
- **Jamie Cooke:** "He's one of our best players, but he is not an NHL prospect anymore."
- **The team's finances:** "Half the teams in this league lose money, but we're profitable. We get over five thousand fans a game. But we're not as profitable as we'd like to be."
- **My proposal:** "I think it's a *great* idea."

Thank God.

As I walk out of Matt's office and back to the hotel I'm thinking about how perfectly comfortable, familiar and welcome I am starting to feel in Bakersfield. I can't wait to get back to the hotel and tell Brooke about how great things went. I still have to play well in practice tomorrow, but even that isn't worrying me so much anymore. Everything is falling into place.

But the moment I enter I know something is wrong. Brooke lies catatonic on the bed in front of the TV. She's gripping the remote. Her eyes are red and puffy.

"I'm sorry," Brooke says. "I can't live here. It's just so . . . so . . . ." She struggles to find the right word. Finally, she adds, "*Boring.*"

* * *

Since the team beat the Ice Dogs 5–4 last night in a shootout (the WCHL doesn't have overtime; rather, teams go head-to-head in a five-shot shootout if the game is tied after three periods), Mack has made the Saturday morning skate optional, which is why Jamie and half the other players aren't in the locker room when I enter shortly before ten o'clock with my giant equipment bag slung over my shoulder. Kid Rock is blaring from the stereo as eight or nine players glance at me the way subway riders do to each other—through me. I just figure they remember me from yesterday–"sex and hockey"–and are accepting me as one of them. Even though I'm not, really.

This might be just another day at work for them; in fact it's probably a shitty Saturday morning that they might rather spend sleeping, or whatever it is pro hockey players do in their spare time. But this is the thrill of my post-tumor life.

This is who I am: An aging jock who thinks that maybe–*maybe*–a tumor was to blame for his career ending too soon. Truth is, the tumor might not have been why I had to quit. My lousy play in college could have been the result of peaking young, or bad coaching, or even bad timing, and playing behind an All-American goalie for two years didn't help matters. It's also possible that the tumor, which had been growing gradually since age fifteen or so, didn't truly hurt my athleticism until after I retired. I simply don't know. All I do know is that I have my body back, and I want–need–to try. To most people, Bakersfield might be an average city shrouded in smog and littered with oil pumps. But, to me, it is a field of dreams.

* * *

Two and a half years ago I lay face-up on a stiff operating table as my surgeon cut through my upper gum, bored through the bone at the base of my skull and then spent five hours plucking a white tumor from my pituitary gland. I have slides of photos that a nurse snapped for research purposes during my operation. Occasionally, when I feel I'm starting to forget just how precious every minute of life is, I will pull the slides out of my desk drawer, tape them to the window and stare at the images of a lifeless-looking man with cardinal blood splattered over his face. An oxygen hose is stuffed down his throat, breathing life into his lungs. At the moment these photos were snapped, no one knew whether my eyes would ever again open, let alone if I would ever again enjoy the glory of a glove save in the final minutes of a game.

Mack walks in and tells me I will be the only goalie at practice today, because "our two guys are resting their bones." I think to myself that the other goalies–Trevor Amundrud and Matt Mullin, both of whom are twenty-six years old–are lucky to have younger bones. To an athlete, time is an enemy–unless you're up by one with a minute left in the game. Then the clock can't tick fast enough. I'd like to be able to tell myself that just suiting up alongside these pros is a triumph; just being alive, a victory. I wish that I could wholeheartedly pledge the Special Olympics oath: "Let me win. But if I cannot win, let me be brave in the attempt."

The truth is that I'm no longer disabled; I no longer have an excuse for playing poorly.

All the other players have donned their jerseys and taken to the ice. The music has stopped. Finally alone, I am able to smile.

What happens over the next hour is a blur of pucks coming at me in a blink of an eye and my body somehow stopping most of them. Into my glove, off my shoulder, off the toe of my extended skate blade. A few even ding off the forehead of my mask. At times my breathing gets so labored that I start seeing stars. I take a deep breath, in and out, and then focus back on the puck.

Occasionally, I'll catch a glimpse of the two black letters—**LB**—scrawled on the front of my Colgate-white blocking glove, the very same glove I wore nine years ago in what I had thought would be my final game. The initials are homage to my father, my biggest fan, the man who had helped me get that far.

Near the end of practice, Mack puts me to the test himself—firing shot after shot as hard as he can. A few go in, but most don't. I feel more in command of my body than nine years ago. Testosterone and having grimly faced my mortality at such a young age not only has made me a more complete person, but also a better athlete.

There's not a soul in the nine thousand seats forming the bowl around me, except for Brooke, who's standing twenty rows up to my right snapping photos. The man she's capturing on film bears little resemblance to the one in those bloody surgery photos.

Overcome

"From our studios in Los Angeles, here again is Stone Phillips."

Stone's face pops on our TV screen. Over his shoulder, colorful graphic lettering advertising the title of *Dateline*'s next story reads, "My Body, My Self." Brooke and I anxiously watch, along with fifteen million other people on this Tuesday night in America. The story is about me.

Stone begins his dramatic introduction of the newsmagazine's profile of a man who learned what it means to be a man the hard way and then wrote a book about it. The book, *Man Made*, hit bookstores yesterday. It is my "coming out," as it were, and once my story is told to a national audience there will be no turning back. I'm nervous in the same expectant way I am before a hockey game: *Let's get this over with.*

The correspondent tells my–let's face it–*bizarre* tale of hormonal dysfunction and how it turned my once promising hockey career into an exercise in frustration: "His teammates were developing faster reflexes, bigger muscles. He was still good, but not quite good enough for first string. Colgate, the school that might have been a triumph, just wasn't. There would be no hockey career."

Finally, they show me after a game in Oakland, skating toward Brooke, who stands just off the ice waiting. I kiss her on the lips and say, "Game over."

As the announcer teases the next story, and I exhale with relief that I didn't come across as a total freak on national television, I realize that the game has only just begun.

* * *

It has been ten weeks since my tryout in Bakersfield, which apparently was a success because Mack or Matt never called to give me the old "thanks but no thanks." But I know I could have done better had I practiced beforehand more than once a week. I was also about fifteen pounds overweight. Even so, Matt told me that, at the very least, a third-string goalie slot awaited me for next season, which starts at the end of September–almost seven months away.

Yet I have not even decided whether I will in fact quit my job, train–on and off the ice–to get into playing shape, somehow find enough ice time in the Bay Area to get ready, and last but not least, move to Bakersfield without Brooke, who has decided that she doesn't want to live in Bakersfield, though she supports my move. (We both agree it's important that in the fall she starts her year-long teacher-certification program at nearby Sonoma State University. Why should she risk ruining her educational plans when there's a possibility that I might get hurt or not even be good enough?)

I am afraid, and I have been scared ever since the first time I stepped on the ice a year ago in Oakland. I am afraid of a lot of things–of getting hurt, of not being good enough, of not having fun once it becomes a job, of losing Brooke over this early-mid-life crisis of mine. But the one thing that is most keeping me from committing to heading to Bakersfield is the F-word: failure.

As I watched *Dateline*, I felt uneasy, and not just because it's a quasi-out-of-body experience seeing your life story being told in that cheesy over-dramatic, newsmagazine sort of way. What really shook me was that I *looked* like a hockey player, I *talked* like a hockey player, and, now that I have seen myself playing, I can better see myself *being* a pro hockey player.

* * *

Journalism has given me more than I could ever want from a career. I ended up in celebrity journalism because I like fun adventures, but I also did it so that I could come in contact with people whose talent I admired. At their best, the interviews are inspiring; the worst ones are, at least, informative. I have interviewed comic geniuses (Robin Williams, Jim Carrey), prolific musicians (Carlos Santana, Chris Isaak), world-class athletes (Alex Rodriguez, Brandi Chastain), and brilliant scientists like Douglas Engelbart, the computer engineer who in the 1960s invented the mouse. I have interviewed an American hero, James Stockdale, a man whose struggles as a POW are never too far from my consciousness. Their stories have become part of mine. Now, thanks to a sluggish economy and The Dream that won't go away, I'm about to risk losing a job that has given me so much. Yet losing my job may finally allow me to admire myself as much as I do the people I get paid to write about.

Quitting—or "taking leave," as I have decided to call it—has just been made easier. My boss called this morning and informed me that, due to company-wide cutbacks, I will lose my staff job in two months unless I move to Los Angeles, where several writers have already been laid off. "Don't look at it like you're being fired," he said. "We're just asking you to relocate to where we really need you, down here in Hollywood."

I can't argue with him. Having a writer, albeit an experienced one, based in San Francisco is a luxury for a celebrity magazine that is suffering at the newsstands. My boss gives me until the end of the week to make a decision.

I could stay in Mill Valley and eke out an existence as a freelance magazine writer while I continue training for my hockey comeback. But I will do so at the risk of financial ruin and professional suicide for someone who has made a name for himself as a celebrity scribe. My boss, who knows I have been considering a comeback, understands that a move to L.A. could mean the end of my dream, which is why he made a point of telling me, "If you come back down to L.A. you will have to make at least a year commitment. You wouldn't be able to play hockey."

I'm weighing my options as I drive across the Bay to Oakland for an eight o'clock game. It takes forty minutes in traffic, and I pass the time by calling my little brother Kris, who is back in Buffalo. I am closer to Kris than any of my four other brothers. From the time he was two, and I was eight, we were virtually inseparable.

A natural athlete in his own right, Kris grew up around ice rinks. He stood on the bench as my team's water boy for some of my greatest moments as a youth player. He knows how much hockey means to me, how happy it makes me, and how incomplete my life has been since I quit. When I tell Kris my hockey-versus-Hollywood dilemma, he doesn't hesitate for a second before saying, "You need to play, Kenny. There's no choice. You are gonna play pro hockey."

But what about the money? The potential financial mess? The fear of the unknown? Or what about the fact that I just turned thirty-one, still have a shred of brain tumor that gives me dizzy spells, and very well could get myself killed?

"All I know is that you had that dream for a reason," Kris says.

"I could always do it next season," I reply.

"No, Kenny, you can't," he says. "Face it, you're not getting any younger."

* * *

The headline on the May 20, 2001, front-page of the *San Francisco Chronicle* sports section reads, "Cheating Father Time: Training, nutrition and medical advances prolonging careers." It speaks directly to me. Last month, I turned thirty-one. No matter how strong and youthful I feel, the reality is that I will be one of the oldest players in the West Coast Hockey League.

> "Advances in training methods, medicine and nutrition—plus spiraling salaries, of course—increasingly lead athletes to push the sporting envelope by staying productive into their late thirties and early forties. . . . Many top athletes already zoom beyond what was once considered customary retirement age. Witness the ongoing presence of Jerry Rice in football, Rickey Henderson in baseball, and John Stockton in basketball. And some players are sustaining or even improving their performance as they head into their late thirties, typically a time of declining skills."

That *Chronicle* story comes as I have been watching two of the oldest goalies in the NHL—Patrick Roy and Dominik Hasek—battle it out in the play-offs. They are both at least five years older than I am, and as such they give me hope that maybe I am not too old, even though the average age in the WCHL is twenty-six and I am thirty-one.

To avoid further injury to my creaky knees, I have opted for the most boring—but least jarring—form of cardiovascular exercise: The Stairmaster. I do thirty minutes four days a week and fight the monotony by wearing a radio headset and reading the newspaper.

Brooke leaves for Italy on June 25, and my goal is to get in the best shape of my life while she is gone for five weeks. She'll be working as a nanny for two kids whose parents can afford such a luxury, and I was supposed to come visit her there for two weeks, but since I have lost my job and begun training for hockey, I have to stay home and save money. I'm not thrilled about being apart, especially since we will be living apart for seven months starting at the end of September, but at least it will allow me to get into shape without distraction.

The lighter I am, the faster I am. As such, my goal is to enter training camp at 170 pounds. Less poundage also will mean less stress on my knees and hips every time I drop down on the hard ice. I weighed 183 pounds in March, and I am down to 177.

The leaner I get, the younger I feel, perhaps because the exercise and healthful diet—two giant green salads with avocado and tomato twice a day, no bread or cereals, and no late-night snacking—has raised my energy level. Father Time ticks, but as that newspaper story said, creative training can delay the clock and prevent injury. So can sitting around for the last nine years doing virtually nothing athletic.

* * *

I have negotiated a freelance contract with *Us* that will net me a little over $2,000 a month for the next twelve months. Considering Brooke will be in graduate school full-time and unable to work, making ends meet will be a struggle.

I won't be able to rely on income from hockey. If I am not at least the team's second-string goalie, I will not get paid by the team; I will also have to pay for my own plane tickets. Brooke has suggested that she and Arthur move into her mom's house in Sonoma, but, since her mom's cats are afraid of our big, black wonder, it's not a realistic option. She will be a full-time student, struggling to pay the rent as I am off stopping pucks. I know it's probably just my machismo, but I feel responsible for Brooke and Arthur. They are my family.

* * *

Thwop, thwop, thwop. I can hear the helicopter blades chopping through the moist morning air, but I can't see the bird of mercy that has come to fly me away. I can't move from the shoulders up; the paramedics have locked my neck in place with a brace and stuck thick strips of medical tape across my forehead. I'm scared shitless.

The pilot circles, looking for a safe landing zone near the base of the mountain to pick me up and carry me to a hospital because, as the EMT who's treating me just told his partner, "I'm afraid he broke his neck." They need to get me to a doctor–fast.

I've seen enough television shows and movies to know that a few minutes can mean the difference between a full recovery and permanent brain damage. I know that blood can seep into your brain, build pressure, cause a stroke, eventually rendering the victim a vegetable or, in the worst case, a corpse. If someone has suffered a blow to the head in a remote area–say, on a forested trail halfway up a mountain as I have–it's standard procedure to call in a helicopter to evacuate the victim, which, in this case, is me.

Brooke and I are supposed to celebrate our one-year wedding anniversary tonight, and I had the bright idea this brilliant mid-June morning to hop on my mountain bike and ride 2,500 feet straight up Mount Tamalpais, the jagged mountain peak that towers over the rolling green hills just north of San Francisco. The season starts in twelve weeks, and I have been training so hard–playing pickup hockey twice a week, working out in the gym every day, doing the Stairmaster–that I decided to do something different today.

It took me almost two hours to pedal to the top, where I took off my helmet and gloves, munched on an energy bar, swigged some water, sat atop a picnic table, and eye-balled the 360-degree view: the fog-shrouded ocean to the west, verdant Sonoma County lying in the hazy distance to the north, San Francisco, Oakland and Berkeley to the south and east. I kept thinking, *It's a great day to be alive.*

The ocean breeze kicked up, so I readied for the high-speed ride back down the mountain. As I climbed atop my seat, a sightseer with his two grandkids tapped me on the shoulder and said, "Excuse me, but you forgot your helmet." He handed me my helmet, which I had left on the picnic table. He may have saved my life.

For ten minutes later came the blur of events that left me lying on a stretcher: *barreling down a narrow straight-away . . . bending over in a tuck . . . my front tire rolling over a softball-size rock . . . the handlebars locking to the left . . . flying headfirst over the handlebars . . . landing on my left shoulder . . . the back of my head slamming against the dirt.*

Blackout.

It's hard to say how long I was unconscious; no one witnessed the wipe-out. I'd later learn that a pair of hikers had found me moaning on the trail, my helmet still strapped to my head but cracked in two pieces. When I came to, I saw two of everything and the ground swayed up and down, side to side, as if I were on a boat. Blood ran down my legs, which were mangled with cheese-grater scrapes made even more painful by the dirt in the fresh wounds. Twenty feet or so down the trail lay my bike, the front tire twisted like a pretzel. I couldn't remember my name. When the female hiker asked me what I was doing, I, for the life of me, couldn't figure out why I was there.

The paramedics check my pupils, ask me to count their fingers, ask questions I don't have the foggiest idea how to answer. They tell me not to move, so I lie here afraid that my second chance at a professional hockey career was indeed too good to be true, that the dream has just evaporated in the split-second twist of a handlebar.

"Is there someone we should call?" an EMT asks me as though I were retarded, which, actually, I suddenly am. "My wife," I mumble. But I can't remember our home phone number.

A few minutes later, Brooke gets a call at home from an unusually calm voice saying, "Your husband has had a bike accident," and she starts shaking.

The four-wheel-drive ambulance carries me down the bumpy trail and a half-hour later pulls to a quick stop outside the emergency room, where I become the star of a scene right out of *E.R.* A nurse cuts my shorts and shirt off my body. A doctor shines a light in my eyes. He asks me to bend my knees; I do. He asks me to wiggle my toes; I do. I raise my right arm, and it's seemingly uninjured. But when I try to lift my left arm off the bed, a sharp pain shoots across my left shoulder blade, the bones grinding against each other. I almost pass out from the pain.

A nurse then wheels me under a giant x-ray machine and tells me to remain still.

A doctor pricks a needle in my toes. "Can you feel that?" he asks.

If I don't feel the needle, more than a hockey career would be over. Luckily, thanks to my helmet, I feel every single prick.

* * *

On the same day that I suffer a nasty mountain-biking accident, there's big news down in Bakersfield that might make my worries about my shoulder all for naught. The Condors have fired Mack and hired a new coach, Topeka Scarecrows head coach Paul Kelly. According to a Topeka newspaper:

> Paul Kelly, who coached the Topeka Scarecrows of the CHL for the past four years, was introduced Thursday as the new coach of the Bakersfield (Calif.) Condors of the West Coast Hockey League. Kelly, who was named the CHL coach of the year last season, after leading the lame-duck professional franchise to the play-offs, left the Scarecrows when they became an amateur team. He replaces Kevin MacDonald, who was fired after three seasons as Bakersfield's coach after a 26–36–10 finish. The Condors, like the Scarecrows, are owned by successful Wall Street trader Jonathan Fleisig.
>
> "It's definitely a good league," Kelly said, "and I'm excited about the opportunity."
>
> Kelly considered several options after leaving the Scarecrows and said that as recently as last week he was contacted by a team that could go into Kansas City and play in the new league formed by the merger of the Central and Western Professional leagues.
>
> "There are drastic changes happening in hockey with the IHL folding and the CHL and WPHL merging," he said. "But I definitely feel this is a very, very sound organization. I never had any problems with Jonathan. He and I were very up-front and honest with each other."
>
> Kelly will have to adjust to a few changes–the WCHL allows teams more veterans and a higher salary cap–but some familiar faces should help ease the transition. Many of last year's Scarecrows could become Condors.
>
> "I've talked to quite a few, actually, and informed them of the situation," Kelly said. "I feel like a good portion of them will probably go with me."

It's not necessarily good news. In pro hockey, everything changes when a new coach comes to town. He brings in new players, sets new rules. He doesn't even know about the goofy writer-guy who wants to make a comeback at age thirty-one with his team. I call Jonathan Fleisig.

"Now that Paul Kelly is the coach, am I still welcome?" I ask.

"It's up to him," Jonathan says. "I'll talk to him."

* * *

The injury report from my mountain-bike accident is nothing short of miraculous: a mild concussion, severely torn muscles in my left shoulder, and scrapes across the left side of my body from head to toe. And a really bad headache for the next week. But I have no broken bones, no skull fractures from slamming my head against the rocky bike trail, no dislocated shoulder joints.

I won't be able to play hockey for over a month. But my dream is still very much alive.

* * *

A week after my accident, I receive a fax from my endocrinologist at the University of San Francisco Medical Center. No matter how many times I get my blood drawn, I always dread the moments before seeing the results of my blood tests. Fortunately, the results show that my hormonal makeup is normal, that there is no biochemical evidence of the tumor growing back. In fact, my testosterone levels are higher than normal, which may explain my recently acquired machismo, in the form of my need to scale mountains, lift weights, and block hockey pucks with my body. If anything, the results confirm that I am wired for hockey, one of the most brutal sports known to man.

* * *

My injured left shoulder actually focuses my training. I become more intent on working out and getting stronger, and the shoulder stretches remind me how vital flexibility is for a goalie.

Throughout the length of Brooke's trip—the entire month of July—I adhere to a strict training regime. When she returns, I have hardly any fat on my body and, while I have a long way to go until my goaltending skills are anywhere near a pro level, I'm in the best shape of my life. I stand naked before our bedroom mirror every morning and hardly recognize the lean body I see. I have transformed myself in a matter of months from a flabby writer to a fit hockey player, and I haven't even had to drink a glass of raw eggs.

Stress has always brought out the best in me. The first time I ever stopped more than fifty shots in a game was the day my father got into a huge fight with my mother and moved out of the house for good. I was twelve. A teammate's dad had to drive me to the game in Rochester against the first-place team. I stopped sixty shots and we won 3–2. The opposing team's coach said he had never seen such a display of goal-tending domination.

I always played better when the pressure was on. It was the games that didn't matter in which I played like shit. Now, with the specter of being athletically unprepared, of going into major debt, of living away from Brooke, I am more resilient and determined than ever. I might have good health, a good job, a nice place, rich neighbors, a wonderful wife, and a loyal dog, but I now realize what has been missing from my Mill Valley life over the last two years: a challenge.

Prepare

Every few days, I check out the Condors Web site to read press releases announcing the acquisition of new players and other roster moves. I'm thrown into despair when on August 14, I read this one:

CONDORS SET BETWEEN THE PIPES
CARAVAGGIO, HAY MAKE THE MOVE FROM TOPEKA

BAKERSFIELD, Calif.–The Bakersfield Condors have taken an important step in solidifying their roster for the upcoming season. Their goaltending tandem is now completed, with the signing of Luciano Caravaggio and Scott Hay. Both have followed Head Coach Paul Kelly from Topeka.

The veteran Caravaggio played 40 games with the Scarecrows in the Central Hockey League last season, compiling a 3.15 goals-against average and stopping 89.9 percent of the shots he faced. He finished in the top five among Central League netminders in wins, shootout wins, and minutes played. Hay appeared in 31 games during what was his rookie season, compiling a 16–12–3 record with a 3.72 GAA.

"Looch (Caravaggio) is one of the most consistent and hard-working goalies that I've been associated with, and I'm pleased to have him back with my team this year," said Condors Head Coach Paul Kelly. "Last year he showed me something–that he could concentrate through adversity. Hay is a fiery competitor who really came into his own last season,"

Kelly continued. "Last year he had a strong rookie season, and showed he could handle the work. I expect big things out of both this season; they give us a quality duo of goaltenders that we can feel confident about."

The 25-year-old Caravaggio was selected by the New Jersey Devils in the 6th round (number 155 overall) of the National Hockey League's Draft in 1996. Before joining Kelly in Topeka last year, Caravaggio led the New Mexico Scorpions of the former Western Professional Hockey League to a 101-point season, and the President's Cup finals in 1999–2000.

Last season was Hay's first as a professional, following a junior career in the Ontario Hockey League. In his last season of junior competition with the Sarnia Sting, the Scarborough, Ontario, native won 16 games with a 4.25 GAA. The duo combined for the sixth best goals against in the Central League last season.

The 2001–02 season opener is 59 days away with the Bakersfield Condors playing the Long Beach Ice Dogs at Centennial Garden on Friday, October 12.

I can't help but think that in fifty-nine days it will be "here we go again" time. In college, I not only battled myself, but the coach always pitted me against other goalies whom he favored. The coach never thought I was first-string material. When I played lousy, he would sit me the next night, but when another goalie stunk up the joint, he would show confidence in them and start them the next game. It's *déjà vu.*

* * *

The games in Oakland and San Francisco with a group of salesmen, stockbrokers, and construction workers have not prepared me enough. I need to face more skilled players before heading to Bakersfield. When the 100 mph slap shots start flying at me in a month, I could very well make a total ass out of myself—not to mention get myself killed.

With nowhere in California offering a high level of competition, I called Kris Hicks, my hockey coach from ages thirteen to eighteen. Kris started Buffalo's only junior hockey team in 1987, in the fall of my senior year of high school. Back then we were called the Niagara Scenics, named after a local bus company, but the team has since been renamed the Buffalo Lightning. Kris had cultivated my talent over the years and in my senior year founded a team that would bring me in regular competition with players from hockey hot beds in Detroit and Canada. But, just as I had lost touch with everyone else in the hockey world after retiring, we had not spoken in about twelve years.

"Sorry to hear about your dad, Kenny," Kris said when I called. A rotund man with a perpetual smile, Kris served as a father figure for me throughout my teens; he saw me endure my parents's divorce, saw me bring a girl to the rink for the first time, and helped me decide where to go to college. But, like the rest of my friends and family, he didn't know that I had been battling a brain tumor since I was fifteen. He didn't learn of my plight until a few months ago when he read about my first memoir in *The Buffalo News*. "We saw your story in the paper," he said. "I wish I would have known what you were going through. Maybe I could have helped."

When I tell him why I am calling, that I am attempting to make a comeback in order to end my career on my—rather than a tumor's—terms, he replies without hesitation, "I will help you in any way I can."

"But," he adds, "You sure you wanna come back? I mean, it's been a while."

That's when I tell him about The Dream, how I am haunted by not ever taking my hockey career to the pro level, that it's not a matter of choice. "I have to try, or I will always regret it," I say.

"Kenny, you know I'm your biggest fan. I've been coaching in Buffalo for twenty years, and you're still the best goalie to ever come out of here. We still talk about you."

He invites me to practice with the Lighting in the first week of September back in Buffalo, where my hockey dream began long ago.

* * *

It's Labor Day weekend and, since my first practice isn't until tomorrow, Kris and Kyle, my two brothers still living in Buffalo, have come over to our mother's house for a cookout. As the sun sets and the mosquitoes swarm, I take a seat on the back porch with Norm, the man my mother married a few years after divorcing my father, the man who taught me how to drive because my father nearly had a heart attack the first time he went out with me. Clutching a can of beer, Norm tells me a story about how he blasted a raccoon with his shotgun a few years ago after a pack of them hissed at my mom. "The little sucker exploded into a million pieces," he says, adjusting his Buffalo Bills cap.

Norm is an electrician at the GM plant in downtown Buffalo; a blue-collar straight-shooter. I figure he will tell me whether I am crazy for trying to play hockey at thirty-one. Norm and I sit alone on the porch, and I ask him what he thinks about my comeback.

"It makes sense to me," he says. "You have a second chance, and you want to go for it. It was your dream when you were young. It was the only thing you wanted."

"I want to play," I say. "But I don't know what I really want out of this season."

"Your goal, you mean."

"Yeah. What is my goal? Like do I want to just see how far I can take it? Or do I really want to have a career and play till I am thirty-five? I'm not sure what I want."

"Seems to me, you have to go back. You have to find out what you want." He gulps his beer. "You have to go back, but make sure of one thing: Don't lose your marriage over it."

* * *

Practice isn't until three o'clock, so I have enough time to drive Mom's car over to the hockey supply store beforehand, where I buy a new stick—lined with Kevlar, the material they use in bullet-proof vests—and a new blocker and catching glove. I've put five hundred bucks that I don't have on my credit card by the time I leave.

"Forever Young," that cheesy Rod Stewart song, is playing on the radio as I pull into the parking lot of Holiday Twin Rinks. I must have played here over a hundred times when I was a kid. I remember stopping then-18-year-old Sabres rookie Alexander Mogilny on a break-away during a summer-league game, back when I was a high school hot shot.

Hicksie is in the locker room when I enter. "Bakes!" He gives me a bear hug, his belly coming between the two of us. "You look great, Kenny."

"What were you expecting?" I ask, dropping my equipment bag on the floor.

"A fat shit like me!" he says with a chuckle.

Then arrives Chris Economou, my goaltending partner in the 1987–1988 season, who now serves as the Lightning's goalie coach. He stops dead in his tracks upon seeing me. "Holy fuckin' shit!" Chris says, slapping me with a high-five. "Looks who's here. Kenny fuckin' Baker!"

When he learns about my comeback, Chris tells me how the five years after I left Buffalo were real tough ones for him, that he spent too much time drinking and, well, just rotting in the Rust Belt. Then, in 1995, he decided to chase his dream of playing pro hockey before it was too late. He ended up dressing for a team in Waco for thirteen games before they cut him. It devastated him.

"When you walk into the rink, you have to be all business," he says. "For those two hours, it is all focus on what you have to do. And they'll fuck with you. Watch your back."

"Who will fuck with me?" I ask.

"The other goalies, the coaches, the guys who don't like you for no good reason. They are there to win, at whatever cost. They won't care about you. You will have to make them care about you. Pro hockey is a tough fuckin' business, Bakes."

Out on the ice, Chris orders me through a series of movement drills to see what I've got. Shuffle to the right, to the left. Drop to the knees. Stack the pads both ways. On my ass and up again. I perform a series of "half-butterfly" pad saves. The half-butterfly is perhaps the most physically awkward and contorting move for a goalie. It involves dropping down on both knees—but not flat on the kneecaps. In order to flare your legs out to the side to cover the lower part of the net, you have to flex the inside knee ligament to keep the inside edge of the pads flat on the ice. The flared out pads look like the two wings of a butterfly.

Chris schools me in the fundamentals that, like any student who hasn't been to school in almost ten years, I have mostly forgotten. He corrects me when my stick is not flat on the ice in front of my skates, or when my glove isn't being held up high enough to cover the upper corner of the net. As I take shots from the guys—their average age is sixteen and a half—he tells me to come out more, cut down the angle, to go down and not stand up so much. "The position has changed," he says. "Back when we played you only went down on your knees when you had to. Nowadays, the guys shoot so fast that you just go down on everything to cover the lower part of the net. The key is timing—not to go down too early so they fire it over you. It used to be a game of reflexes. Now it's all about positioning." By the end of the two hours, I am spent and my right groin aches.

In the parking lot, I learn why Chris is so enthusiastic about helping me make a successful comeback.

"Let's face it, Bakes," he says. "I screwed up. After you left for college, I played another year with the Scenics and then tried out at Buffalo State. Then I flunked out because I didn't go to class. Then I didn't do anything for two and a half years. I was working in a liquor warehouse on the night shift thinking, 'What am I doing? I'm not an idiot. I can do something with my life.'

"But, first, I wanted to have peace with hockey and try to go pro. So I got in shape, skated, and played a little. When they cut me in Waco, I had five hundred dollars to my name. I was crying, just totally messed up. I was driving north out of Dallas on I-35 and pulled over. I got out of my piece-of-shit car and started breaking my goalie sticks over a guard rail. The people driving by must have thought I was a fucking nut, which I was. I lost it, dude. I thought it was the end of the world, but now I realize it was the beginning of a new one. I see more of the game as a coach, get more out of it. Now I want to make it to The Show, as a coach. That's my goal: the NHL."

Before the Lightning practice the next day, my little brother—who is excited to see me play after almost ten years—and I stop by the Pepsi Center, the Sabres practice facility north of the city, to watch a pre-training camp scrimmage. The spanking new four-rink complex didn't exist when I was a kid. All the rinks back then were dark and musty and you'd never have more than two rinks under one roof.

A young goalie prospect, Tom Askey, who is from Buffalo, is in the nets. He's only twenty-five and has the flexibility of a gymnast, two qualities that make me burn with envy and awe. *If only I could turn back the clock.*

The Sabres' first-string goalie, Martin Biron, the 25-year-old who backed up the departed veteran and all-time-greatest goalie Dominik Hasek last season, walks past our spot on the bleachers. Biron, a Frenchman, is over 6 feet tall and not much more than 160 pounds soaking wet—a beanpole compared to myself. I am down to about 165.

"See, Kris," I say. "I'm not too skinny."

"But, Kenny," Kris replies. "He sucks." *Good point.*

At practice, Economou runs me through an even more intense series of drills. Afterward, my newfound personal goalie expert hands me a thick pamphlet he calls "the bible." It's called *Mitch Korn's Goaltender Manual,* written by Mitch Korn, the former goalie coach of the Sabres who now coaches the NHL's Nashville Predators. Mitch is a "goalie guru," one of the dozen or so true scholars of the position. He helped Hasek win his four Vezina Trophies as the NHL's best goalie. I had attended Mitch's goalie camps as a teen-ager, but had since lost contact during my nine-year hiatus from the sport. Chris is Mitch's protégé, or, as he calls himself, "Mini-Mitch."

"Mitch has helped me as a coach," he explains. "If you follow his bible, you will have success."

While at my mom's house that night stretching my sore legs and reading Mitch Korn's seventy-six-page goalie bible, the phone rings. It's Economou, and he doesn't sound quite as fired up as he has been the last few days.

"Hey, Bakes," he says. "I was thinking today how it's too bad L.B. isn't here to see you come back."

"L.B." is what my friends used to call my dad, short for Larry Baker, because he was the cool-guy kind of father who never fit the "Mr. Baker" moniker. On bus trips, my dad would sit in the back and shoot the shit with the players. Like most of my friends, Economou was good buddies with L.B., who died six years ago when he was only fifty-one. It was tragic. "I really miss that guy," Chris continues. "He was a piece of work."

"Yeah," I say. "The problem was that he was too much of a piece of work. The chain-smoking did him in."

Even after my miserable senior year of college hockey, Dad pushed me to play pro. "You're still young enough to play, you know," he'd say in our near-daily phone conversations in 1993 when I was living in Washington, D.C., working as a grunt at ABC News. Dad was almost always at home on the couch, suffering from neuropathy, a diabetic condition in which the nerves in his arms and legs were dying; unable to work due to the pain, he had recently started collecting Social Security disability payments. He was living on Vicodin and an assortment of other pain pills and, after he was diagnosed with emphysema, he couldn't breathe without the help of an oxygen tank. He would only take off the mask to steal a puff of a cigarette. "I would play if I could," he'd say. But it was easy to dismiss his urging as being more about his own self-regret than mine.

But three years after I left hockey even *his* encouragement went away. It wasn't the diabetes that got him. My father, who had smoked two packs a day of unfiltered Pall Malls since he was thirteen, came down with lung cancer. Within a few months it had spread to his back and neck. He died on a blustery afternoon in February 1995. So did his dream that he would someday see me play pro hockey.

When The Dream came to me nearly five years later, and I began my comeback, it wasn't for my father. In fact, until I got to Buffalo I hadn't thought much about him. Now that I'm here, and he isn't, I realize that I'm angry that he won't be able to see me realize the dream we shared for so many years. I'm angry at him for smoking himself to death.

"I wish he were here to see me," I tell Economou.

"He is, Bakes. He is."

Economou adds, "You're going to have success this year, I feel it. Just wait for your chance. Remember that luck is preparation meeting opportunity. Prepare, and when the opportunity comes you will have luck. I know it."

"But don't you think I'm a little old?"

"Bakes," he says, "Hasek is thirty-seven. Patrick Roy is thirty-six. They are the two best goalies in the world. Goalies get better as they get older."

A few days later, on my flight back to San Francisco, I take stock. After my first full week of practice in over nine years, I'm better prepared for Bakersfield than when I left, but it has come at a price: a sore right groin, sore left hamstring, a bruised knee, a sore lower back. In Bakersfield, where the training camp starts in just twenty days, I will skate nearly every day for 218 straight days. I will have to play through injuries, play when I am sick and when I am tired. It will be my job. Before I start feeling too defeated, I read a quote from rookie NFL quarterback Quincy Carter in *ESPN The Magazine*: "Who wants it easy? If everything was easy, everybody would be doing it."

* * *

My little brother wakes me up with a phone call at six-thirty in the morning. "Turn on CNN, Kenny," he says breathlessly. "You won't believe what's going on."

A few minutes later, Brooke and I lie on the couch in tears, holding each other as horrifying images of the World Trade Center towers crumbling to the ground rock our senses. Thousands wander the sidewalks amid a post-Apocalyptic fog. Airports are shut down. Our president is in hiding. A local TV station reports that National Guard troops are stationed at the Golden Gate Bridge. It's a living nightmare.

If I can see anything clearly through the dust billowing over Manhattan it is the thousands of dreams that died with those thousands of victims. All of us wake up every day with dreams that we let die. In a world where your life can be ended in a sudden act of terror, chasing dreams seems more important than ever.

Trust

The average player in the West Coast Hockey League makes $13,000 a season. The average player in the National Hockey League makes $1.64 million a season. And there's a good reason NHLers make so much more money: They are better.

The giant talent chasm separating guys like me from guys like *them* doesn't stop me from wondering if I could someday be as good as they are. So I've spent the last few weeks phoning the ice rink in San Jose where the Sharks practice, trying to find out when Sharks players are playing in pre-training-camp scrimmages. I want to play against them, just to see how I compare to real pros.

But no one from the Sharks ever calls me back. Finally, with the help of the team's P.R. guy, I contact the Sharks' goalie coach, Warren Strelow, one of the most revered goalie coaches in the history of the game. Strelow coached Jim Craig when he won the gold medal in the 1980 Olympics and has coached every U.S. Olympic team goalie since, in addition to Martin Brodeur of the New Jersey Devils.

I left several messages on Strelow's cell phone explaining who I am and how I want to meet him. He never called back. But this morning I read on the Sharks Web site that the team was holding an intra-squad scrimmage this afternoon and it was open to the public. Immediately, I phoned Brandon, my eleven-year-old "little brother" in the local Big Brother program. Brandon, who has met his father only a few times, has been raised by his mom still. He is a sports nut. We've gone to Warriors basketball games, a 49ers game, played street hockey at the playground by my house. He's yet another person I am going to miss when I head down in a few weeks to "B-town," as the locals call it.

My plan is to sneak my way into the Sharks locker room and find a way to meet Strelow. In case he's interested in seeing what I got, I pack my equipment in the car. Strelow is a legend, the kind of guy who, if he thinks I have potential, could put in the right call to the right person and get me a tryout with an NHL team.

Inside the rink, I walk the perimeter trying to pull open closed doors. Finally, one opens. "You sure we're allowed in here?" Brandon asks.

We slink down the hallway and the next thing we know we're standing just outside the Sharks dressing room. The carpeted room makes Bakersfield's look like a utility closet. A few muscular guys in light-blue long johns walk past us, and since I recognize one of them as Owen Nolan, the team captain, I ask him where I can find Warren Strelow.

"Right there," Nolan says, pointing to a gray, balding man with the build of John Candy.

"That guy?" I ask.

"Yep," Nolan says. "In the giant flesh."

Ever the fifth-grade jokester, Brandon looks at Strelow and mutters, "He's so fat, he's from *both* sides of the family."

Warren is sitting in a windowless room alone watching a video-tape. When I enter, Warren strains to see us through his thick glasses and I glance at the TV and see it's the 1991 NHL All-Star game. Mike Vernon and Patrick Roy are the goalies. Wayne Gretzky is playing. It's a classic. But why he's watching it alone in a room is anyone's guess.

"Hey, Warren," I say. "It's Ken Baker, the goalie."

Warren looks at me askance, like I'm speaking Swahili.

"Huh?" Warren grunts.

"I'm the goalie who called you."

"Yeah," he says plainly. "O.K."

He strains his eyes to identify me and then quickly turns his focus back to the TV screen. "I know who you are," he says. "You played at Colgate. I think I scouted you a few times."

Warren apparently is more interested in a game from ten years ago than this stalker standing before him, so to break the ice I tell him I watched the Buffalo Sabres training camp last week. When he doesn't seem to care, I ask, "Do you know Mitch Korn?"

"He's in Nashville," he says. "I know who he is."

"He used to coach me," I say.

"Oh," Warren says, obviously uninterested. "What does he have to say?"

I reply, "Mitch said the position has changed a lot in the last ten years."

"The position changes *every* year," he snaps, his eyes still fixed on the TV. Warren is either really shy or really annoyed that I found him hiding out in the coach's room.

Then in walks Darryl Sutter, the Sharks head coach and a former star with the Chicago Blackhawks. Sutter is as friendly as Strelow is not. Sutter shakes Brandon's hand and smiles. "Hey, there, son," he says to Brandon, who blushes when he realizes that he has just met Darryl Sutter, who promptly shakes my hand. "Nice to meet ya."

Sutter tells Brandon to look over to the other locker room at the goalie who is getting dressed. "That's Evgeni Nabokov, last season's rookie of the year," he says with a faintly British-Ontario accent.

I am awed for the first time since I stalked Tom Barrasso for his autograph after Sabres games when I was in junior high school. In fact, in my five years as a celebrity journalist I have never been so starstruck—and I've met every Hollywood bigwig. Since the NHL expanded beyond the Original Six franchises in 1967, only four other goalies have won the NHL's rookie of the year: Tony Esposito (1970), Ken Dryden (1972), Ed Belfour (1991) and Martin Brodeur (1994). I am in the presence of greatness.

As I watch Nabokov, who also made the All-Star team last year, get his gear on, Strelow introduces me to Sutter as "Steve" Baker, and explains that I am a goalie trying out for Bakersfield this year.

Sutter smirks, as if it's amusing to him that someone so old and skinny thinks he can be a pro hockey goalie. "Great," he says. "Well, good luck to ya."

Warren struggles to his feet and grumbles, "I have to get upstairs and scout the goalies for the scrimmage. Sorry, but I can't let you skate. Insurance issues. I can't help you. But you're more than welcome to watch the game."

"Just watch Nabokov," he adds. "He is the real deal. All you need to do is watch him."

I thank Warren, and as Brandon and I turn and head back to the stands, Nabokov, now fully dressed, bounds past me. He's 6 feet tall and absolutely imposing in his bulky equipment. Being from Kazakhstan, an old Soviet republic, he speaks broken English, and I'm not sure if I should even bother talking to him. But this might be my only chance to ever speak directly to an NHL goalie. Maybe he will give me that one bit of brilliant advice that inspires me to NHL greatness.

Fortunately, Warren shows some charity and chimes in, "Nabby, I want you to meet someone. This is Steve Baker. He's a goalie, trying out for Bakersfield in the West Coast League." (I let it slide that he keeps calling me Steve.)

Nabokov played three seasons in the AHL and IHL before making the Sharks in 1999. He has to be aware of the WCHL. He takes off his blocker and kindly shakes my hand. He looks at me not like a peon, but like a member of a fraternity, that of pro goalies. With respect. I feel I'm in the presence of royalty, which I am.

"How's it going?" I ask nervously.

"Getting ready," he says. "It should be good year. We see."

"Got any advice for me?"

"Any *what*?" Nabokov asks Strelow. "What duz he say?"

Warren saves the conversation from sinking into total absurdity, shouting on my behalf, "DO-YOU-HAVE-ANY-ADVICE-FOR-HIM?"

Somehow, Warren's nurseryschoolspeak works.

"Oh, oh," Nabokov says apologetically. A few seconds later, he looks me in the eye and says, "Stop da puck."

* * *

Cliff is my barber. He cuts hair at a shop in downtown Mill Valley. I don't even know his last name, but every time I come in he knows everything about me by the time I leave.

"Hey, Cliff. You know, this will be my last haircut here for the next seven months," I say as he snaps a smock on me.

"Why?" he asks, snipping away.

"I'm moving to Bakersfield."

Cliff puts his hands on his hips and glares at me as if he just found head lice.

"Bakersfield?" he says. "No one goes to *Bakersfield.*"

* * *

I am set to leave in two days, and rarely has a day gone by when I haven't wondered whether quitting my job, moving away from my wife and dog in order to move to a dusty oil-and-agriculture town to play minor-pro hockey is the most idiotic thing I could ever do.

Nevertheless, I go to the gym every day, climb the Stairmaster, lift weights, stretch my increasingly pliable muscles, all in an effort to make sure I am strong enough to endure the marathon that is a seven-month, seventy-four-game minor-pro hockey season.

In college, amid the hockey-playing days when I would make a fitful search for the strength to recapture my on-ice brilliance, I searched for inspiration in the essays of Ralph Waldo Emerson. Unaware that a brain tumor was subverting my attempts at self-improvement, I nonetheless hoped Emerson's words would improve my "inner" game. I remember reading Emerson's words, "Trust thyself: Every heart vibrates to that iron string," and then going out the next day to practice, infused with a newfound faith in myself, only to fail. In Bakersfield, there will be forces working against me, but not a tumor. This time, I will truly be able to trust myself.

At night, I lie in bed with Brooke and talk ad nauseam about my ever-expanding list of insecurities. Only Brooke knows how scared I am. She always dutifully listens to my verbal neuroses. *What if I get hurt in the first week? What if the coach doesn't like me? What if I don't pass the physical?*

When we go to the Sweetwater Cafe, Mill Valley's hipster hangout on Friday nights, our friends pepper us with even more questions: "How will you guys handle being apart?" "Who will watch Arthur?" (He has grown up for the last two years by my side virtually day and night, and certainly will miss me.) "Aren't you too small for pro hockey?" We respond to all of them as convincingly as possible, even though we don't know whether the answers are right.

* * *

Brooke hasn't been looking forward to my leaving for Bakersfield. Yesterday, the phone company turned off my work phone, which for me, as a writer, has been my single most important piece of equipment other than my computer; tonight, Brooke's throwing a going-away party for me; tomorrow, home delivery of the *Chronicle* ends. Monday, I will pack up the car and leave.

Our closest friends show up at the party. As I supervise operations at the barbecue, Brooke secretly takes Polaroids of everyone and pastes their picture in a photo album, next to which they scribble *bon voyage* notes.

—I've got one word for you, kid: adventure. Keep it up.
—Knock 'em dead, Ken! We'll miss you.
—I trust you'll make Bakersfield, finally, a destination place.

Later, after everyone has left, Brooke and I cuddle on the couch. Arthur lies on the ottoman. I'm gonna miss that guy, too. "You know," Brooke says, "there are a lot of girls who are going to be after you down there."

I tell her not to worry, that they're all probably ugly, and to remember that, even though I'm moving away for a while, she is still my wife. I don't mention the newspaper story I read last month about a recent Oregon State University study, titled, "When Sports Heroes Stumble," that found that infidelity and general extramarital hanky-panky is rampant among professional athletes. Among the report's findings were that "a culture of adultery" permeates professional sports and that pro athletes often have a "fast-food sex mentality." The study analyzed the marriages of basketball, baseball, football, and hockey players. "Not all of the husbands were having affairs," the study concluded, "but the fear of the possibility that he might have an affair was there, and that's very stressful."

It's our last night together, and I hold her tightly, knowing that tomorrow I will let go of someone I love for the next seven months in order to pursue something else I love. I want to feel whole, so I can hold her as a strong, satisfied man with no regrets. Right now, I am not yet that man.

FIRST PERIOD

SEPTEMBER 24, 2001

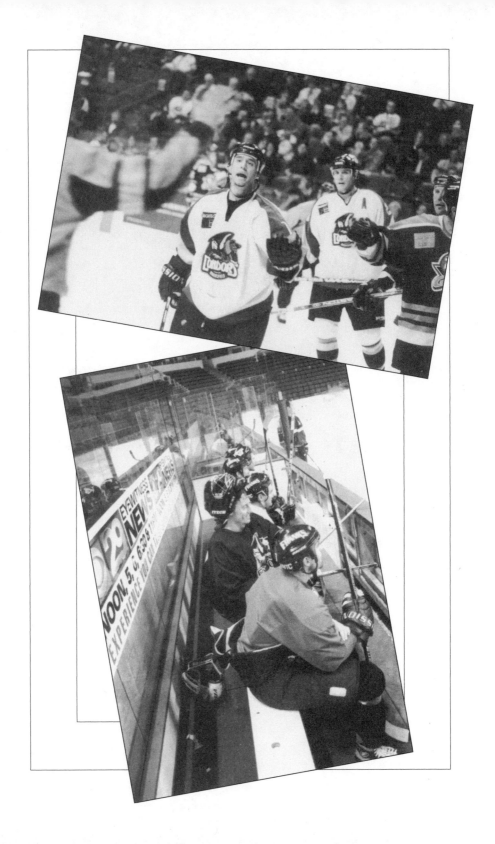

Remember

When I wake, Brooke is gone. We decided it would be easier on both of us if she left for school and avoided a tear-jerking, Hollywood-style goodbye. She took Arthur with her. I had that hockey-playing dream twenty-one months ago and, were it not for Brooke's support, I still might be sitting on the couch watching ESPN, wondering "what if?"

I load the used truck I bought with all of my book-advance money (working at home for the last year, I haven't needed a car). I will carry down the bare essentials: two suitcases, a backpack and, of course, my hockey equipment. It looks more like I'm going on a week-long vacation than a seven-month journey on the minor-league hockey circuit, but I will soon learn that I am bringing twice as much stuff as most of the other players, young men from Canada who pack lightly, partly because they don't have much and partly because, as minor-league hockey players, they know they can be fired and sent home at any time. Before closing the front door—the same door through which my old hockey equipment arrived almost two years ago, starting this anachronistic odyssey—I stand in the living room and look around. I glance at my empty writing desk, Arthur's sleeping blanket, a wedding photo of me and Brooke on the book shelf. I'm glad she's not here. If she were, I might change my mind. Leaving feels like a slap shot to the gut.

* * *

The bone-dry tumbleweeds dancing across the freeway is the closest I will come to a welcoming parade today. Tornadoes of dust spin wildly in the distance as I roll up the windows when a truck carrying onions passes me.

Bakersfield sits amid a mostly barren, flat-iron plain and is home to the highest airborne ozone levels in the United States, thanks to local industry. The backbone of Bakersfield's economy is oil and carrots. The city produces more oil than any other county in the United States and it supplies about 90 percent of the nation's carrot supply, which explains why the city is surrounded by irrigated green fields. When you combine the summer dust kicked up from the agriculture industry with the soot of the oil-refining process you get air the color of mud.

To many of its residents, though, Bakersfield is a hidden gem. It's laid-back and has nice weather year-round. Its housing costs are a third of those in L.A. Even so, the city has a serious P.R. problem with the rest of the state's population. Although local boosters accurately tout the tight-knit community feel of the three hundred thousand-resident city, the low real estate prices and the simplicity of life there, other Californians look at it like an ugly stepchild. The local newspaper recently published the findings of a survey that concluded, "The overwhelming majority of Californians have no interest in visiting Bakersfield, moving to Bakersfield or relocating their businesses to Bakersfield." Yet here I arrive, greeted by a pungent waft of hot, steaming manure blowing in from the fields.

The city's nine thousand-seat ice arena, Centennial Garden, is the only shiny new building in what is an otherwise aging downtown. The downtown's second-newest building, the Holiday Inn Select, is an eight-story concrete box, and will be my home for the next couple of weeks of training camp.

When I arrive at the hotel shortly before six o'clock, the thermometer on a bank down the street reads ninety-two degrees. Hardly hockey weather.

Training camp doesn't start for another three days, but I have come early so I can skate in pickup games with some of the team's other early arrivals, including Jamie Cooke, who has lived here year-round since he arrived three years ago after a season with the Idaho Steelheads. Any doubts I might have about why I'm here are further justified when, after handing me my key and informing me that my roommate is scheduled to arrive in two days, the pipsqueak hotel clerk chirps, "You don't look big enough to be a goalie."

When I call Jamie he invites me for sushi at a mini-mall (a common part of the Bakersfield landscape) out by the oil fields just west of downtown. I knew that Jamie and Beth had five kids, including two-year-old girl twins, but even so I am taken aback when I walk into the restaurant, and Jamie is sitting on his chair like a human jungle gym for three of his daughters as another daughter climbs atop the table. The kids are as cute as they are rambunctious. Beth, who I haven't seen in ten years, apologizes for the "controlled chaos" and gives me a warm hug. It might only be a polite hug to Beth and a firm handshake from Jamie, but they make me feel part of a family–of Colgate grads, of pro hockey vagabonds, of "old" guys still playing a kids' game in a place far removed from where we learned the game.

Jamie tells me he is looking forward to seeing how the new coach will do, especially since Mack suffered two losing seasons in a row before they fired him. Jamie admits that he almost retired after last season because Mack, who liked to shout and intimidate players, had taken the fun out of the game.

"The guys just didn't want to play for him," Jamie says. "He was too intense. At this level you are dealing with twenty different personalities. So many guys are here for so many different reasons. Some guys are here for fun, some want to make it to the next level, some are just wasting time before they quit, some are here to make money, some make nothing and just play to avoid the real world. Mack might be good at the junior level, where he could bark at the guys and light a fire. But it just didn't work with us."

"What's Paul Kelly's reputation?" I ask.

"From what I hear, he's a player's coach, one of the guys. He was a pretty good player in his day, drafted by the L.A. Kings. He's only thirty-four, which should help. He's a real character."

"How?"

Jamie cracks a smile and chuckles, "He likes to throw back a few with the boys."

Drinking was always one part of the game I didn't like; I have never been much of a drinker and was always amazed by the amount of alcohol some of the best hockey players can consume. My doctor says I shouldn't drink alcohol because, as the warning label on my antitumor medication reads, "It may aggravate side effects of this drug." Then again, the label also warns that I shouldn't perform "tasks requiring alertness," yet I am willingly playing one of the most dangerous positions in all of sports.

Jamie, having played AAA in the early nineties, talks a lot about "this level," as in, "most guys *at this level* aren't going to make it to the NHL" and, "even the best guys *at this level* only do one thing really well. If they did everything well, they would be *at the next level.*" Jamie has been at the next level, but he knows he will never return there. There's a hint of resolution in his voice. I suppose ten years of minor-league hockey does that to a player.

I tell him that I hope I can compete "at this level" because there is no pro level below this level. "But I'm worried about being a third guy," I admit. "I hear that teams hardly ever carry three goalies. I'm afraid I'll just get in the way."

"Well, you never know how the other goalies will react," Jamie says. "Goalies can be pretty insecure and territorial. They might let you work in, or they might not. At the end of the day, it will be up to Kells. I'm sure you will at least get some ice time before and after practice."

Before one of his twins snatches it, Jamie grabs the last California roll from the platter, and swallows it.

"Listen, Kenny," he says. "If you just show up, work hard, and be patient, you'll get a shot. Even if you don't make second string, there are always injuries. Always. I have yet to play a season where a third goalie wasn't brought in at some point. Just be patient, and I'm sure you'll get a shot."

Back at the hotel, I lie in bed hoping the TV will lull me to sleep. It doesn't. Around ten o'clock, I call Brooke. Knowing we faced the potential for massive cell phone bills (which we cannot afford) over the course of the season, we've signed up for a two-way radio plan where the calls are free; it's like using walkie-talkies. This technology will serve as my tether to the outside world, as well as the glue keeping our young marriage alive. We miss each other and tell each as much. But I don't get too sappy. This is my first night. I have to stay strong.

Finally, around midnight, I fall asleep with Mitch Korn's goalie bible in my hands. At 4:37 A.M. I pop awake and, unable to fall asleep, drive to an all-night diner near the interstate for breakfast. On the way I hear a sports-radio announcer report that Michael Jordan, 38, is expected to announce his NBA comeback later today. At 31, I might be old and crazy, but at least I'm in hallowed company.

The team has open ice at 10 A.M. for guys who want to scrimmage to get in skating shape. Around nine, I walk over from the hotel with my hockey bag slung over my shoulder, reminding myself of my self-imposed guidelines:

- Don't tell anyone about the shred of tumor still in my head. (I don't want sympathy or a built-in excuse for not being good enough.)
- Have fun, unlike the last time I played in college.
- Stay positive and work harder than the other goalies.
- Remember what Chris Economou warned: Watch my back.

I'm the first guy to arrive, except for the team's trainer, a chubby, buzz-cut Midwesterner named Larry, who tells me that only half the players will be skating today. Larry was the trainer for the Topeka Scarecrows last season and, along with eight players, was hired by Coach Kelly, whom he calls "Kells," which sounds like "Kellz."

"Dickie is the equipment guy," Larry says. "He'll get you set up." Larry walks me from the training room, a tiled room with a hot tub, and some padded benches, down a hallway to the locker room.

Dickie—Dick Earle is his full name, but, as I am learning, everyone in pro hockey has a nickname—is as grouchy as Larry is pleasant. Dickie has a thick mustache and furry eyebrows that curl downward on his forehead like a couple of crawling caterpillars.

"Put your stuff over there," he orders me, pointing at a corner stall. "This is your locker."

The location and size of each player's locker reflects his perceived value. As such, the two goalies from Topeka each have two stalls at the entrance to the ice. They already have their name plates glued on them. Luciano Caravaggio has the two stalls closest to the door, signaling that Kells has already pegged him as the number-one guy. Scott Hay, Caravaggio's backup last year in Topeka, is right next to him. My stall is directly across the room from theirs. Above me is the wall-mounted television, at such an angle that it is impossible to watch, and in front of me is the room's only plastic trash can. The cinder-block wall is stained from tobacco spit, and the carpet is stained from god-knows-what. As I hang up my gear on the hooks, other players trickle in.

The team's captain, Paul Willett, a minor-league hockey legend who was the West Coast league's MVP two years ago, takes his seat in the corner near the training room. Entering his twelfth season as a pro, "Willie" has pictures of his two little girls taped on the wall like it is his office, which it actually is. Willie is only a year older than I, but, like Jamie, the hockey grind has taken a toll on his scarred face and body.

Most of the stalls in my row are reserved for rookies and younger players, who, unlike the veterans, are fresh-faced and buff. I pull the brim of my baseball cap down toward my eyes and try to fit in.

I pretend not to notice when the goalies, Scott Hay and Luciano ("Looch") Caravaggio, walk in. I'm a little annoyed that Kells apparently has already decided who will be the number one, two and three goalies, making it clear that this team is not a meritocracy. Although Jonathan, the owner, had phoned me over the summer and said that I will have as much of a chance to play as the other goalies, Kells has already relegated me to the third string, even though he has never seen me play.

When Jamie walks in, I go over and shake his hand, happy to see someone I recognize. A group of Topeka guys–forwards Peter Brearley, Mark Edmundson and Jeff Goldie–are sitting near each other and get dressed, ignoring me and the rookies.

A few minutes later, Kells walks in and looks my way–"Hey, Baker," he says harshly–before moving on to crack jokes with the Topeka guys, muttering something about getting "shit-housed" last night at the bar. Everyone is Canadian except for me, Ryan, a defenseman from Minnesota, and Glen Mears, a veteran defenseman from Alaska, who has played in Bakersfield for the last five years. I overhear a few players talking about how the perpetually sunny weather in Bakersfield is tripping them out. "It's like that fuckin' movie *Groundhog Day*," Kells quips.

Kells reminds me of the actor Russell Crowe, but more the chubby tobacco executive Crowe played in *The Insider* than the svelte warrior in *Gladiator*. Kells dangles an unlit cigarette in his hand. "I'm going to smoke a dart," he tells Brearley and Edmundson, rubbing his belly fat.

"But it's training camp, Kells," Eddie says.

"I don't give a fuck," Kells says. "I ain't in training."

Clearly.

A player turns on the stereo to the local country station. The speaker is above my stall and it's SO LOUD that I just zone out and mind my own business as I get dressed. I will do a lot of zoning out for the next few days, minding my business like a good, little rookie.

The first one dressed, I grab my mask and walk across the locker room to the entrance to the ice. I walk past the other two goalies, who have been ignoring me the entire time, but I decide to break the ice and introduce myself.

"Are you trying out?" Looch asks as Hay laces up his skates and ignores me. Looch, who majored in math at Michigan Tech before getting drafted in the sixth round by the New Jersey Devils and going pro in 1998, is obviously the more talkative of the two tenders. Both are twenty-six. Looch is an inch shorter than I am and more muscular, while Hay is an inch taller and thirty pounds heavier. *Lucky I came in shape.*

"Did Kells mention me?" I ask.

"Not really," Looch says.

"I'm spending the season here," I say.

Looch says that he and Hay are both from the Toronto area and drove across the country together, arriving last night. *Great, they're friends. Two against one.*

On the ice, I mask my nervousness by playing the role of pro-hockey goalie: head up, shoulders back, a cocky swagger, projecting an image of confidence and competency even though I have not faced a 100 mph slap shot in almost ten years.

A half-dozen players form a semi-circle about thirty feet in front of me to fire "warm-up" shots. The pucks fly at me so fast and hard that a part of me (the sane part that has been sitting on my ass for the last nine years) doesn't want to get in the way. When I catch a puck, it stings my hand. I try not to think about how much it will hurt if I get hit in the neck. I'm not in Oakland anymore. These are pro shots–hard, fast and accurate.

Only a dozen or so guys come out for the scrimmage, many without shoulder pads and a helmet. When Looch and Hay take the ice, the guys shoot the stray pucks into the nets to start the scrimmage. Since I was the first goalie on the ice, I take one of the nets, which only seems fair. But that means one of us three must sit out.

Being a rookie and, well, something of an oddity who desperately wants to fit in, I don't want to piss off guys. So when Hay skates by I ask, "You wanna go in?" He shakes his head no and heads to the bench.

They decide to play a game up to five, meaning the first team to score five goals wins. It takes fifteen minutes or so, but my team loses 5–2, yet the goals are good ones. Looch simply outplayed me. Hay then hops the boards to take over for me. As I skate to the bench and pass Hay (who ignores me) I feel a sharp pain shooting through my right inner thigh. *Shit, my groin. I yanked it. Lovely. It's only Day One and my old body's already breaking down.*

We play three more games up to five goals, but neither goalie comes out of the net. It is normal rotation in scrimmages for goalies to replace each other after every game.

Finally, after my spending a half hour on the bench, Kells, who has been watching from the stands, walks down and says, "Baker, get in there." Being the number-one goalie, Looch is entitled to stay in the other goal until he wants to take a break. So I hop the boards and skate toward Hay, who pretends not to notice my return to the ice. *I'm baaaack.*

"Kells wants me in," I say abruptly.

"He's the boss," Hay snips, skating back to the bench.

I play solidly in the scrimmage, trying extra hard to impress Kells, who out of the corner of my eye I can see watching me. When I make a nice pad save, Mears chirps, "You're getting pretty fast in your old age."

No matter, though. Looch is just too damn good. Looch is not particularly fast and isn't much better on his feet as I am, but he plays solid positional goaltending, and thus he is almost always in the right place. Though I keep it close with some impressive saves, we lose 5–3. Nonetheless, I leave the ice having earned respect, if also the scorn of Hay.

"You looked pretty sharp out there today," Willie tells me afterward in the locker room. "You'll get in a couple games this year."

"Thanks, but talk to him," I say, pointing across the room to Kells.

Over the next two days we scrimmage, with more guys arriving and the games going quicker. A few of the guys are in great shape, obviously having worked out over the summer, while others, especially the older players, are flabby and sucking wind after a one-minute shift. In the NHL, players are expected to arrive at training camp in perfect shape. They get paid millions of dollars a year to be fit. But this is the WCHL, where players, almost all of whom will never even get a sniff of NHL action, make an average of five-hundred bucks a week. These minor-leaguers, like me, didn't have the luxury of working out all summer. They had jobs. Eddie worked at a golf course. John Vary mowed lawns. Ryan Hartung, one of only two Americans on the roster, tended bar in Minnesota. Jamie Cooke sold real estate. Mears, who is married and now lives in Bakersfield year-round, woke up every morning at four to inspect oil pumps. David Milek, a rookie who graduated from Guelph University in Ontario in the spring, worked as a lifeguard. Josh Maser worked on his family's cattle ranch in Alberta. Some taught at hockey schools. It's safe to say that none wrote magazine articles.

Ryan Hartung is a third-year pro, and it's immediately clear to me that he is also one of the nicest guys on the team, staying out late after practice each day and firing pucks at me. As Americans and college graduates, we share two things in common that I don't with most of the others. And, like me, he is on the small-ish side. At 5' 9", he's the shortest player on the team.

The goalies, however, aren't going out of their way to be friendly. Hay makes sure he takes the net before I can. I don't fight him on it; I can't. He's a second-year pro, and I am a rookie.

Back at the hotel one night, I plug my laptop into the phone and write Mitch Korn, with whom I started corresponding via e-mail after my training mission in Buffalo. I ask for advice on how to handle the politics of the three-goalie system.

> "Whether I play or not, I will be around these two guys for the whole season, presumably, and I don't want them to hate me," I write. "What should I do?"

In his reply, my goalie guru explains the concept of "goalie math":

> Mitch writes, "They are probably bonding because you are a common enemy . . . but that's just a guess. On most teams

that carry three goalies, number one gets along great with number three because number three aspires to be like number one and number one is not threatened by number three. But number two feels threatened by number three and he doesn't like him. Just be patient. Pro hockey is political. That's just the way it is. But the coach can't deny talent. Keep in mind: You are good, but you've been away from the game a long time."

Hit

The entire team gathers in the locker room for a seven o'clock meeting, the first team meeting of the year. Training camp officially starts tomorrow morning and the atmosphere is tense, like the first day of school when you don't know the teacher or other students very well. Kells walks in about ten minutes late, having been smoking on the loading dock with John Vary, a veteran defenseman who played for Kells in Topeka. Obviously, Kells won't be enforcing a strict training regime.

Kells breaks the silence with a joke.

"Eddie," he says looking with mock disgust at Edmundson. "You must have packed on thirty pounds over the summer. You have more chins than a Chinese phone book!"

The guys laugh. It worked. Kells broke the ice.

The training camp squad consists of twenty-four men ranging from ages twenty-one to thirty-seven. Three of the six rookies in camp will get cut. Teams can only carry twenty-one guys, and the league requires that three of them be rookies. Since I will likely serve as a practice goalie–at first, at least–and not be part of the roster, unless I play, I will not count as a rookie on the official roster.

Only three players are older than I am: Willett, Jamie, and Chris Felix, a former NHL defenseman who, at 37, is the oldest player in the WCHL. Felix, whose nickname is "Cat," is about 5' 9" on his tippy toes and his receding hairline has claimed half his skull. Felix's sunburned skin has the texture of an old leather shoe.

"Who's the old guy?" whispers Jason Sexsmith, a 21-year-old rookie from Manitoba.

"Chris Felix," I say. "He played for the Washington Capitals in the eighties and was on the '88 Canadian Olympic team."

"Holy shit," Sexsmith says. "*That's* Chris Felix? I remember watching him on TV when I was little."

After glancing at his notes, Kells clears his throat and begins his speech.

"Listen, I like to have fun as much as the next guy, but we are here for one reason, and that is to win," he says, pacing the carpet. "All we got is each other. This is a family, and we help each other. From the trainers, to the rookies, to the vets who have been here for years. You're not going to like everybody. But once you walk in the locker room, you treat everyone with fuckin' respect, you know what I mean?

"One of the rookies just asked me what the curfew was. There ain't no curfew. I'm not gonna baby-sit you guys. If you're out boozing the night before, I'll be able to tell. Some guys can do it, some can't. You have to be a pro, police yourself. Just remember: no drinking and driving. Take a cab. Fuck, I don't care if you call me at two in the morning because you are too shit-housed to drive home yourself."

At which point, Willett chimes in, "What if *you* are shit-housed?"

Kells doesn't miss a beat. "Then I'll have my wife pick you up!"

"But, seriously," he adds, "if you do get pulled over, don't pull this 'I play for the Condors' shit, because they don't care who you are around here."

Later, I ask one of the guys from Topeka why Kells is so worried about guys driving drunk. "He had a buddy die a few years ago in a car wreck," he said. "I guess it fucked him up pretty bad."

As I look around the room I think about how lucky I am just to have made it this far. Sure, this isn't the NHL, but it is pro hockey. It beats sitting on my ass all day along.

Hockey is a team sport. One of the most fulfilling aspects of team sports is the camaraderie. Our individual goals might be different, but we'll all need each other to get what we want. Some guys still dream of making it to the NHL, while others know they will never make it. Some guys will play their first pro game this season, others will play their last. I might play both.

Kells continues, "We have to have goals. There are eight teams in this league, everyone makes the play-offs. But we want home ice in the play-offs. That's our goal. So we want first or second place in our division."

The San Diego Gulls have won first place in our division for the last several seasons and are the defending league champions. They are the glamour boys of the WCHL. They have the highest attendance and the guys live near the beach. If Bakersfield is to win its first championship since joining the league in 1997, we will have to beat San Diego.

"I don't have a lot of rules," Kells says. "I want you to show up. Even if you're sick, you show up. None of this phoning in and going, 'Oh, I'm sick.' No, get your ass down here, we'll see if you're sick, and then you can go home. We've had some success in the past, but this town is starved for a winner. You guys are gods in this town, but you have to conduct yourself with class."

At times, Kells comes across as a driver behind the wheel of a big rig that he doesn't have a license for, and he doesn't do much to dispel this hardscrabble image when a Bic lighter falls out of his pocket. Yet the more the guy talks, the wiser he sounds. Under his drinkin'-buddy demeanor is a man who has learned most everything he knows about life by playing and coaching hockey, the only jobs he has ever had. And it's that school of education that I have enrolled in, and from which Kells, who played ten seasons of minor-pro hockey, appears to have learned some valuable lessons.

Kells then turns the floor over to Jamie, whom everyone calls "Cookie."

"It is a small town, and everyone knows your business," Cookie says. "So if you are out whoring around, people will know. So do what you do, but be careful about it."

"You know any good whores?" asks Brearley, an ape-ish forward with a beer gut. Everyone laughs.

Kells turns serious.

"Listen, guys," he says. "This is *a game*. The best fucking game in all of sports. Don't forget that. We're all getting paid to play a sport that thousands of kids only dream about doing. But you gotta be humble. Sure, you're playing pro hockey. But big fuckin' deal. Remember, you're playing the world's fastest sport at the eighth-highest level. We ain't a bunch of big wheels. We're minor league hockey players. This isn't the NHL; this is the WCHL. If we were good enough, we'd all be in the NHL. But, uh, guess what, guys? We ain't that good. Some of you might think you deserve to be up there, and some of you don't give a fuck anymore.

Whatever you think, I just ask that every time you show up to the rink you give me everything you got. If you don't, you're not only cheating yourself, but you're cheating me, my family, your teammates, the organization, and the fans. And I guarantee you, if you don't give a hundred and ten percent, you won't be around for long."

The meeting breaks and we line up for our preseason physicals. First up, the dental exam. Dr. Rimmer has the guys sit down one at a time on a bench in the training room. When my turn comes up, I ask him why he's checking our teeth—who cares if we have cavities?

"We check the fillings," he tells me.

"Why?" I ask.

"So when they get knocked out we know what was there in the first place."

Dr. Rimmer also checks our faces for scars and each is noted in our records. Felix has a six-inch scar across his neck that looks as if someone tried to behead him with a machete. Vary has several lumpy scars all around his chin; it takes Paul Rosebush, an otherwise good-looking guy, about a minute to show the doc all his scars. The longer they've played, the more scars they have. I don't have any. I peek over the shoulders of the guys as they fill out their dental forms and most check "yes" to having dental plates and crowns. Truckers get hemorrhoids, mail men get dog bites, and hockey players get scarfaces. I have the face of a writer.

I tip the scales at a trim 168 pounds. Larry then checks my blood pressure—a very healthy 118/78. And my pulse is a calm sixty beats a minute. Larry arches his eyebrows, impressed.

"Kells, this is embarrassing," Larry says to our coach, who is watching a baseball game a few feet away in the training room. "Check this out."

Larry promptly hands Kells my medical sheet. "Look," Larry says. "Baker has the lowest pulse on the team."

Kells hands it back to Larry. "So what," he says. "Baker should have the lowest pulse. He's dying of brain cancer!"

I think about correcting Kells, reminding him that I once had a *benign* brain tumor, but that I am—except for the little nugget left over—healthy now. But I don't. He wouldn't hear me, anyway. He's too busy laughing at his own joke. So I just smile.

In addition to a general health form—on which I don't mention the brain tumor, just in case the team decides I would be too much of a lia- bility—we all sign waivers acknowledging that we understand that play- ing hockey "can cause serious injury and/or death." Playing against old guys with 45 mph shots for the last year and a half, I have yet to experi- ence that side of the game. Undoubtedly, I will now.

Each of us also must be examined by Chris Hamilton, a local ortho- pedist, who surprises me by asking about my brain tumor.

"How'd you know?" I ask him.

"They told me," he says evenly. "It's kind of a big deal."

"Well, it's gone," I say.

"All of it?" he asks.

"Basically."

Somehow, I pass the physical.

After the physicals, Kells hands players white envelopes, inside of which is a wad of cash. Since this is training camp, in which all players are technically on a tryout, the league requires every player get paid meal money. "Here's your fuckin' money," Kells abruptly tells me. I don't know him well enough to know whether he is being mean or just kidding around. "Eighty-four bucks," he adds. When I offer a friendly "thanks a lot," Kells snaps, "Don't thank me. If it was up to me, you'd get shit."

* * *

The first few days of training camp we practice twice a day, with two- hour sessions in the morning and afternoon. On the first day, I patiently waited along the boards next to the net of both Hay and Looch as they took shots. Every so often, one of them would get tired and let me re- place them. It seemed to be working fine until Kells skated up to me and informed me, "I was thinking last night that these guys are going to wanna see a lot of rubber, so you should probably make sure you are getting out there early and after practice to get your maximum workout. Because I don't think you're gonna get it during the practice."

* * *

One benefit of doing nothing most of practice is at the end, when we do sprints for the last half hour, I have a lot of pent-up energy. I always beat the other goalies. If the coach won't give me a chance to beat them in the net, I will find other ways to score small victories. While skating during a really hard sprinting drill today, Brearley, huffing and puffing, skated up to me and quipped, "You still want to be a pro hockey player?" I skated harder and lapped Hay.

I refuse to complain. In college, I spent a season and a half riding the pines before I walked into the coach's office and asked why I wasn't starting. I have always felt that a coach must have authority and the players should respect that. But what makes my situation now so frustrating is that (*a*) I'm too old to waste time standing around picking my ass and (*b*) if Kells were smarter, he'd use me to motivate his goalies, especially Hay, who, as harsh as it sounds, tries as hard in practice as he does in dieting.

It's Saturday night, and I've just tasted my first two days of professional hockey, both an encouraging and discouraging venture. On one hand, I have proved that I can compete at this level. On both days I stayed out after practice and took shots from Willie, Cookie, and Jason Firth, a veteran and former Detroit Red Wings property. And I stop more than I let in. Yet while many of the players realize that I am the real deal, Kells has forced me to go out early and stay out late. During practice, I just stand around and stretch and work on various movement drills I have read in Mitch Korn's goalie bible. If this isn't annoying enough, I miss Brooke, whom I won't see for another week when she comes down for our first exhibition game at home against the Tacoma Sabercats, a game that I have very little chance of playing in.

If there ever was a good time to toss back a stiff drink, this is it. So I round up all the other rookies at the hotel, including my roommate Josh, a twenty-two-year-old who grew up on a farm outside of Medicine Hat, Alberta. He chews tobacco by the cheek-full, wears tight blue jeans with a giant metallic belt buckle, and he's always got on cowboy boots. Josh, technically, is not a rookie; he played his first year of pro last year in Austin, Texas, for the Ice Bats of the Western Pro League, which merged this summer with the Central Hockey League.

One indisputable fact: Josh sleeps a lot. After lunch, he will take an hour cat nap. In the evening, he will conk out for another two hours, get up and eat, usually a steak, and then go back to bed and sleep for ten hours.

One afternoon in our hotel room as Josh lies on his back watching cartoons, I read the training camp roster. According to the roster, Josh is

6' 1" and amassed 275 penalty minutes last season. Usually, if players receive more than 200 penalty minutes in a season, they're often so violent that they end up in jail. And this is my roommate.

"Two hundred seventy five penalty minutes?" I ask him.

"Yeah, so?"

"You're a goon?" I ask.

"Depends what you call a goon," he chortles. "I'm a fighter, if that's what you mean." He expertly spits his tobacco juice into a plastic bottle, simultaneously grossing me out and impressing me. "But I'm not a goon," he adds sharply.

"What's the difference?" I goad.

"I grew up boxing. That's an art."

"So you're an artist," I say.

Josh's bursts out a staccato "HAH!" and adds, "I don't know about that. But I'm not a goon."

Later, I get a good look at Josh's right hand and see that he has no visible knuckles. Instead, where a normal person, say, someone whose living doesn't involve pounding faces with fists, has five distinct bony knuckles, Josh has a heinous mound of scar tissue.

"Doesn't that hurt?" I ask.

"Nah," he says, punching his left palm. "Well, at first, maybe it did." That he would admit it hurt must mean it *really* hurt. "But eventually it's just like having cushioning, like a permanent glove."

I ask him what's the key to winning a hockey fight.

"Well, a lot of guys will tell ya, 'Oh, you gotta yank the guy's jersey over his head,' or 'You have to rip off his helmet,' or some shit like that. But it's actually more simple than that. Basically, it's hit or be hit. No one can punch you when they're getting their face smashed in."

Josh and the rookies hop in my car and we head to a nearby Outback Steakhouse. It's been a grueling first two days, the hardest since I quit the sport. It's sad knowing that at least three of these guys will not make the team, because they're good kids who are here chasing their own dreams. They've all been getting pretty beat up in scrimmages–except for Josh, of course.

Chad's the youngest player in camp. He just turned twenty-one and is from Moose Jaw, Saskatchewan. I'm not making that up. Look it up, it's a real place: Moose Jaw. When our waitress, a brunette cutie with a

Bakersfield drawl (very Texas), takes our order, Chad sincerely asks, "Do you have steaks?"

Keep in mind, we're in an Outback Steakhouse. The place reeks of red meat. You can hear the beef sizzling in the kitchen. There's even a sign on the front of the building on which giant letters announce, "STEAKHOUSE."

The waitress assumes no one could be so stupid as to think the Outback doesn't have steaks, so, naturally, she thinks she's being played the fool. "Oh," she says sneering at Chad, "I think I could find you a steak if I look *real hard.*"

"Oh, great, thanks very much," Chad politely replies, ordering a strip steak, medium-rare. The waitress rolls her eyes in disgust and walks away.

Back at our hotel room, Josh kicks off his cowboy boots, sending them flying against a wall. Josh had a few tall glasses of beer at the Outback and is a little drunk. He puts a pinch of tobacco, his fifth of the night, under his front gum and plops onto the bed next to mine.

"That guy from Moose Jaw is pretty green, eh?" Josh says. "He didn't know they had steaks. What an idiot."

The third day of practice is open to the public, the first chance to see all the new players Kells brought in from Topeka, as well as the hometown heroes Paul Willett, Jamie Cooke, Glen Mears, and Paul Rosebush.

I notice the goalies are trying harder than usual to stop the pucks. "The fans can be very unforgiving," one vet told me the other day. "If they get a bad first impression, they will talk shit about you on the boards."

"What boards?" I asked him.

"On the Internet," he said. "They get on there every day and talk like they know what the fuck they're talking about, which, 99 percent of the time, they don't."

I do my best to look competent on the ice. I feel pretty good about myself, almost as if I fit in here. The guys have been friendly and supportive, except for the goalies, even though, judging by the way Kells is treating me, I have as good a chance at taking their jobs as they do mine at *Us Weekly.*

It's ninety-seven degrees outside, which must have motivated a lot of fans to come inside, if only for the air conditioning. Within the first fifteen minutes, two thousand people–men in white, red, and green Condors jerseys, teen-age girls with photos to sign, adult women in miniskirts and tight tops snapping photos of their favorites–are milling about the stands. Mind you, this is only a practice, and we are not in the NHL. We aren't even playing for an NHL farm team. Yet they still come.

For most of the one-hour session, I work on movement drills and shoot pucks and a few times get to face a couple of shots after Looch heads to the bench for water. Mostly, I just stand there watching and learning, playing my "role" on the team.

With a few minutes remaining, Kells runs a breakaway drill, then sends the team off to work out at the 24 Hour Fitness gym, where we will have free season passes, but where most of our lazy guys–especially the team's nine smokers–will work out less than a half-dozen times. A few guys stick around for more breakaways, and I am the goalie. I usually stop at least two-thirds of breakaways, but this time I am lucky to stop half the shots. The guys are trying harder in front of the fans.

Players stand just off the ice and sign autographs on photos and sticks and just about any other paraphernalia. No one asks me for my auto-graph, but as I leave the ice a cute, plump teenage girl with bottle-blond hair runs down the aisle to greet me. She's wearing a Condors jersey with a photo of Paul Rosebush pinned on the front.

"Who are *you*?" she asks.

"Ken Baker," I say. "Who are *you*?"

"Breanna," she says with folksy twang. "You ever gonna play this year?"

"I hope so," I reply. "I'm working on it."

* * *

The whole team shows up to a backyard barbecue being thrown by a couple of team boosters, John and Judy, who, like most rabid fans, are nice to the point that they literally would do anything for the Condors.

The city has never had a championship hockey team, even though hockey has been played in Bakersfield since 1940, when the semiprofes-sional Bakersfield Oilers played in the California Ice Hockey Association against teams like the Santa Rosa Bullets and the San Diego Rowers, until World War II forced the league to suspend operations. Hockey didn't re-turn to the southern San Joaquin Valley for another twenty years, when, in 1962, the Bakersfield Kernals, sporting green jerseys and named after the area's plentiful corn crop, began play in the Bakersfield Civic Auditorium. The Kernals played their first game against the Burbank Stars before an impressive crowd of two thousand fans and tied the game 3–3. According to Mike Griffith, a local newspaper reporter and Bakersfield hockey historian, "The Bakersfield players got a reputation of being the bad boys of the league with goaltender Phil Headley leading the team in penalty minutes midway through the season." But the team folded after just two seasons, a brief existence that might have had something to do with the fact that, according to those who witnessed games, the auditorium, originally built for concerts and stage plays, may have been the most bizarre rink in the history of the sport. A tiny ice rink lined with chicken wire, it was constructed on the theater stage. Half the time the auditorium was so warm the ice would melt, forming half-inch water puddles throughout the "ice" surface, and nearly all of the theater seats were located behind the visitor's net. Imagine 90 percent of the fans at a New York Knicks game watching from behind the basket, and you get the picture. It was definition bush league.

Hockey wouldn't return to Bakersfield for another thirty years when, in 1994, the Bakersfield Oilers began play in the semipro (meaning the players also had real jobs), Pacific Southwest Hockey League, competing against teams from Fresno, Las Vegas, and Anchorage. Many nights, the contests looked more like boxing matches than hockey games, the game little more than an opportunity for oil-field workers to vent their rage. The Oilers played in the very same auditorium as the Kernals. The rink still had chicken wire instead of glass.

Bakersfield's rink remained the wackiest in pro hockey until 1998, when the new Centennial Garden was built for the Condors of the West Coast Hockey League, a professional league formed out of the now-defunct Pacific Southwest League. New York millionaire Jonathan Fleisig promised to bring a newer, more polished brand of hockey to town. With no other community entertainment options, the franchise was an instant success, averaging over five thousand fans a game. Even though the team has never won a championship, attendance has increased every year. As a local reporter once told me, "Jonathan Fleisig put Bakersfield on the map."

The team's booster club has a membership of about five hundred fans who donate everything from pots and pans for players' apartments to cars. Some women even offer their bodies. Most, though, like John and Judy, just like to party with the guys, who are unique in a city composed of Mexican-Americans and mostly transplanted Oklahomans who came here during the Dust Bowl of the thirties to work the fields.

By the time I arrive at Jack and Judy's house, Kells is holding court by the pool. He's wearing his partying uniform of a golf shirt and Bermuda shorts, and holding a baby bottle in one hand and a beer bottle in the other. "I'm back on the bottle," he cracks.

His two daughters, a seventeen-month-old and a six-year-old, play with other kids in the house with his wife, Eileen, a sweet-faced woman who met Kells when he was playing in the American Hockey League for the New Haven Nighthawks. She was the bank teller where he cashed his checks from the L.A. Kings. She's followed him around the country, from Utica, New York, to Muskegon, Michigan, to Topeka, and now Bakersfield. "It's like working in the circus," she tells me. "You're in a different town every year."

"Isn't it hard?" I ask.

"On the kids, but even they get used to it," she says. "It's a good way to see the world."

There's an old-but-true saying that hockey is Canada's national sport, but drinking is its national pastime. Accordingly, the players stand in the yard and drink, drink and, well, drink. Willett seems to swallow half a bottle with every gulp. A few guys have drunk more than twelve beers yet still act stone sober. It's impressive, actually.

"Cat" or Felix, is more mature than the rest, which makes sense since he is thirty-seven. I ask him why he's still playing the sport, even though it's at the lowest pro level, and, without even thinking about it, he replies, "Because I can."

Cat has the gift of gab, especially when it comes to reliving the glory days. "The '88 Olympics," he says. "Now that was a high point. Everyone was coming up to my mom and dad back home in Toronto. They were so proud. Our goalies were Sean Burke and Andy Moog—the best goalies I've ever played with. Burke wouldn't ever give up. Even if it was a 3 on 0, or some impossible shit that never happens in a game, he would try hard. He hates to get scored on. After practice, he'd always be taking shots, working on things. It paid off. That's why he's a fucking all-star today."

Cat, who has two kids and an attractive wife he met when he was a teen-ager playing junior hockey in Ontario, acknowledges that this could be his final season. "See, I'm on my way down from the top," he says. "Most of these guys are trying to get where I have been or won't ever get there. I've been there. And I'll tell you what: Everyone thinks The Show is so much faster, so much better, so much this or that. It isn't. Sure, it's fast. But the biggest difference is everyone does their job. There are very few breakdowns. When mistakes are made, that's usually when a goal is scored. And NHL players aren't nearly as fuckin' tough as the ones at this party. At this level, it's much more physical, more brutal, you know? It's part of the whole show of it all. The fans like it, and since there are very few guys who can excel on skills alone, the physical part of the game is more important. You'll see a lot of crazy shit this year."

As we talk, Kells—several beers later—stands on the edge of the pool. His wife wisely snatches the car keys from his shorts' pocket as he announces to the party, "I swear, I'm gonna jump!" Kells rises to his tip toes and leans forward. As he's about to plunge facefirst into the pool, he falls back on his heels.

A wife standing next to me rolls her eyes. "Great," she says. "We've got one of *those* coaches this year."

* * *

The next few days of training camp go by in a blur, though an exhilarating one. Back in the Bay Area, I would play once, maybe twice, a week, and if I pulled a muscle or took a hard shot to a part of my body unprotected by padding, I had a week to heal. Now I don't have that luxury. I am learning a lot about the pro-athlete art of warming up properly and treating minor injuries before they can become major ones.

Still, my right groin is constantly sore, a recurring injury that, during my years of inactivity, I had forgotten I ever had. The injury dates back to a tournament in Montreal in 1986, when I did a full split while stretching to stop a puck passed across the crease. I didn't stop it, but I did tear my groin muscles from my femur. But that wasn't the worst of it. I truly screwed up my leg forever when I played the rest of that game, essentially, on one leg; the following day, after popping half a bottle of Tylenol, rubbing Ben Gay all over my right thigh and wrapping an ice bandage tightly around the muscle so it wouldn't tear any further, I played the next night. It was a big mistake. I walked with a limp for the next three weeks and couldn't run without throbbing pain for the next five years.

Fifteen years later, I am paying the price for my youthful idiocy. When I wake in the morning, I can barely walk without wincing, but then, like magic, after placing a heating pad on it in the training room, stretching and then warming up with light skating when I hit the ice, it loosens up in time for practice. I've learned that the key to making sure it doesn't get worse is to ice it immediately after practice. Unlike my Bay Area days–when I would peel into the parking lot fifteen minutes before game time, suit up and start playing–I have to arrive an hour early. I spend a half hour treating my sore muscles and wrapping my hand with padded tape as extra protection from the pucks. Then I take the ice about twenty minutes before anyone else and take shots from the other early birds, usually Jason Ralph, another rookie. Practice usually starts with a five-minute warm-up of sprints, with Kells blowing the whistle as an alert to skate hard laps, and a second whistle signaling to slow down. For the first few days, I got winded doing sprints, but now I can keep up with the other guys. *Baby steps.*

After the sprints, practice starts with players taking long shots on the goalies from the blue line. This is also when I assume my position as the third-string old fart chasing his dream and who, as charity, the coach lets come out on the ice probably because the owner told him so.

I stand along the boards and work on movement drills, dropping to my knees, poke checking, moving side to side to simulate actual action. A few of the players make fun of me by shooting pucks my way, but I ignore them. Rather than act pissed, I will just keep working hard and wait for my chance. I only take shots when Looch or Hay get tired, hurt or break a stick. Unfortunately, this only happens a few times a practice. But I'm paying my dues. I hand them water bottles, gather pucks for drills, hand guys sticks when they break. Since I'm not being treated just like anyone else, I will earn their respect. "Aren't you bored?" Willett asked me in the middle of practice the other day. "Go take some shots."

"Kells doesn't want me to," I said.

"Fuck him," said Willett, who is thirty-two, has scored 323 career goals, is the captain, and has played in 727 pro hockey games; Kells is thirty-four and has coached only 357 pro hockey games.

But Kells is the boss, and, as a result, I remind myself that if I was able to wait nine years to come out of retirement, I can wait a few more weeks, or even months, to get my big break.

* * *

In preparation for our exhibition game against Tacoma, Kells is trying to put together forward lines—a center and a left and right winger—and his two-man defensive pairings. Most teams at this level feature a scoring line, consisting of at least two of their best offensive players and a hard-checking forward. The second line usually consists of solid all-around players who can score and play good defensive hockey. The third line is a checking line used primarily as a defensive unit that can create scoring chances by throwing hard checks and skating their balls off. In addition to the three lines, there will be one or two extra forwards, one of whom is usually a goon. Our goon, of course, is Josh Maser.

Kells has players wearing black, yellow, red and green practice jerseys to differentiate the lines. Some guys will wear three different colors over the course of a practice as Kells tries to find the right mix. Our number-one line is Willett, Cookie and Jeff Goldie, a lanky left-winger who played for Kells in Topeka.

By the sixth day of camp, the players, except for the eight Topeka guys who have played together, are still getting used to one another. They are tentative. At one point, Kells gets pissed when Firth, who, at thirty years old, has more points (1,092) than any other active player at the AA level, passes the puck to his linemate rather than taking a shot at the net.

"Firthie, shoot the damn puck!" Kells shouts, his voice echoing through the empty arena. "I know you are getting used to each other and don't want to piss off the other guy, and so you are passing the puck. But fuck it! You get close to the net, you shoot. It's not about making friends; it's about scoring goals."

Kells can go from happy-go-lucky to livid in a matter of seconds. And his rant isn't over yet.

"This ain't rocket science, boys," he continues shouting. "It's not even football. This is a simple game. You skate, you pass, you check, you shoot the puck. It's not a complicated game."

Kells's hockey philosophy is an old-school one. Rarely does he pull out a chalkboard and diagram a play like a lot of more technical-minded,

European-influenced coaches. Rather, Kells is *laissez-faire*. "It's about finding the right mix and letting guys play the game," is how he describes his approach. That's why he has a reputation as a "player's coach." He wants the guys to play by instinct. As such, he doesn't do much x-and-o coaching, which makes players happy, since most of them just want to play. In the past, his approach has worked. Ever since he began coaching in 1996, helming the Muskegon Fury of the UHL, he has amassed a winning record of 183 wins, 140 losses and 35 ties.

But while Kells obviously knows the game, he doesn't profess to have any special knowledge of goaltending. While standing next to him yesterday during a drill, he asked me what I thought of Looch and Hay. "Looch is much better, obviously," I said.

"Why's he better?" Kells asked.

"He's usually in the right position. So pucks just seem to hit him. He makes it look easy. But with Hay, it's like he's always diving or doing the splits because he hasn't moved with the play. His angles are off, leaving huge parts of the net wide open. And he gives back too many rebounds."

"Makes sense," Kells said. "Truth is, I don't know dick about goaltending."

* * *

The Tacoma Sabercats will be the only team we play in exhibition. Following the game, Kells has said he will make cuts, winnowing the roster down to twenty-one guys, plus me. I'm coming to grips with the reality that I will probably serve as an unpaid practice goalie unless Looch or Hay get hurt or suspended or play so badly that Kells puts me in a game out of desperation.

Our regular season will start when the Long Beach Ice Dogs come to our rink on October 12, and the Tacoma game is a chance for Kells to play the five younger guys who are vying for two available slots, as well as an opportunity for the veterans to get the kinks out.

Even though I'm not at all happy about my standing around, at least Kells has been nicer to me lately, joking and asking me what I think about different things he is doing. He doesn't have an assistant coach, so I am usually the only other person on the ice who is not occupied. That's not to say that he hasn't stopped with the brain tumor jokes. At the beginning of practice the other day he stood in front of the net pretending to play goalie.

"Why don't you put on my mask?" I asked.

He replied, "I don't want to catch a brain tumor."

* * *

The rookies are starting to get nervous. Chad has been about as sharp as he was that night at Outback. His passes are sloppy and he isn't scoring. Add to that the fact that he is the only player wearing a plastic visor to protect his eyes (few pros wear the visors, partly because they think it inhibits vision and partly because it's just not cool) and it's becoming clear that he is not adapting very quickly to the professional game.

At the free hotel buffet lunch, I sit next to him.

"I don't think I am going to make it," he tells me under his breath, careful not to broadcast it to the other guys. "I have dreamed of playing professional hockey my entire life, but I feel like I am just shitting the bed."

Rather than tell him I agree, I just say that Friday night is his chance to shine, to just focus on that game.

Jason Sexsmith, another rookie tryout who is from Calgary, joins us. Rookies sit together at lunch. Jason has a better shot, even though he, too, is small and not a very strong or fast skater. But Jason has put less pressure on himself to make the team. "I don't know if I will play one game, two, or whatever," he says. "I am just taking it a day at a time. I could be out of here tomorrow."

"What if he cuts you?" I ask.

"I'll probably become a cop up in Edmonton," he says. "I've always wanted to be a cop. You know, after twenty-five years you get a full pension."

I ask the same question of Chad, who stares sullenly into his strip steak and says, "I don't know. I guess I'll just go back home and hang it up."

Improve

Brooke tells me that our faithful dog Arthur keeps waiting for me to come home. "Whenever he hears someone in the driveway his tail starts wagging and he runs to the door like daddy is home," she says.

Having an understanding wife and loyal dog five hours up the interstate keeps me sane—as sane as someone who gets pelted with hard rubber every day. Brooke is taking the train down on Friday, before that night's exhibition game. It's just three days from now and I can't wait.

The guys are getting bored with practice and are itching to play in a game. As for me, I am just itching to practice. Game time would be nice, but I am starting to fear playing because, without any practice time, I might make a fool out of myself.

At least I break a sweat and take about a hundred shots before practice and twice that many after practice. Hay and Looch are usually too spent to stay out late, so I am the only goalie. My goal every day is to be the first guy on, last guy off. It's a goal that I don't need Kells to make happen.

I have improved a lot in the last week, and my body feels looser and my reflexes more reactive. But I'm feeling that I'm not developing as quickly as I could be because I never face game situations. In games, players clog the slot, blocking the goalie's view, rebounds have to be controlled because pesky forwards are waiting to swat the puck in, and you have to have your stamina built up because the play can be in your end of the ice for minutes at a time with no break. Moreover, in games, one mistake by a goalie can result in a goal, the difference between winning and losing. And playing under pressure is entirely different from the nonpressure of practices. Even so, I play practices as if they are my games, even though I know the players aren't trying nearly as hard as they do in games.

I ask Josh to stay out with me. Though a goon, Josh knows that Kells expects him to sit on the bench and, when an opposing player is roughing up one of our guys, skate out, drop the gloves, and pound the living shit out of him. But Josh wants to get better, acquire actual hockey-playing skills, which is why he works on his skating, passing, and shooting after practice with me.

I have him line up twenty pucks about fifteen feet in front of the net. "Shoot as hard as you want," I tell him with a cocky glare and bet him five bucks he won't score more than five times. Josh lets out his cowboy guffaw and orders me to "shut up and get in the fuckin' net."

Until now, I haven't faced much rapid-fire shooting, especially slap shots. That might explain why I have suffered only a few minor bruises—on my forearm, my inner thigh, the palm of my catching hand. Josh may not be a goal scorer, but a life spent bailing hay and hog-tying calves has given Josh a pair of Popeye arms that can send a puck flying at over 100 mph.

As Josh lines up the pucks in a straight line, I fasten my gloves extra tight and strap on my mask.

"Ready, goalie?" Josh asks.

"Just fuckin' shoot," I say.

Thwap.

Thwap.

Thwap.

Thwap.

Josh's stick launches pucks at me like a batting-cage machine wildly spitting out balls. His shots are hard, but not accurate. One sails over my right shoulder and smashes against the glass. Another smacks me in the gut. I get the feeling Josh has no idea where the pucks are going, but that he figures if he shoots them hard enough at least six will go in. Of the first five, only one gets by—a low shot along the ice. At this distance, I have less than a second to react. If he places it to a corner, I have to kick out instantly to stop it.

Thwap.

Thwap.

Thwap.

Thwap.

Thwap.

By his tenth shot, he has scored only once.

Thwap.

The puck takes off from his stick and it heads straight for my chin–no, make that my neck!–a part of my body that is vital to sustain human life and that happens to be unprotected by the fiberglass chin of my mask.

Some goalies wear clear plastic throat guards, but I don't; they tend to fog up and block your vision when you look straight down. The new throat guards are better than they were when I last played, but I am a stubborn old goalie. Brooke urged me to buy one when she saw a goalie wearing one in the Oakland beer league, but I blew it off. I had been hit in the neck back in college and high school, but I was always fast enough to twist my neck, or duck, so the puck didn't crush my windpipe, an injury that I had heard happened to goalies all the time but that I had so far evaded.

Needless to say, Josh's bullet has caught me off guard. At the last millisecond I manage to cock my head to the left, enough to save my larynx from getting crushed, but the puck still impacts the side of my throat. I tumble face down to the ice like a pile of dirty laundry.

Josh rushes over.

"Sorry, Bakes," he says urgently. "You all right, old man?"

My face is planted into the ice. I'm seeing stars. Though I can already feel the swelling build on my neck, I can breathe. At least I'm not dead.

I struggle to my knees and lift off my mask. "Fuck off," I say, to no one in particular.

Josh taps me on the pads with his stick. "I knew you weren't a pussy."

I grab my stick and put my mask back on. Dad always said if you don't get back in the net after taking a wild shot to the face, you'll be "gun shy" and flinch. Goaltending is as much a position of nerve as it is one of reflex. Mitch Korn once told me that hockey is 90 percent mental, but goaltending is 99 percent mental. If I leave the ice now, I may as well just head back home because I will have lost the mental game.

I return to the crease and assume my stance: knees bent, stick blade on the ice in front of my toes, glove held waist high, eyes fixed on the black rubber.

"No, man," Josh protests. "You're hurt. Let's just finish tomorrow."

"No," I grunt. "Let's finish this now. Shoot the fucking puck."

Half-heartedly, Josh skates to the line of pucks and flicks them at the net, keeping them on the ice. He scores just once, and I don't flinch.

Breathe

Seven days after the start of my first professional hockey training camp, eleven days after leaving my wife to move into a Holiday Inn with a cowboy from Alberta, four years after brain surgery freed me to explore my athletic potential, one day after a puck to the neck nearly aborted my supposed comeback, I wake up relieved. Tonight is the exhibition game, which means, since I have as much of a chance of playing as Anthony, the team's "stick" boy, I can rest. My body needs recovery time, anyway. Plus, Brooke has taken the Amtrak down from the Oakland station (she's able to study during the five-hour train ride), and I'm looking forward to spending a few days with her.

Then, as I stretch on the ice before our pregame morning practice, Kells skates up to me with some surprising news. "You're going to play the third period tonight," he says bluntly.

Convinced he's pulling my leg, I just smirk–but not too much just in case he is serious. *But what if he's not kidding? I haven't had enough practice. Until a month ago, my competition consisted of thirty-year-old bankers and ankle-bending welders. I want to play, but I need more practice.* My stomach tightens.

"Is that OK?" he says.

"Hell, yeah," I reply.

I have to focus, be ready to play, Sure, it's only an exhibition game, but there will be five thousand people in the stands, my team will be relying on me, my dream of playing pro hockey is–sort of–coming true. I was not expecting this.

Kells skates over and tells Looch, who will play the first period, and Hay, who will play the second, that I will be playing the third. They react unemotionally. This is their job. They seem annoyed enough that I have been around the rink. Now I am going to play when they could be fine-tuning. Too bad for them.

"Make sure you rotate in for shots today," Kells tells me. "Get loose."

I don't ask him why he decided to play me, whether the owner urged him to, or if he just wants to see what I can do. For the next hour, I face hundreds of shots and experience game situations–two-on-ones, breakaways, three-on-ones, breakouts, power-play drills. I try not to think about the welt on my neck from yesterday. For the first time since I arrived, I'm being treated like any other.

At the end of practice, Kells calls everyone over to the net I will be guarding tonight. We all huddle close in a semicircle.

"Tacoma has a lot of new guys this year, and they'll have a lot of guys fighting for spots tonight, so they're not going to just roll over," he says.

Kells looks straight at the guys wearing blue jerseys, the rookies: David Milek, Jason Sexsmith, Chad, Kelly and two Finnish guys. And me. None of us has ever played a single second of pro hockey. "This is a good chance for you guys to show what you got," he tells us. "But this ain't gonna be practice. Keep your head up. If you don't, someone will knock it off."

Back in the locker room I notice that the buckle on the right toe of my leg pad has broken off. If I don't get it replaced, I can't play because my pad will slip off at the toe whenever I move. I panic and head straight to the equipment manager's office, where Dickie is sewing torn socks and jerseys.

"Sorry," he says. "Can't help ya."

"Why not?"

"I'm not a fucking shoemaker. I don't have the equipment to sew leather. You'll have to find a shoemaker."

"Where?"

"I don't know." He goes back to his sewing. "Look in the phone book."

Of course, if this were the NHL, I would have three extra sets of pads and a competent equipment manager would stitch on a new buckle. But this isn't the big leagues. This is Bakersfield. In NHL, a team of gofers carries players' bags onto planes and buses; we carry ours. NHL players get as many sticks as they want, over five hundred a season. We're allowed a few dozen, and if we go over that, we may have to buy them ourselves.

Annoyed, I carry my pad back to the hotel, where Brooke has arrived and is waiting.

"I'm playing tonight," I tell her.

"Really? I thought the coach didn't like you."

"I guess not."

*　*　*

Ever since The Dream, I have known that the only way to feel true adrenaline-pumping, endorphin-secreting thrill is by getting back in between the pipes. And, now, in eight hours I will get my first taste of that thrill.

After the pregame meal, Brooke and I speed over to "Hollywood Luggage," a curious name for a shabby shoe-repair shop a few miles south of the rink. By the looks of the items in the shop, the store repairs luggage and cowboy boots. The stocky Mexican-American woman behind the counter stares at me when I walk in carrying a bulky white-and-red leg pad. "I never see this before," she admits. Nevertheless, with the help of Brooke, who speaks a little Spanish, I explain what I need fixed. She nods, and I hope she doesn't mess it up.

My plan: Drive back to the hotel, take a nap, or at least try, visualize making saves, stretch, have Brooke pick up my (hopefully) repaired pad, and head over to the rink around five o'clock.

Brooke drops me off at the Holiday Inn. She wants to give me space and heads off to the mall for the afternoon. Josh, at my request, moved into a room with another rookie yesterday so Brooke and I could sleep together like an actual married couple. So, inside, I close the curtains, lie in bed and thumb through Mitch Korn's goalie bible, hoping I will doze off. And I do.

Bling, bling, bling!

Aw, fuck.

Bling, bling, bling!

Damn phone.

"Yeah," I groggily answer.

"Is this Ken?" the chipper voice asks.

"Yeah."

"It's Dylan from *Us Weekly* in New York," he says. "I have a question about a story you helped write last week."

Dylan, a fact-checker for the magazine, reminds me that two weeks ago, before leaving for Bakersfield, I interviewed Matthew Perry, the *Friends* star and native Canadian, about the death of L.A. Kings scout Ace Bailey, who died in one of the planes that crashed into the World Trade Center three weeks ago.

At first, I am annoyed. I have already forgotten about the story and moved on to my hockey career. That 9/11 story was the last I wrote for the magazine before taking leave. But the call actually calms me, reminds me that this hockey-playing adventure isn't to be taken too seriously. It isn't life and death. It's fun, and I'm blessed enough to be chasing a dream.

Dylan checks the spelling of someone I quoted.

"Where are you?"

"Bakersfield, California."

"Where's that?"

"The middle-of-nowhere, California."

"Why are you *there?*"

"I'm playing my first professional hockey game tonight." Just hearing myself say it makes me nervous.

"Good luck," he says.

"I'm gonna need it."

I'm too excited to sleep. When I think about how much this game will mean to me, how far I have come since my surgery three years ago, and how great it would be to play well, even though it is just a preseason game and not one for the record books, my eyes fill with tears.

After Brooke returns with my pad, which the boot-repair lady has fixed perfectly, I phone my little brother, who's working at the record store back in Buffalo. Ever since we were kids, Kris and I used to play make-believe pro hockey games in our living room. I would be on my knees and he'd shoot a balled-up sock at me, doing play-by-play. Granted, the teams were usually teams like the Sabres and Bruins and Rangers, not Tacoma and Bakersfield. Even so, tonight is going to be something of a dream come true for both of us.

"Record Theatre, Hamburg. This is Kris, how can I help you?"

I disguise my voice. "Yeah, Kris," I say in my best redneck voice. "I need a roll of toilet paper."

"O.K., sir," he says, not recognizing my voice. "Why do you need toilet paper?"

"Because I'm crapping my pants. I have to play a pro hockey game tonight."

"Seriously?" he enthuses.

"Yeah, isn't that cool?"

"I told you this would be different than college," he says. Kris then does nothing to calm my nerves. "Just don't fuck up," he says. "This is your chance."

* * *

In the locker room, hard-rock music blares over the sound system as the guys stretch, drink coffee, sit in the hot tub, ride stationary bikes, rub Atomic Balm on their sore muscles, and perform their various pregame rituals.

For some, like Cookie, a veteran of almost six hundred pro games, this contest will be an unemotional moment, just a warm-up game to get the body back in playing mode after a six-month layoff. But to me and the five other rookies, this is monumental. From the time we were little more than cartoon-watching pipsqueaks we've played the game, working our way up the ranks with the goal of someday getting paid to play. And, finally, here we are: pro hockey players. No matter what happens tonight, we can say that at least we made it this far.

Chad and Jason are ghostly white. Kelly Kilgore, a beefy kid from North Dakota wearing a ball cap that hides his eyes, feverishly chews tobacco and keeps to himself. I'm quiet, too.

Looch and Hay get dressed on the other side of the room, chatting with each other and ignoring me. *They probably wish I'd just go away.*

Kells announces what fore-check system we will use tonight (2–1–2, meaning we will send two forwards skating in hard up front, with the one center hanging back and the two defensemen staying in the rear) and announces the lines, then the goalies.

He looks at his notes and says, "Looch, the first, Hay, the second, and Baker, the third." He pauses. "Baker, just don't die on me," he deadpans. His joke relaxes me, and I have to laugh along with everyone else, even though I wish this coach with the smoker's cough and a chip on his shoulder would stop fucking with me.

While every other player has a black game jersey hanging from his locker, I do not, so I hunt down our grumpy equipment manager and ask for one.

"I don't have any extra goalie jerseys," he snaps. "Looch and Haysie have the only two goalie jerseys . . . ."

"So what am I supposed to wear?"

Dickie doesn't like to do any work he doesn't absolutely have to, so he grudgingly steps over to the closet and pulls out a jersey with number twenty-three on the back. I have never in my entire life seen a goalie with a number twenty-three, but I have no choice but to take it. "Twenty-three," I say. "That's Michael Jordan's number." Dickie gives me an I-don't-give-a-fuck glare. The parallel—Michael J. and I both are coming out of retirement this season—apparently is lost on him.

In the warm-ups, we skate out to "The Boys Are Back Are Back in Town," and a few hundred fans already have arrived for the game. About three thousand, half of the average regular-season crowd, have come. Too many fans would make me nervous, so I am glad the arena, which holds almost nine thousand, is mostly empty. With five minutes left before game time, Kells enters the room with a bounce in his step to deliver the final pregame ritual: the calling of the starting lineup. He's chosen our third line, our checking line, to come out hammering the Sabercats. "Eddie, Rosie, Maser, Hartsy, Cat. All right, Looch. Let's go!"

The game night is also a run-through for the off-ice folks who put on the show. The team's flamboyant announcer, a deep-voiced guy with flowing blond hair named Chris Peace, introduces the starting lineup. A spotlight illuminates each player as he steps on the ice to Peace's pro-wrestling-style intro. *And number thirty-threeeeeeee, Luuu-uuciano Caravaggioooooo!* I take my seat at the end of the bench, trying to stay relaxed as I watch the other two goalies for the next forty minutes.

From the drop of the puck, we come out flying and dominate the play. Cookie and Goldie are in total sync on the wings, passing the puck crisply back and forth. Kelly Kilgore gets some time on their line, but he circles around invisibly, clearly out-skilled by his linemates. I feel bad for him.

Five minutes into the game, Cookie, who seems to glide effortlessly through traffic, pops in a goal on the power play on a feed from Goldie. The place erupts when they realize their local hero has scored.

Peter Brearley, who scored 44 goals last year in Topeka, is dominant. At 6' 3", he's the tallest guy on the ice, and can use his size to place himself in scoring position. At the end of the first, he steals a pass from a defenseman up the middle and, turning on the turbos, speeds to net, fakes a shot and lifts the puck over the goalie on his backhand. A brilliant play.

Brearley, who played up at the AAA level two years ago, looks like he's too talented to be here. And, at twenty-six years old, he still has a few years to make it to The Show. Sexsmith, however, looks out of place, a step behind everyone. With five minutes left, he takes a stupid penalty, tripping a guy instead of skating harder to catch up to him. Rookie mistake.

Looch makes several impressive saves before letting in a rebound that gets away from him. At the end of the first period, we're up 5–1. *Good. The bigger the lead when I go in, the less pressure. I will have a cushion.*

As guys return to their stalls during the first intermission, Kells storms into the room with a fake scowl and yells, "Fuck, guys. Is that the best you can do? Awful." Of course, he's joking. We just made Tacoma look like a Pee Wee team.

Hay starts the second period. From the start, Tacoma, who must have been chewed out by their coach in between periods, is gunning for revenge. Their goon, Aaron Plumb, a big bastard who can hardly skate, lines up against Josh at the opening face-off. Before the ref even drops the puck, Plumb and Josh have tossed off their gloves and, with fists up like boxers, square up. This is a common minor-league hockey ploy. In order to throw the other team off their game, the losing team will pick a fight, both to fire up their own team and distract the other one. The odd thing is that it usually works.

Josh, who's six feet tall, is a couple of inches shorter than the towering Plumb, but Josh's boxing background—he won dozens of boxing tournaments as a kid—makes up for his lack of size.

Josh, who stares down his opponent with the face of a psycho-murderer, goes right to business, grabbing Plumb's collar with his right hand and throwing a flurry of left knuckles to the nose, cheek, and eyes. Plumb drops. Kells grins, relieved that he has found his goon.

Hay stops eleven of twelve shots, the one goal a shot from the point that was tipped by a forward who sneaked behind Hay and deflected it in. He played well, but he didn't look like a superstar. We're up 7–2 at the end of the second.

The entire time, I sit patiently, not wanting to get too excited too soon because it, well, would exhaust me. And, though I am aware of Brooke up in the stands proudly snapping photos, I do my best not to think about anything but the game.

During the second intermission, I chow down half a Powerbar for energy and start stretching.

"You cold?" Josh asks me.

"No," I reply, "I'm burning with desire." Josh flashes his cool-cowboy smirk.

I've been sitting on the bench for almost two hours waiting. After nine and one-half years of retirement, it's nothing. I'm ready.

Up in the stands, I know that Brooke is a bundle of nerves. Not that she doesn't believe in me, but she's afraid that I will mess up. She has never seen me play a real game. There are a few thousand fans in the crowd, and Brooke and I have rearranged our lives in order for me to chase The Dream. It's time to play well. I once heard Cal Ripken Jr. say that if you want success you have to be willing to fail. And I am. It sure beats sitting on my ass wondering, "What if?"

The red-lettered digital clock on the wall reads five minutes until the start of the third period—my period. *Just don't let in a bad goal. Make them earn their goals. Shot by shot.*

"Bakes," Kells announces. "You're up."

I slide my hands into my gloves, strap on my mask and walk down the hallway leading to the ice. At the end of the tunnel hangs a black curtain fluttering in the cool breeze. I stood here for the first time ten months ago, nervous about trying out for the team, not even believing that I had it in me to make it this far. Now here I stand. *I've already won.*

Brearley, standing at the curtain, peeks his head out and sees the refs have taken the ice, our signal to go out. The goalie always goes first.

"Ya ready?" Brearley says.

I stomp down the tunnel past Brearley and leap onto the ice, skating toward the net and turning for a lap. When I make the turn back toward the bench, I see that I'm the only player on the ice. Brearley let me come out alone, playing a trick on the rookie. He finally comes out, laughing. "Hey, rookie! Lonely out here?"

The joke keeps me from being too nervous, as does Hay, who charitably offers his first advice of the season, "Just relax and have fun," as I stand in the goal crease and ready myself for the start of the period.

Live in the moment. Breathe.

My heart is racing. I can't slow it, no matter how many deep breaths I take. If it weren't for the bulky leather gloves on my hands, I could see them shaking like a Parkinson's patient. Sweat is pouring down my face, dripping onto the ice—and I haven't yet even faced a single shot.

Calm down. We're up 7–2. I can let in four goals and we'll still win.

I hear a male fan in the stands to my right yell, "Go get 'em, Baker!" Finally, I smile.

Meanwhile, Brooke overhears fans around her talking about me, wondering who is this little goalie.

"I think he's the writer guy."

"He has a brain tumor."

"I bet he's nervous."

I can't hear him, but Kells is barking to the guys on the bench to protect me. "He's been out of the game for a while," he shouts. "Give him support."

The puck drops and, just like that, I am playing pro hockey, albeit an exhibition game.

The worst thing for a goalie is to let in his first shot on goal. It not only can ruin your confidence, but it doesn't let you get a feel for the puck and ease into the game. My aim is to stop the first shot, and, if I do, I am convinced I will be fine.

The first thing I notice is how much faster the game is than practice. If practice runs at 30 mph, then games cruise along at 80. And my heart is going a hundred and fifty.

Two minutes in, I face the best first shot I could want, a slapper from the point. As Chris Economou instructed me, I drop to my knees, laying my pads flat; the puck hits my stick and deflects into the corner. *One for one.*

We take a penalty, then another, and suddenly we are playing three against five. This will be my first real test. It won't make it any easier to keep the puck out of the net with Kells benching the veterans so he can get a look at the rookies.

Seven minutes into the period, after a flurry of shots on the power play, a Tacoma winger digs the puck out of the corner and passes it out front to a speedy forward, Todd Esselmont, who fires a low wrist shot to the left post. I drop to my knees and kick out my toe, just missing the puck, which hits the inside of the post and goes in, making the score 7–3. The building falls into a cathedral-like quiet.

A minute later, we take another penalty and end up spending eight minutes–almost half of the entire period–killing penalties. But I come up big, making a glove save, a nice leg save on a rebound, and poke check a guy on a breakaway. The fans cheer loudly. I've won them over.

Still, I am nervous, never finding a comfort zone. Sweating like a pig, I drink an entire bottle of water in the first fifteen minutes. Then, with about three minutes left, a nifty forward darts out of the corner to my left and fakes a shot. I take the bait and go down to my knees. He curls around the back of the net and, as I dive to block the open side, he stuffs the puck into the net.

Shit.

It's 7–4 now. To preserve the win, Kells sends out Cookie, Willett and some of his other best veterans. You never want to lose, even in exhibition.

But I make a few saves on some long shots, finally feeling sharp and relaxed, and we get the victory. The crowd cheers.

At last, I can breathe.

I stopped ten out of twelve shots, letting in two goals. They weren't bad goals; they earned them. But I could have done better. Admittedly, I think Looch and Hay played better. Even so, this game wasn't even for the record books. It's only the beginning.

My teammates skate off the bench to congratulate me, butting their helmets against mine and tapping me on the pads. Even Looch and Hay tap me. "Good job, Kenny," Looch says.

It's not the realization of that dramatic dream I had almost two years ago, that nocturnal fantasy that propelled me to this city in the middle of California. But it's a good start. *Who knows? This could be my first step toward the NHL!*

In the *Bakersfield Californian* the next morning Kells will be quoted as saying, "We were hoping he'd get the shutout. He's in good shape and did a good job."

I hustle out of my gear and shower, so I can go see Brooke, who's waiting for me in what the players call "the hen house," a room down the hall from the locker room where wives and girlfriends gather. Inside, I give her a hug and hold on. "You were great," she whispers, sending my faucet of tears streaming. I hold on to her as tightly as my dream.

Dance

The day after my professional debut, Kells comes over to the Holiday Inn and hands out the keys to our apartments. It's "move-in" day and our first day off from skating since camp began eight days ago. Good thing. My right groin is aching more than ever from last night's game. The married guys have been living in the complex, the sophisticated-sounding Cambridge Apartments, a cluster of modern buildings with tennis courts, a swimming pool and outdoor hot tub that is located in the irrigated suburbia ten miles southwest of the arena. The rest of us have been itching to get out of the hotel. Buffet breakfasts, buffet lunches, dinners at Denny's and the Outback, cheap mattresses. It gets old after a week and a half.

I had hoped Kells would keep Josh as my roommate, but when Kells hands me the key he tells me, "You're with Hartsy."

"What about Josh?" I ask.

"He's staying in the hotel for a little longer," he says. "Him and the rookies need to show me a little more before I move them in."

"You'll like Hartsy," Kells adds. "He's a good kid."

Ryan Hartung, or "Hartsy," is a polite, friendly Midwestern kid who majored in accounting from a Minnesota college. Ryan has the distinction of being the only guy I've seen reading anything other than the sports section. The other day at the hotel, I even spotted him reading a novel.

Brooke and I drive over to my second-floor furnished apartment, a two-bedroom suite with a kitchen, tiny dining area and a living room with a balcony that overlooks a courtyard. Each apartment costs $900 a

121

month, but the team covers the rent for players; under the agreement I made with Matt Riley, I'll pay the team $450 a month as long as I am not on the roster. It's your typical generic modern apartment, but it's a home.

The other residents are a mix of young families and students from Bakersfield State, located a mile away. This will be my home for the next six months—without Brooke, who must head back to Mill Valley for another three weeks before her next visit.

The apartment is empty, but Ryan has already dropped off his bags and left a note on the kitchen counter reading, "I put my stuff in the smaller bedroom so you can have more space." Hartsy is apparently as religious as he is polite. The only thing he has unpacked from his suitcases is a wooden cross and a Bible that he has already set on his nightstand.

Later, Rhonda—an elementary school teacher and Condors booster club member who is pretty, single, blond, and enjoys wearing short skirts around the guys—drops off a few boxes containing sheets, blankets, a toaster, silverware and some cleaning supplies. "Just call if you need anything," she says sweetly in a raspy smoker's voice.

Rhonda adds with a flirtatious smile, "Good game last night. You're a damn good goalie for not having played in so long. I would know, 'cuz I'm an expert on goaltending." That's an understatement. I later will learn that Foxy Rhonda's e-mail handle on the Condors message boards is "GoalieLover."

* * *

Our regular-season opener against the Long Beach Ice Dogs is in five days and Kells has to cut at least four guys before the Friday-night home game to get the roster down to the league-mandated maximum of twenty-one.

After an upbeat practice—the guys were in a good mood about beating Tacoma and, of course, moving into the apartments—I stay out late taking shots from Josh and Ryan. Even though I played well on Friday night, it doesn't seem to have changed Kells's mind. I spend the entire practice standing by myself along the boards. "Hey, poet," Willie shouts to me. "I thought you'd go home already."

At least the Condors fans are impressed—sort of. In the chat room over the weekend, a fan cyber-named Dante46 wrote, "Even our third goalie didn't look too bad. 12 shots, 10 saves is pretty solid for a guy who hasn't played at a major level since 91–92." It was a backhanded compliment. Mr. 46 continued, "But if we had kept Caravaggio in there we probably would've won 7–2 or 7–3."

In the locker room after practice, the rookies–Chad, Sexsmith, Kelly Kilgore, Dave Milek and the two barely-English-speaking Finns, Ossie and Tom–are standing outside Kells's office. They're as ashen as funeral-goers.

"Kells wants to talk to me," Sexsmith says. "He just cut Chad."

One guy who has a shot is Dave Milek, a 6' 3" defenseman who just graduated from the University of Guelph. The others are vulnerable. Kelly Kilgore, who last year played for the University of Minnesota at Crookston, looked fairly solid in Friday's game, even though he was markedly slower than the other guys.

Chad is already cleaning out his locker when I get to my stall. Then, a few minutes later, Sexsmith walks in with tears in his eyes.

I had a feeling Jason was going to get cut when he fell into the boards during practice today during a breakout drill. He got up, broke his stick against the boards, and stormed off carrying his shattered stick.

One player quipped, "Where's he going?"

To which Kells replied, "I know that he's heading back to fuckin' Calgary tomorrow."

"What did Kells say?" I ask Jason now.

"Pack your bags," he sniffles.

"That's all?"

"No, he said I was being put on waivers and some other team in the league might be able to pick me up. But maybe not. Either way, he said I have to go home. He asked me if I had a return flight, and I said I did. So I guess I gotta go home now."

The death march continues when Kelly slinks in with his head down; he looks stunned, like someone just told him he has cancer.

"I'm outta here," he says, dropping into his seat next to mine.

I'm shocked. I thought Kells might give him a chance. Plus, Kelly is a good kid. Before Friday's game, he handed Brooke his camera so he would have pictures of him playing pro hockey to show his mom and dad. At least he has a memory of his big game.

"Well, I gave it a shot," he says, obviously holding back tears.

But I don't share my thoughts. At a time when he thinks his dream has just died, the last thing he needs to hear is a lecture on the musings of a Roman philosopher. I shake his hand and wish him luck.

The smile on Milek's face tells a far different story. He has made the team—for now. I head for the shower feeling lucky that I'm sticking around. Better them than me.

I can't help but feel sorry for the cut rookies. For them, this might have been their only shot, the end of a long line that started when they were kids. But back at the apartment, Ryan, who in his rookie season two years ago played for five different teams—The San Antonio Iguanas, Missouri River Otters, Toledo Storm, Tallahassee Tiger Sharks and Mohawk Valley Prowlers—expresses little sympathy. "It's just part of the game," he says. "If they're good enough to go pro, someone will pick them up."

* * *

Kells makes the mistake of giving Willett the team credit card so we can celebrate our newly formed "family," as Kells has starting calling us. Most of the guys take it as an opportunity to get wasted for free, and Cat, ever the jokester, uses the gathering as an opportunity to show off to some of the new guys his favorite bar trick.

"Hey, Ramona," he barks at the young barmaid, who dutifully hustles over to his table. Cat then points to the crotch of his jeans, where there appears to be a red smudge of material stuck to his pants.

"There's gum stuck on my pants, Ramona," he says with a straight face. "Can you get me some ice and rub this out for me?"

Ramona strains her eyes and bends over to see the red speck, which she instantly recognizes as a part of Cat's scrotum, which, somehow, he has stretched out of his zipper and pressed down like gum.

The guys, most of whom are already boozed up, though it's only three in the afternoon, howl like brothers in a fraternity, which we're becoming, only our school is an untraditional one.

The day after the party, guys reek of cigar smoke, vodka, spiced rum, and cheap beer when they arrive in the locker room for our team-systems meeting.

As a goalie, you don't need an intricate understanding of the team's systems—breakouts, fore-checks, defensive-zone formations, power play, and face-off setups—but it does help to know where guys are supposed to be at any given point. For example, if I go behind the net to get a puck, it helps to know that our wingers stand along the boards at the hash marks for the breakout. That way, I can send the puck around the boards, where a forward should be waiting.

Kells has stuck white tape on the carpet in the shape of a rink, including lines and face-off dots. He has balled up white and black pieces of hockey tape to use as players. In the NHL, players are given 100-page playbooks and expected to know them inside and out. But this is the WCHL, a league that one of the veterans, after a few too many beers last night, called the "Who Cares Hockey League."

"This is just a foundation," Kells explains. "Guys who played for me in Topeka know my philosophy: Hockey ain't that complicated."

Kells proceeds to go through various situations and asks the guys to align the "players" in their proper position for each scenario. (Not much of a strategist, it's the last time Kells will draw out strategy for the next four months.)

- **The fore-check:** "Center always supports the wingers."
- **The breakout:** "Wingers, you have the easiest job out there; get your ass on the boards. We need to win the battles on the wall."
- **Defensive zone face-offs:** "When we win it, you have three choices: Get the puck over the blue line, fuck off, or fuck off." (In other words, just get the puck out of our end.)
- **Power Play:** "Shoot the fucking puck. It's all about getting the highest-percentage shot you can get."
- **Communication:** "You gotta talk. If you go to an NHL game, all you hear are guys chirping."

After going through a dozen or so different game situations, Kells goes around the room and asks each player to give an example of something "we need to do to win on Friday." A few numbskulls can't think of anything, but most have one:

Jason Firth: "Limit shots."
Peter Brearley: "Give 100 percent."
Chris "Cat" Felix: "Do the little things well"

Looch: "Communicate."
Mark Edmundson: "Shoot the puck."
John Vary: "Block shots."
Dave Milek: "Get it on net."
Steve Zoryk: "Good D is good O."
Ryan Hartung: "Stand up for your teammates."
Paul Willett: "Limit turnovers."
Scott Hay: "Good dumps."
Josh Maser: "Fore-check hard."
Glen Mears: "Finish your checks."
Me: "Play shift to shift."
Quinn Fair: "Stay off spiced rum at the cigar bar."

Quinn's comment gets a good laugh, but Kells returns the focus to business. "We're keeping it simple," he says. "Some of the best teams I have seen have no systems. They just go out and play. This is pro hockey, but it's still hockey, you know what I mean? I can map this play out and that play out, but we may never use it. You are here to play hockey. If you are too worried about what system you should be using, then you are fucked. Dancers dance. Singers sing. Do your job and play within your strengths. Our goal is to win. Plain and fuckin' simple.

"We're not a favorite to win in this league. If they say we're the underdog, I say, 'Fuckin' fine with me.' That means we got something to prove."

For some of the players, this will be their last season, and others will have another ten years to toil in the deep minors, hoping to graduate to the next level. As for me, I'm not sure if this will be both my first and last year of pro; I haven't decided. For now, I just want to play.

Work

It's only two weeks into the season, and my foray into the "play" world of pro hockey—which has already caused me to shed five pounds from my already thin frame—at times, especially in the morning when I hobble out of bed, feels like a repetitive grind. If I'm going to keep this from feeling like work, I will have to pace myself, because as Kells said the other day, "A season is a marathon, not a sprint."

Mark Twain called the play-versus-work conflict "a great law of human action," and I'm growing to appreciate what he meant when he wrote that "work consists of whatever a body is obliged to do and . . . play consists of whatever a body is not obliged to do. There are wealthy gentlemen in England who drive four-horse passenger-coaches twenty or thirty miles on a daily line, in the summer, because the privilege costs them considerable money; but if they were offered wages for the service that would turn it into work, then they would resign."

The six-month-long regular season consists of seventy-two games, plus the play-offs, which can tack on an extra twenty games if we make it to the finals. Half will be at home, half on the road. Since there are only eight teams in the league, and since this is a business in which the more seats that are filled the more owners make, we will play some teams far too many times for anyone's liking. We will play the WCHL's other California-based, Southern Division teams—the Fresno Falcons, Long Beach Ice Dogs and San Diego Gulls—thirteen times each. For these games, we will travel by bus. It's an hour and a half to Fresno; two and a half hours to Long Beach; and four hours to San Diego. But we will fly to play Northern Division teams—the Anchorage Aces, Idaho

Steelheads, Tacoma Sabercats and Colorado Gold Kings—whom we will battle eight times each (four at home, and four away).

* * *

Tonight is the first edition of "Coach's Corner." Every Thursday night for the rest of the season, a local radio station, KGEO, will broadcast the hour-long show hosted by Kells and the Condors play-by-play guy, Kevin Bartl. Such shows, in which fans call in and ask questions of the coach and a guest player, are a staple of every minor-league hockey team's P.R. efforts. "When the team's doing well, it's a love fest," defenseman and six-year pro Quinn Fair told me. "But when the team's stinking up the joint, the fans just abuse us."

This is the first season as "voice of the Condors" for Bartl, a twenty-seven-year-old native of Rochester, New York. He's got the classic, deep, radio-guy voice, but he has just enough of a folksy, Bakersfield drawl to fit in here. The weekly show will be held in the lobby-bar at the Holiday Inn next door to the rink. When we're on the road, Bartl will interview the coach in his hotel room. About thirty fans, including my first-ever fan, Breanna (in her Condors jersey again), have come to see the inaugural show.

After a few minutes chatting with Kells, Bartl opens the floor up for questions. Breanna confidently steps up to the mike.

"Who's gonna be our starting goalie?" she asks.

"Well," Kells begins, hesitantly. "We've got two good goalies. Both Looch and Haysie played for me last year. Looch is a real solid veteran, and Scott showed a lot of improvement last year. But Looch will get the start tomorrow night."

"What about Kenny Baker?" Breanna follows. "He did good last week."

"Oh, Kenny?" Kells says, cracking a smile. "I hear he writes a good book."

* * *

As I stretch on the locker room floor the morning before the pregame skate, a solidly built guy with wavy black hair who looks vaguely familiar is sitting at a stall across from me. He's taping his stick and, since the music is blaring and everyone is ignoring him, he's keeping to himself. I ask Larry who the new guy is. "Todd Esselmont," he says. "He's a forward. Kells picked him up from Tacoma on waivers."

I knew he looked familiar. Esselmont scored on me in last week's exhibition game—the low shot to my left. The bastard is now one of us.

It's tough being the new guy. Rookies are afraid he might take their job, and veterans are afraid that, if he is good, he could take away their ice time. Economou told me to watch my back, and I am starting to see why. As long as he's not a goalie, he can't bother me—unless he takes joy in shooting pucks at my head or nuts.

"Hey, Bakes," Josh says to me during our warm-up sprints. "That new guy is thirty years old. Another old fart."

During the drills, which the guys skate through lazily since it's a game day, Esselmont shows that he has some serious wheels. He's a winger with speed, able to cut from the boards to the net in a flash. So why is he a thirty-year-old rookie? After practice, as he stays out to shoot on me, I have to ask him.

He explains how he went from playing major junior hockey as a teenager to working as a truck driver in British Columbia and Alberta. He hauled cement in an 18-wheeler and drove a Coke delivery truck. Last year, he started working as a bartender at the Shark Club, a nightclub directly across the street from the arena where the NHL's Vancouver Canucks play. He says, "The players would come in flashing wads of cash, cocky as hell, and I started thinking, 'I can play in the NHL. I could be these guys.'"

Twenty-five pounds overweight from drinking and smoking, Esselmont, who is from the British Columbia mountain town of Kamloops, started skating every day and working out at the gym. He then wrote every NHL team asking for a tryout. When none wrote back, he contacted the Tacoma Sabercats, which was the closest pro team to Vancouver, and they promptly cut him earlier this week after they brought in a rookie in his early twenties with more long-term promise. "Kells said he liked what he saw of me in the exhibition game, so he's giving me a shot," he says. "We'll see."

"I'm basically doing the same thing," I say.

"You looked pretty good against Tacoma," he says. "Even though I scored on ya."

As Esselmont fires a few more pucks into the net, I learn that his story is not so different from mine.

He says, "I didn't want to wonder 'What if?' the rest of my life, you know? My New Year's resolution last year was to ask the universe for some answers to what I am supposed to be doing with my life. I wanted stability. And within a month I met my fiancée. Her name's Lesa. She has two little boys, eleven and seven, and I consider them my own. They look up to me like a dad, and I realized that I wanted to be someone they could admire.

"Lesa and the kids would come watch me play in the rec league, and she would say, 'You're really talented. You should do something with your talent.' At first, I said, 'Fuck off, it's not that easy,' but she just kept on me. She would tell me, 'When I was a little girl I dreamed that I would marry a husband who was a hockey player.' She made me believe in myself. So here I am."

"Where is she?" I ask.

"Back in Vancouver. She can't move here until I have some stability," he says. "I'm just taking it day by day."

He rapid-fires the last few pucks. His snap shots are low and accurate–dinging off the posts.

"I want to take this as far as I can," he says. "I think I have at least five good years left in me."

* * *

Kells doesn't have to tell me; I know I'm not going to play tonight. Sure, I thought the same thing before last week's exhibition game, but that was just that, an exhibition. It wasn't for the books. This one will count.

Both goalies, especially Hay, have improved dramatically over the last two weeks. It's predictable: The more shots you face, the stronger you get, the quicker your reflexes, the better you become. Likewise, the fewer shots you face, the less you improve. It's tough to see the other goalies find their groove amid a sea of pucks while I scrap to see any action I can. But it's a long season. Be patient, I tell myself. Things can change.

When I return to the apartment after our pregame meal of chicken and pasta at a restaurant near the rink, I begin what will become a ritual. Ryan is on the couch watching TV. I sit in the armchair. A little later, he throws me the remote and heads to his room for a two-hour nap. I will read or watch TV for the next few hours. Then, at 4:30 P.M.–two and a half hours before game time–we will drive together to the rink, arriving shortly before five o'clock. A few dozen fans are already lined up in the plaza in front of the arena.

The mood inside the locker room is workman-like. The guys have had the last six months to rest, and tonight they will start their jobs. As they tape sticks, stretch, and have Larry tape their ankles and wrists, I read over the pregame notes that Kevin Bartl has prepared.

Expectations are high that we are going to give Bakersfield its first championship team. We have a new coach, new goalies, and a slew of new players from the Central Hockey League. And we kicked some mighty ass last week against Tacoma. The team's advertising slogan—"Bring it On!"—is reflected in the confident attitude of the players and the fans, hundreds of whom are now outside, even though the doors don't open until 6:00 P.M.

Yet no one expects tonight's match to be a cakewalk. The Long Beach Ice Dogs are loaded with talent. While we have defensemen who are well under six feet—Chris Felix (5' 9", 190) and Ryan (5' 9", 180)—the Ice Dogs defensemen have NHL size: David Kudelka (6' 4", 215), Todd Kidd (6' 3", 210) and Lloyd Shaw (6' 3", 215). Long Beach also boasts the tallest player in minor-professional hockey in left-winger Jeff Ewasko, who is NBA-sized at 6' 7" and 242 pounds. Meanwhile, our goon, Josh, is only 6' 1". This could be a problem.

The Ice Dogs are expected to be physical. Their General Manager, Jon Van Boxmeer, is a legendary NHL goon who played for the Buffalo Sabres in the eighties. "Boxy" is known for his equally hard-nosed hockey teams.

At 5:30 P.M., Kells calls a quick meeting to go over the lines and our three defensive pairings. Esselmont is dressing, but he will be our extra forward, meaning he will sit on the bench most of the game with Maser. The pregame pep talk is when most coaches, especially in the NHL, diagram plays on a dry-erase board or maybe review video of the opposition. Not Kells. True to form, Kells sticks to his fundamentalist, old-time hockey mantras.

"Keep 'er simple, boys."
"Do your job."
"Play within yourself. Get the puck on net."
"Short shifts. Win the battles along the boards."
"Have fun out there."

After Kells's pep talk, the guys disperse into their pregame rituals, activities that they will repeat consistently for the next six months. Maser stares at the floor, a giant pinch of chewing tobacco under his lower front lip. Jeff Goldie and Looch ride the stationary bikes. Cookie squeezes a tennis ball to loosen his stiff hands and rubs Atomic Balm on his sore back. Cat sits naked in the hot tub watching TV. John Vary, Mark Edmundson, and Scott Hay smoke cigarettes out back on the loading dock, where Kells eventually joins them.

A third of the team smokes cigarettes. As one of the training-camp rookies observed, "It's right out of *Slap Shot.*" But since Kells also smokes, they don't have to worry about its hurting their playing time.

The owner, Jonathan Fleisig, has flown in from New York for tonight's game. Kells didn't know whether he would make it because Jonathan lost his best friend in last month's World Trade Center collapse. His office was two blocks from the towers, and as a result, we're the only team in the league that has the letters "WTC" painted on the back of our helmets in memoriam. Jonathan has a boyish face for a multimillionaire Wall Street investor. He firmly shakes my hand and says, "Great game last week. I saw the videotape. You look like you can actually play."

I pretend not to be insulted by his surprise.

He then invites me into Kells's office under the stands, where I can hear the fans starting to file in above us as Kells sits filling out the night's lineup card.

"I know I've told both of you this separately," Jonathan says, "but since we're all here, I'm going to say it again." Jonathan is direct, in that unmistakably New York manner that makes everything sound like he's barking directions at a cabbie. He points at Kells and says, "He's the boss, Kenny. If it's not working out here, you're out. It's his team, and it's his call." As Jonathan talks, Kells uncomfortably shuffles through some papers on his desk. I look Jonathan right in the eyes and say, "Of course, he's the boss."

Fortunately, for the first time since I met him, Kells—inexplicably—shows some affection for me and says, "We like having Kenny around. I'm sure it'll work out."

* * *

Welcome to the hockey capital of the West. Everybody, on your feet!

The announcer, Chris Peace, introduces every player under a spotlight, after which they line up on the blue line. Some carry American and Canadian flags onto the ice. The crowd of 5,370—who have paid anywhere from nineteen bucks for a seat near the ice where you can can count the stitches in the players' faces, to five bucks for cheap seats in the upper balcony, where it's like watching ants play—stands and cheers as each player steps on the ice, Cookie receiving the loudest cheers. I'm sitting about twenty rows up behind our net. No Bakersfield player has ever graduated from the WCHL to the NHL, but, to these fans, most of whom will never attend a big-league game, this is The Show.

Just before the singing of the Canadian and American national anthems, Cookie skates to center ice and, speaking into a microphone, reads an opening-game prayer to the hushed congregation:

"Lord, we ask that you continue to heal our nation in this time of tragedy and conflict. We ask for your eternal peace on behalf of all those who perished in the terrible events of September 11th. May the promise of your word comfort those who have lost loved ones, and console their grieving hearts. Grant your divine wisdom to guide our leaders, and we ask for your care and protection for all those now called to defend us. For this, we humbly pray in your name. Amen."

With homage to God and Country out of the way, followed by Queen's "We Will Rock You" booming from the overhead speakers, the crowd is adequately prepared to see thirty-six men punch, elbow, slash, body-slam and bloody each other on a sheet of ice for the next two and a half hours.

The rink announcer, Chris Peace, attempts to get the fans even more fired up with a charge right out of the pro-wrestling-announcer handbook: "I know we have patriotic Americans here tonight. But do we have any *Condors fans* here tonight?" It works. The crowd cheers wildly.

The opening ten minutes are impressive ones in which we keep Long Beach pinned in their end. If it weren't for some big saves by their nimble young Swedish goalie, Marten Engren, we could easily be up by three goals. But the twenty-four-year-old goalie stymies our best attempts. Engren, who is about two inches shorter than I am, wears giant white pads that are three inches taller than mine. I have pad envy. I really need bigger pads.

Brearley looks even stronger and faster than he did against Tacoma. He has the size of the Los Angeles Kings's Jason Allison and the niftiness of Mario Lemieux. He could be a potent force at this level.

The speed of the game is twice that of practice—not to mention about ten times more physical. No one carries the puck on his stick for more than a few seconds without a slash coming down on his arms or a two hundred-pound body checking into him.

Halfway into the first period, Cookie sends a crisp pass to Brearley, who cuts sharply to his right to evade the approaching defenseman. Just as

Brearley is about to scoot past the defender and go in one-on-one against Engren, the defender sticks out his knee, which smacks against Brearley's left knee. Brearley drops to the ice, wincing in pain. The crowd falls quiet.

As the play continues, he struggles to his feet and limps to the bench, where Larry assists him down the hallway and back to the training room.

By the time I get there Brearley is lying back on a training table as Dr. Hamilton gently tugs and twists his leg to determine what part of his knee is injured. Brearley bites his lip when the doc stretches on the media collateral, or MCL.

"I'm almost positive you strained your MCL," the doctor says.

"How long will I be fuckin' out?" Brearley asks.

"Probably four to six weeks," Hamilton says to the guy who has been looking like our team's best forward.

When Hamilton leaves the room, Brearley, choking back tears, turns to me and says, "This fuckin' sucks."

Brearley's misfortune, however, is Esselmont's gain. As soon as Brearley limped off the ice, Kells put Esselmont in his place on the right wing. It's his first ice time as a pro; too bad his fiancée and her two boys aren't here to see him do it.

On his second shift, however, Esselmont receives a harsh welcome to the pros when a Long Beach player inadvertently slashes him in the mouth. The blow smacks his lip against his upper front teeth, two of which crack. His teeth cut into his lip, blood squirting onto the ice like ketchup.

Esselmont can only look down to the ice on all fours as he tries to regain his composure. As the pool of blood spreads, the referee blows the whistle, and Larry sprints out to Esselmont and presses a towel to his face to sponge up the blood. In between the first and second period, one of the doctors, without using Novocaine, will sew the cut on his lip with five stitches; the two chipped teeth will be capped next week. Nonetheless, Esselmont returns to the ice for the rest of the game. In most walks of life, if you get smashed in the face so bad that you need stitches and dental work, there's a good chance you'll take, at least, a week off from work. Esselmont only misses ten minutes.

After two periods of dominating the play, we hold a 2–0 lead. Looch has made several great saves. If it weren't for Looch, in fact, the game could easily be tied.

In the locker room at the end of the second, Cookie, who has scored our two goals, is spent. As soon as he gets into the room, he takes off his skates and hobbles into the training room, climbs up on the edge of the hot tub and dips his feet into the steaming water.

"What's wrong?" I ask.

"Cramping," he says with a cringe.

Ten years ago, Cookie's body would never cramp. But he's thirty-two now. Eventually, your body wears out.

Hockey players learn from a young age not to show pain. So when they do show it, they're almost always suffering, which is what Cookie's clenched-teeth grimace indicates. But while Cookie might feel like walking back to the locker room, taking off all his equipment and heading home, the reality is that he can't. He has five mouths to feed. He has started selling real estate in the off-season, but that doesn't come close to the money he makes punishing his body for six months straight. That's why once his foot cramps loosen, he towels off his feet, carefully steps back to the locker room, rolls his sore feet on a golf ball, slides back into his skates, squeezes a tennis ball, and returns for the third period. This is the Cookie the fans don't see. To them, he is a machine, the most reliable, consistent player the franchise has ever seen. He is seemingly effortless on the ice, making it almost look easy. But, behind the scenes, it's anything but. I've been writing about entertainers for most of my journalism career, and when I see his private struggle to keep his body functioning I realize that while minor league hockey is much more brutal, pro hockey and Hollywood share at least one common ethic: the show must always go on.

But Cookie might as well have stayed in the room. Within the first few minutes, we take several stupid penalties. A minute and a half in to the penalty-kill, Long Beach scores off a rebound that Looch sloppily allowed to pop out front onto the player's stick. A few minutes later, Long Beach scores another two goals, less than a minute apart, both long shots that Looch saw the entire way. Suddenly, we're down 3–2. More than a few fans, fueled by several cups of beer and the disgust of seeing their hometown boys stinking up the joint on opening night, start booing. The Bakersfield honeymoon, apparently, is over.

A part of me–the competitive part that thinks I can be as good as Looch and deserve to play–is happy to see Looch let in some soft goals because it could make it possible for me to get my shot. But the other part of me–the loyal team player–feels terrible for the guys, especially Looch, because, while he's my competition, he's also a fellow goalie.

Just when things are looking grim for our season opener, they get even grimmer. Thirty-five seconds after their third goal, Long Beach scores a fourth goal on a breakaway after Vary coughs up the puck to an Ice Dogs forward. Suddenly, Bakersfield's church of hockey falls as silent as a real one.

Kells immediately sends Maser, who has only seen a few shifts the entire game, out to try to stir things up a little and pick a fight. But since the Ice Dogs are up by three goals, none of the Long Beach players will take the bait.

Our peskiest forward, Paul Rosebush, then tries to fire up the crowd with two minutes left by picking a fight with the 6' 7" Ewasko, but his efforts are useless. Ewasko, whose arms seem as long as Rosie is tall, just holds him at arm's length and pummels his face with his free hand.

We lose 5–2.

Afterward, Kells walks into the locker room and glares at every player. "You guys just ran out of fucking gas," he says calmly. He's not so much angry as he is disappointed. "We played forty solid minutes, and then we didn't even fuckin' show up for the final twenty. Luckily, you all have a chance tomorrow night against Fresno to show me that tonight was just a fluke. See you all here in the morning."

Less than an hour after the game, the fans have gathered in the Condors chat room to offer a harsher assessment of their team.

Dante46: Depressing . . . simply depressing.

Tuffstuff: I hear ya. The dogs got a hold of some kibble and mauled the Condors bad.

Droeskefan: For some reason our Condors just stopped checking!!! We were flat in the third . . . How many times do you see a team score not one, not two, not three, not four, but five unanswered goals against a team in the third period? Also, I hope Brearley is O.K.

Brearley is not O.K. He needs crutches and, depending on the results of an MRI, he might need surgery. He will miss, minimally, the next ten games.

In pro sports, it's useful to remember that failure often precedes success. Michael Jordan was cut from his high school basketball team and went on to be the most dominant player in the history of basketball. The New England Patriots went from the cellar one season to winning the Super Bowl the next. Now I'm a third-string minor-pro hockey goalie even though I had a pituitary brain tumor two years ago.

* * *

The night after getting spanked by Long Beach, we play the Fresno Falcons, at home again. Jonathan wants to address the team before the game. Jonathan, a baseball nut who openly admits that his knowledge of hockey is scant, wants to get a few things off his chest after seeing last night's contest.

The players sit obediently at their stalls, on their best behavior since Jonathan has the power to fire everyone in the room.

"Look," he says. "I want to win just as much as the next guy, probably more." "I'm competitive, and this town is starved for a winner. You saw last night how quickly they can turn on you. When you win, they are the best fans in the world. But if you lose, they will let you know they don't like it. But, you know what? A month from now, no one is going to remember you lost last night, but they will remember you visiting their school, or signing an autograph, or saying hi to them at the Holiday Inn after the game. I am big on community, guys. It probably sounds odd to you, but that means a lot to me, maybe as much as winning.

"I know some of you might think this community stuff is a bunch of crap, and that's fine. But what you need to remember is that, as a pro athlete, you have a unique opportunity to make a difference with people. People will listen to you. Kids look up to you. Most of all, I want you guys to have fun. This is a special time in your life. You know how many guys would give their left nut to be in your position? You get paid to play a game you've played since you were kids. It's special. So have fun while you are here. And if your dream is to move on to the next level, we won't stop you. If that's your dream, I will support you."

Jonathan then asks the guys if they have any questions, complaints or concerns. No one speaks up, even though I've heard a lot of the guys complaining that they haven't yet received a paycheck, which they will start receiving every Tuesday, which is not for another four days. Ryan has been bumming rides because he has no money for gas. Many guys have empty refrigerators because they can't afford groceries. But no one dares speak.

I am impressed by Jonathan's sermon. He seems to have a good perspective on sports and its role in a community, and to me he comes across as a businessman with a heart. Not all the players agree. "What a dick," one veteran murmurs after Jonathan's speech. "He thinks signing autographs is as important as winning."

Kells opts not to deliver a pregame speech, apparently figuring the guys know what they have to do: play hard for sixty minutes, not just forty like last night. He thought most of the lines played well together. He was not, however, impressed with Looch's performance, even though he stopped thirty-one shots. Scott Hay will get the start; Looch will back up. I'll be in the stands trying not to be too selfish in my hoping that Hay lets in some stinkers.

About five thousand fans, a few hundred less than last night, show up for the game. As I take my seat behind our net, the usher quips, "The place would be packed if they'd won last night."

Unlike last night's game, we don't come out flying. This being its first game of the year, Fresno is riled up, and a few hundred rowdy members of its fan club are sitting in the sections near Hay cheering on their team and chanting at Hay, "You suck!"

Our team is loaded with experienced offensive talent–Willett, Firth, Cookie, Goldie, Vary–but we're having trouble getting any shots on net, let alone the kind of high-quality ones from the slot that it will take to beat the Fresno goalie, David Mitchell, the league's rookie of the year last season.

When a Fresno defenseman blows a slap shot past Hay, who looks sharper than he does in practice, but still unsteady, Goldie takes it upon himself to pick a fight. For the first time since the national anthem, the fans rise to their feet and cheer.

It might have been smarter, though, if Goldie had chosen a weaker opponent than Kory Murphy. The fight gets off to a bad start when Murphy is able to rip off Goldie's helmet without losing his. Hitting a hard-plastic helmet tends to break the bones in your hand, which is why the player who gets the other guy's helmet off has an advantage.

Goldie is a tough guy, and he is able to pop Murphy in the face five or six times, but Murphy, whose shots have more weight behind them, gets in his own punches. A few to the cheek and nose, and, finally, a blow to the side of Goldie's head. Goldie, however, punches Murphy's helmet as many times as he hits flesh. When Murphy starts pounding Goldie mercilessly, the linesmen jump in and stop the fight. *Amen.* (That night, Maser, who the minute he finally moved into a team apartment taped a poster of Muhammad Ali on his wall, offered his assessment of the fight: "The problem was that Goldie had no defense. He got off a lot of punches and connected, but his head was fucked. If you do that in The Show, when you have a 220-pound guy with big fucking hands pounding you, you're not going to last long. You'll get knocked out.")

At intermission, Goldie sits dazed at his stall with multiple knuckle marks all over his face. He keeps sniffling to keep the blood from running out of his nose and has stuck both hands into a bag of ice. This sport, I am reminded, is fucking brutal.

By the midway point of the second, the shots on goal are even—about twenty each—yet we are down 2–0 due to another soft goal let in by Hay. I tell myself, I could have had that.

The Fresno fans point at Hay and chant in unison, "You suck! You suck! You suck!"

Jonathan fidgets in his seat across from our team's bench.

I watch.

Kells nervously paces the bench and barks at the players. "If you're not gonna skate, get the fuck off the ice! . . . Hartsy, look before you pass! . . . This is fuckin' embarrassing." In an effort to get us back in the game, Kells keeps putting out the veterans. Meanwhile, Maser and Esselmont sit on the bench, getting only a shift or two each period. But Kells keeps playing the vets because they are making the big money, they are the ones who are expected to lead the team. Never mind that the oldsters are sucking wind like asthmatics.

Goldie—swollen knuckles and all—gets us back in the game with fifty seconds left in the period by swatting in a rebound off Mitchell. But it's not enough to keep Kells, whose voice is already growing hoarse from hollering at just about everyone on the bench but Anthony the stick boy, from laying into the guys at intermission.

"Where's Cookie?" Kells asks no one in particular. Larry, who is checking to make sure the stitches in Quinn Fair's upper lip aren't falling out, replies, "In the tub."

Kells's face is tomato red. "Well, get him the fuck in here!"

When Cookie hobbles in a few minutes later, Kells doesn't draw up any new plays on the board, he doesn't switch up the forward lines or devise a new forechecking scheme that might give us more scoring chances. Instead, he simply issues a warning: "Some of you need to ask yourselves why you are here. Are you here just to fuck off and avoid getting a real job? Are you here because you want to get laid by dirties? Or are you here to do your job and play hockey? Because there ain't a lot of guys doing their job. There are a lot of good players out there, and I could call any of them tomorrow. I have a stack of résumés on my desk. I could have ten new guys in here tomorrow who will skate their balls off. Some of you need to show me something, any-thing–a shot on goal, a hit, pound the piss out of somebody. I don't care what you do. Just do something."

Kells spits his gum into the trash can and sighs.

"All I know is that if I don't start seeing something, I can guarantee you some of you won't have a job come Monday morning."

Kells storms out the back door to have a smoke, leaving the guys sit-ting alone, sweaty and quiet, in shock. Twenty-four hours ago, we were the "Bring it On" Condors that were going to–finally–bring a cham-pionship to Bakersfield. Now, after a hundred minutes of hockey, we're just a bunch of losers who may soon become unemployed losers.

Rather than light a fire under their asses, Kells's speech has the op-posite effect. The guys play scared, afraid to make a mistake that will get them fired, and just a minute and a half into the period Fresno has scored again–on a clean slap shot from the top of the face-off circle that slides along the ice to Hay's right. They score a power-play goal ten min-utes later to extend the lead to 4–1.

The boo birds in the stands start chirping. We look tired, out of shape, which, of course, we are. Kells has not skated us very hard in practice, and the lack of conditioning is showing, especially in the smokers, who are desperately sucking in air as if they're atop Everest.

Then, the referee hands us a gift, calling tripping on a Fresno player. We've already had seven power plays tonight, yet we have no goals to show for it. Kells puts our offensive guns out: Cookie, Willett, Goldie, John Vary and Jason Firth on the point. Willett, who still has not lost his summertime pudge and has reeked of alcohol nearly every morning since training camp, starts showing flashes of the brilliance that has made him a Bakersfield hero, and won him the league's MVP title two years ago. He handles the puck as though it's on a string, weaving around defenders with quick cuts and fakes, popping in a rebound past a diving Mitchell.

For the last few minutes of the game, we give it our best–Cookie, ever the warrior, even scores with five minutes left–and the crowd comes back from its funeral break. Still, we lose 4–3.

The locker room is silent but for the sound of players ripping tape off their shin pads and hanging up their gear. Hay, who must have sweat off ten pounds tonight, stares angrily at the floor. I take a seat at my locker as Kells walks in.

"We have fuck-all to be proud of," he shouts. "I thought I had put together a good team, but guess what? Every team in this league is good. We have to be better. Maybe I was misled into thinking we were good. I don't know." He's pacing. Blood pressure is turning his cheeks lipstick red. You can see the fear on the faces of players, who, being on day-to-day contracts, face the real possibility of getting fired.

"This should be a wake-up call to everyone in this room," Kells says, settling down a little. "There are no easy games in this league; this ain't the Central Hockey League. You should be embarrassed about tonight. Five thousand people paid money to come here and see you guys shit the fuckin' bed. Come Monday, we're going to do more conditioning, more skating. Some of you look slower than me out there. We're 0 and 2. As professionals, that should burn you up inside. It's a fuckin' disgrace."

Just as he's about to leave the stunned-silent room, Kells turns and angrily points his finger at us. "Nobody's job is safe," he says. "Nobody."

Turn

When someone in the real world of work does a bad job, only a few coworkers and his boss know about it. When a pro athlete screws up, it happens in front of thousands, sometimes millions, of fans. Then he may be pilloried in the press and criticized by couch potato know-it-alls on talk radio and television. His value as a human being is even debated inside Internet chat rooms.

I've published some poorly written stories in my journalism career, but there's no page in the sports section dedicated to showing just how many lousy stories I've churned out, no Web sites keeping a permanent record of it, certainly no talk-radio show dedicated to the subject.

But for a pro athlete, even one in the deep minors, public accountability is a fact of life. Even our elected politicians conduct the majority of their business, and make their mistakes, in the cocoon of closed-door sessions. In Hollywood, where I've spent a career documenting the personal lives of public people, actors and actresses are known mostly for their fictional characters. But jocks are out there naked, playing out all of our strengths and weaknesses for everyone to see. A helmet and bulky pads can't even hide you.

Considering the pressure, it's understandable why pro athletes cope with the stress in some extreme ways. For hockey players, it's often with booze, and after just a few weeks in Bakersfield I realize that beer bottles are a common therapist.

A couple of days after our loss to Fresno, the Condors host a golf tournament at the Rio Bravo Country Club to raise money for Kern County fire fighters. Fans spent ninety-five bucks for an afternoon of golf with the players. We all are asked to put on team-issued black golf shirts with a Condors logo and be paired up with eager fans. Since it is sunny, over ninety degrees, and most guys would rather be sitting at the bar, most of the players use the tourney as an excuse to guzzle beer. By the end of the day, almost everyone is smashed—even I am. I rarely drink, and it only takes me four beers to get drunk. Fortunately for the players, we don't have to give a speech to the fans that night at a post-tournament dinner banquet. Unfortunately, Kells does.

Obviously inebriated enough to flunk a roadside DUI test, Kells wobbles up to the podium and slurs, "What can I say? We lost both games this weekend. We sucked. People are down. But don't worry, 'cuz I got a joke for ya."

Oh, no. Someone stop him.

"Okay," he begins, his impaired brain trying to remember the joke. Most of the fans are older, local business executives. Classy rich guys, not hockey players. Kells doesn't care.

Please, don't tell a dirty joke.

"Fifty years from now, a father takes his son to New York City, and at the southern tip of the city the son sees a giant parking lot and asks, 'Daddy, why is there a giant parking lot in the middle of Manhattan?'"

The September 11th attacks happened just last month. Almost every guy in this room had an American flag on their car; a few of them are military veterans. Kells is a Canadian hockey coach whose closest brush with war has been bench-clearing brawls.

"And the dad says, 'Well, son, the World Trade Center used to be here.'"

The room has turned so uncomfortably quiet, you could hear an ant fart. Oblivious, Kells continues. "The son asks his dad, 'What's the World Trade Center?' And the dad says, 'It was a giant building that the Arabs knocked down a long time ago.'

"His son asks, 'Who were the Arabs?'

"The father puts his arm around his son, smiles and says, 'Oh, you don't have to worry about them anymore.'"

A few people laugh, but most stare into their emptied plates. I was just relieved no one socked him. As Kells went back to the bar for another one, Felix took away his car keys.

* * *

My little brother, Kris, can't understand why, after my playing respectably in the Tacoma game and after the team lost two straight with mediocre goaltending, I'm not only sitting in the stands but not getting regular practice time.

"It's complicated," I tell him over the phone. "Pro hockey is not a meritocracy."

"It should be," he says fiercely.

"But even if I was better than the other two guys, they've both been hired to play here. So the team is gonna give them every chance to improve. It's political, man. I just have to put in my time."

"Kenny," Kris says. "That's the problem. You don't have time."

* * *

The day before our third game, against the Colorado Gold Kings at home, at a time when we really need some inspiration, Willett, our hard-partying captain, steps up and acts like a leader when he calls a players-only meeting on the ice after practice.

"O.K.," he says, "I know I played like horse shit last weekend, a lot of us did. We need to hit and move the puck. We were awful last weekend. You probably saw on the Web site that a lot of fans saw how bad we were and are saying it. Me included. So let's show 'em tomorrow night. They don't know hockey that well, but they know when we lose, and it hurts the team. So let's get it together, boys."

Before the game, I write "Fun!" in marker on the dry-erase board. It is as much a motivator for the other guys as it is a reminder to myself not to get so down for not playing.

I don't know if it's my uplifting admonition, which is doubtful, or Willett's pep talk yesterday, or just luck, but after the first period we are up 2–0 over Colorado and having fun, leading with goals by Goldie and bruising winger Steve Zoryk. But Colorado, which has a lot of fire power up front, evens up the score just five minutes into the second.

To cool Colorado's momentum, Kells pulls one of his old-time hockey tricks: He puts Maser out to pick a fight. As soon as the puck drops, Maser skates over to 6' 1" Colorado forward Chad Cabana, a muscular guy who in 1993 was drafted by the NHL's Florida Panthers, but who has played most of his career in the American Hockey League. Cabana racked up 250 penalty minutes last season. Safe to say, Cabana could inflict some serious damage on the less-experienced Maser.

It's Maser's first fight of the season, and, since Kells is paying him over three hundred and fifty bucks a week to be our designated goon, this is his first big test. The two heavyweights drop their gloves and sticks and shadowbox each other at center ice. For a lot of hockey fans, this kind of boxing-like standoff is one of the most exciting moments in a minor-league hockey game. Two grown men with their fists up, readying to pound each other. Raw, pure brutality. Yet, unlike boxing, the gloves are off and there are no written rules–only that both players will receive a five-minute penalty for fighting, and the officials won't break it up until one guy is clearly losing, or both guys tire out.

Hit or be hit.

Maser charges at Cabana like a frothing pit bull and grabs Cabana's jersey with his left hand, throwing several right hooks square on his jaw. Cabana "turtles" up in a shell–his hands defensively up in front of his face–and the refs step in and hold back Josh. The fight is over. Josh dropped him in eight seconds.

Kells's strategy works. A minute later, Steve Zoryk stuffs in a rebound off the goalie's pads and we go up 3–2.

Yet for the rest of the game Colorado dominates play. Like in last week's games, our players look dog-tired, out of shape. But Looch makes several outstanding saves and keeps us ahead by one goal. Glove saves, pad saves, he even stops one with his head. We can smell victory; we are about to shake the monkey–our winless record–off our backs.

With a minute left, announcer Chris Peace riles the crowd with his bravado: "Everyone on your feet! It's time to do it–Bakersfield style."

The fans, perhaps convinced that if they shout loud enough they will inspire their team to hold on for the win, rise and clap in unison. The players on the bench stand and slash their sticks against the boards.

Fifty seconds left.

A Colorado defenseman takes possession of the puck and dumps it into our zone. The fans cheer louder as John Vary retrieves the puck from the corner and shoots it up ice, hoping to get over our blue line.

Forty seconds left.

Vary, however, fails to execute any of Kells's three breakout options–get it out, fuck off or fuck off–and the puck ends up on the stick of Colorado defenseman Aaron Boh, who skates in to the top of the face-off circle. Every player on the ice charges to the front of our net–their players trying to block Looch's sight or tip it in and our guys doing everything but rape them in an effort to prevent a goal. It's a scrum-on-ice.

The crowd collectively holds its breath as Boh fires a wrister at Looch, who is crouched low, fighting to see the puck through the maze of legs and sticks and wide bodies. The puck heads upward and, as if it has eyes of its own, sails into the back of the net, both tying the game at 3–3 and instantly sucking the life out of the crowd.

In the WCHL, there is no overtime. Rather, a shootout is held in which each team is allowed to send five players down one-on-one against the opposing goalie. The teams alternate shots. The team with the most goals after five wins the game and gets two points in the standings. The loser gets one point.

Colorado shoots first, but Looch stops the Colorado player cold with a left toe save. Kells sends the crowd favorite, Jamie Cooke, out first, and the cagey veteran calmly skates in and pokes a shot between the goalie's legs.

After Colorado's fourth shot, we are ahead 1–0. Kells sends Willett out and the fans go nuts because, if our captain scores, we will win the game.

Willett coolly fakes a shot, freezing the goalie, who drops to his knees as Willett skates across the goal mouth, flicking it over the goalie's outstretched arms and into the net. And we win! Finally!

Afterward, Kells is sporting the widest smile I've seen since he almost drunkenly jumped in that pool. "This was huge, boys," he says. "Drink a lot of water, get a good meal, because tomorrow morning we get right on the bus and head down to San Diego for another one. It's their home-opener. And fuck it, we're gonna take that one too!"

* * *

Being a lowly rookie, I have to share a seat on the four-hour bus ride to San Diego. Further, being a rookie, my seat is in the back row of the bus, directly in front of the shitter. Jason Ralph, a red-headed rookie fresh out of Union College whom Kells picked up last week, is my seat mate. In addition to rookies sharing seats, I've just learned the two most important road rules on a minor-league hockey team.

- **Road Rule Number One:** There is absolutely no crapping allowed in the bus bathroom.
- **Road Rule Number Two:** There are no exceptions to Road Rule Number One.

* * *

There are few places in America as geographically close yet culturally far apart as Bakersfield and San Diego.

Bakersfield is an oil and farming town. It's landlocked and often stinks of manure and oil-refinery smog. In the summer, it's hot as an oven; in the winter, it's foggier than a summer in San Francisco. Bakersfield residents talk with a twang that is more Texan than Californian. In Bakersfield, you'll find a lot of young women with high hair and heavy makeup, girls to whom the word "hip" is only used to describe the part of the body at the top of their legs. One of Bakersfield's most cherished institutions, besides high school football, is its hockey team. In short, Bakersfield is a "heartland" kind of town, the kind of place people on the Coasts imagine when they think of the simple, American life.

Meanwhile, just two hundred and fifty miles to the south, sits San Diego, a coastal paradise, a city known for its year-round summer weather and beaches with beautiful babes in bikinis. People talk with surfer-dude accents and wear the hippest fashions. There's no shortage of entertainment opportunities in San Diego. In addition to enjoying the ample beach scenery, one can see the NFL's Chargers or Major League Baseball's Padres, or even take in a play in the downtown theater district. The hockey team, the Gulls, is just another sideshow attraction to an urban citizenry with, if anything, too many social options. And, still, San Diego averages a thousand fans more a game than Bakersfield.

This goes a long way toward explaining why Bakersfield Condors fans love to hate the San Diego Gulls. And as soon as we walk into the locker room at the San Diego Sports Arena most of the players come up with some reasons of their own to hate, if not envy, the Gulls.

It's bad enough that the defending WCHL champions are walking around with a cocky swagger the minute we carry our bags into the rink, but they also have the most attractive cheerleaders in the history of minor league sports.

They're called the "Gulls Girls." Most are models or dancers who aren't good enough to make the Chargers cheerleading squad, but who would out-do most NFL cheerleading squads in other cities.

The Girls prance back and forth in front of our locker room in their tight black pants and cleavage-enhancing blue tops, carrying their

148

little glittery pom-poms and Crest smiles. Of course, almost all of them are blond.

Bakersfield doesn't have cheerleaders. Jonathan considered forming a cheer squad a few seasons ago, but after looking into it concluded he would have to ship in most of the girls from Los Angeles, which was not financially realistic. That doesn't stop the guys from coming up with some names of this nonexistent Condors cheerleading squad. *We'd call 'em the Bakersfield Bimbos . . . no, how about the Screw Crew! . . . or the Puck Sluts!* This is the kind of creativity you get when you throw a pack of sex-starved, pregame-testosterone-pumped pro hockey players together with a gaggle of sexy beach bunnies whose dressing room is right next door to ours.

But the Gulls Girls, who, when not performing on-ice gymnastic routines at intermission or jumping up and down the aisles, are a talented bunch. And we hate the Gulls Guys for having them while all we get is a teen-age boy dressed in a bird outfit.

As the players get dressed, I mill around the locker room and strike up a conversation with San Diego's long-haired goon, Ashlee Langdone, who's sitting outside their locker room watching the Gulls Girls rehearse. In the NFL, it's against league rules to date a member of any team's cheerleading squad. So I ask Langdone if the Gulls have a similar no-dating policy. Just then, a petite Girl scampers by.

"Hey," Langdone grunts at the girl. "Where you guys going out tonight?"

"Pacific Beach," the blond cutie replies.

"So I'll see you there?" Langdone says with a devious smile.

"If you come," she says, giggling flirtatiously.

Langdone turns to me, shrugs his shoulders and flashes a guilty-as-charged grin.

* * *

We have very few rational reasons to think we're going to beat San Diego. First of all, there's the history. Last season, Bakersfield lost eleven of its thirteen games against San Diego, a team returning nearly all of its top players from last year. Plus, in the San Diego team's six years of existence in the WCHL, it has never lost its first game at home. Furthermore, over twelve thousand fans will pack the arena to see the WCHL championship banner raised to the rafters above the rink. Winning will be a daunting task, as if playing in front of this many hostile fans isn't intimidating enough. Just an hour and a half up the freeway in Anaheim is an NHL team, the Ducks, that commonly draws crowds less than tonight's in San Diego. Unlike the Bakersfield fans, the bright-eyed Gulls fans filing in don't hope their team wins; they *expect* them to win.

Luckily, pro hockey is not a rational sport.

Coming off our first win last night, and with the odds stacked against us, the mood on the bench is looser than the first three games at home. We've got nothing to lose and everything to gain. It's the ideal sports psychodynamic. We're so loose, in fact, that when the ceremonial dropping of the puck is conducted by a bombshell model, Willett opens his eyes wide and gawks conspicuously at her ass as she steps off the ice. Our bench breaks into laughter.

The gaiety pays off. In the first three minutes we score two easy goals against San Diego's MVP goalie, Trevor Koenig, who played for Union College in the same league as Colgate, but after I had graduated. Koenig easily should have stopped all of our goals.

Minor league hockey crowds are moodier than unmedicated manic-depressives, and, predictably, the massive arena grows conspicuously quiet. Even the Girls aren't as peppy with their pom-poms.

But, once again, our cigarette-puffing, beer-swilling team runs out of steam in the second half of the game, and we end up being out-shot 42–16. But thanks to several acrobatic saves by Looch, we manage to end regulation in a 3–3 tie. And, once again, thanks to Looch's not letting in any goals in the shootout, we win the shootout when Goldie beats Koenig with a quick wrist shot. Dejected, the Gulls Girls put down their silver pom-poms and head for the showers.

But for us, it will be a pleasant bus ride home.

Around three in the morning, as the bus winds its way back to Bakersfield, most of the players, exhausted from playing two tough games in two nights, sit quietly in their seats sipping beer and watching the California mountain scenery, relieved that they have six days before the next game.

When the bus descends out of the mountains and into Bakersfield's valley, Kells, who is smiling for the first time in a week, pulls the microphone from the driver's dashboard console. "Here's a little Bob Seger for ya," our thirty-four-year-old coach announces. He clears his throat and croons like a country singer . . .

Out there in the spotlight, you're a million miles away
Every ounce of energy, you try to give away
The sweat pours out your body, like the music that you play

Nearly every guy joins in a chorus of drunk men . . .

Here I am, on the road again
There I am, up on the stage
Here I go, playing star again
There I go, turn the page

Todd Esselmont and Quinn Fair sing through the stitches in their lips. Jeff Goldie, knuckle marks on his face from last week's fight, sings along. Peter Brearley, his busted knee locked in a brace, softly taps his foot. Jamie Cooke, father of five, stares groggily ahead. Paul Willett leans against the window belting out the tune. I sit in the back seat, happy that we have seventy more games, seventy more games to chase my dream, seventy more games in which I hope to play star again.

SECOND PERIOD

OCTOBER 21, 2001

Talk

"**W**hy didn't you call me last night?" Brooke says over the phone the morning after our San Diego win.

"I forgot," I say in a dry, hung-over voice.

"But you promised you'd call."

"I didn't have time anyway," I explain, rather unconvincingly. "We had to load up the bus right after the game, then we stopped for dinner. And it was late."

"You still could have called," she insists.

"Not from *the bus*."

"Why not?" she replies. "Cell phones work on buses."

"But I was with the guys."

As soon as I say it I realize how immature I sound, even though it's true. But, remembering what my stepdad Norm told me–*Just don't lose your marriage over it*–I back down and utter those two words that tough-guy hockey players don't say, but good husbands do: "I'm sorry."

* * *

Willett is throwing a "Monday Night Football" party at his house. His wife, a waitress at a local bar, has to work, making him a free man, though he does have to watch their two daughters. "Still," he tells the guys, "we can light it up." But my roommate, Ryan, is not up for going because he doesn't feel like drinking, and it's not just because of his Catholic faith.

Being the smallest guy on the team just got tougher when he got on the scale today and found out he has lost ten pounds since training camp started. He's down to 169. It doesn't help that as a speedy, offensive defenseman he has no goals or assists in his first four games. Worse, he tore some muscles in his right shoulder during the San Diego game when he got slammed into the boards by a beast. Now Ryan is sprawled on the couch watching football in a foul mood.

"You should come anyway," I insist. "You don't have to drink."

"But you do," Ryan says. "It's just the way it is in pro hockey, if you want to be accepted."

I decide to stay home with Ryan.

For the next few hours, we sit in our living room and talk about what it was like for him growing up in Minnesota, about his nightmarish first year of pro two years ago when he played for five different AA teams: four games with the San Antonio Iguanas of the CHL, then twenty-eight games with the Missouri River Otters in the UHL, followed by one game with the Tallahassee Tiger Sharks in the ECHL and twenty-one games with the ECHL's Toledo Storm before finally ending the season in the central New York town of Utica with the Mohawk Valley Prowlers in the UHL. Besides their being the strangest team names I've ever heard, Ryan makes them sound like terrible places to spend your first year out of college. Ryan was twenty-two years old and living away from home for the first time. "It was hell," he says. "I almost quit, like, fifty times."

But he's glad he didn't quit. The following season–last year–he hooked up with the Topeka Scarecrows in the CHL, where Kells was the coach.

Ryan now realizes that in his rookie year he forced the play, trying to make up for his lack of size. But last season Kells, by pairing him up with veteran Chris Felix, gave him the confidence to play his game– smooth, quick, smart.

"We had fun in Topeka last year," Ryan says. "Kells wasn't as serious as he is this year."

Considering that I haven't yet figured out Kells's hot-and-cold personality, I ask Ryan to explain.

"Kells is way more tense this year," he says. "He used to party with the guys more, and he wouldn't threaten to fire guys like he is this year. I think he's feeling the pressure of coming to a new city."

We're bonding in that way only guys do: We're talking while never taking our eyes off the football game.

"You've lived in a lot of different places, haven't you?" Ryan asks.

I tell him that in the span of seven years I went from Colgate to Washington, D.C., to Manhattan, back to Buffalo for a summer, then down to Newport News, Virginia, out to Los Angeles, up to the San Francisco Bay Area. Now I'm in Bakersfield.

"I've never been to San Francisco," Ryan says, "but it must be nice compared to here."

"San Francisco is nice," I say. "But I've lived in beautiful places and been miserable, and lived in ugly places and been happy."

Before our conversation turns too serious—we are hockey players, after all—I decide to give Ryan some shit.

"Ryan?"

"Yeah, buddy?"

"On the stat sheet it says you're 5' 10". I'm 5' 11", and, well, you're a good two inches shorter than I am."

"I hate being 5' 9"," he says. "I always put 5' 10" in the program. I like having that double digit."

* * *

If, as Kells believes, a big reason why our team is tiring in the third period is that other teams are simply physically tougher than ours, then thirty-year-old former NHL goon Sasha Lakovic might be our savior.

It's not hyperbole to proclaim Sasha Lakovic one of the most infamous hockey players in the recent history of the sport. Most of us were shocked when we learned about his acquisition in a newspaper article this morning with the headline, "Condors Add Muscle by Signing Veteran Lakovic." The Condors beat reporter, Mike Griffith, called Sasha "a true heavyweight," and Kells is quoted saying he doesn't expect Sasha to spend too much time in Bakersfield because "there's some interest from both the NHL and AHL."

Sasha played thirty-nine games for the New Jersey Devils and Calgary Flames before injuries relegated him to the minors in 1999. But, as all of us will soon enough find out, there's much more to Sasha's story of how, in just two seasons, he has gone from making half a million bucks a year in the NHL to about twenty thousand dollars in the WCHL.

In the locker room before practice, it's already clear that Sasha is a different breed of hockey player—and human being. First of all, he doesn't look like your typical hockey player. Hockey players generally have distinctive bodies: lean but not overly muscular torsos, thick but not overly sculpted arms, and thick but not overly shapely legs. But Sasha, who has a pit bull tattooed on his right thigh, has a body-builder's physique. Now I see why his nickname in junior hockey back in Vancouver (where he played with Todd Esselmont) was "pit bull."

Sasha's body looks like the chiseled ones you see on the cover of *Men's Health;* he's the only player on our team with abdominal muscles you can see rippled beneath the skin; and his shaved head, thick, black eyebrows, and menacing dark eyes are the stuff of *America's Most Wanted.*

With the market for goons saturated, Sasha's agent was unable to get him into an NHL training camp, so he spent the start of the season at home in Vancouver. He didn't play any hockey; instead, he practiced kung fu, which, despite the cans of various protein and supplement powders already stacked on his kitchen counter, is how he claims he has created his Mr. Universe body.

He still has NHL skills. Not only is he the fastest guy on the ice, even faster than Ryan, but his passes are always crisp and on the tape. He fires a wrist shot that strikes me in the arm with such force that my entire arm grows numb and a bruise immediately forms on my bicep. In the NHL, he is not even considered a "skills" player, but at this level Sasha has talent almost none of our players has.

But he's a little bit of a lunatic.

After practice, I walk over to his apartment. Kells has put him in a three-bedroom place with rookies Dave Milek and Jason Ralph. "This place is a fucking pig sty," I hear him shouting. He's maniacally sweeping the kitchen floor when I walk in.

When I tell him I'm a writer he puts his broom down and plops down on the couch. "Oh, boy," he says, "do I have a story for you! You wanna know how fucked up pro hockey is? Cuz I'll tell ya."

Sasha turns down the rage rock on the stereo and unleashes his own rage against the pro hockey machine. "I almost quit hockey altogether this year," he says. "I was sick of the politics. I was doing my kung fu and hanging out with my son, but then Pittsburgh called and said they might want to call me up this season. They have a bunch of pussies and need some toughness. So my agent called Kells. I'll be here for a while, until I can get back up to The Show."

Sasha may be known as a fighter, but he doesn't pull any verbal punches, either.

"These other veterans on this team are losers. They're boozing, not taking care of themselves. They are on their way out, dude. But I'm on my way back up. It's a waste of my time here. I can't stay too long. It'll drive me crazy."

I ask him what went wrong in New Jersey.

"Lou Lamoriello [the Devils G.M.] didn't like me," he says angrily. His right eye is starting to twitch. "In '99, I was with the team recovering from an eye injury–I took a stick to the eye and only had 70 percent vision–and I wasn't playing. It sucked, big time, eh? It was driving me crazy. My wife was driving me crazy! We were going through a separation battle that year, and I needed to get my mind off all that shit. So when my eye got better I went into Lou's office and told him I was going *crazy* and wanted to play. So he sent me down to their farm team in Albany. I went there, but I was still under contract with the Devils, eh? Things were fine for a while, but, then, the players turned on me and started making up lies about shit I was supposedly doing."

I ask what kind of "shit."

"When I signed a contract with the Devils, there was a stipulation that I couldn't drink or do any drugs while with the team. When I was in New Jersey, I had to go to Alcoholics Anonymous meetings. *They* thought I was an alcoholic, and I said I would do anything to stay in NHL. So I did it. That was the only way they would sign me. But then I told them I'm not going to the AA meetings anymore and stopped going. When I went to talk to the players in the locker room the next day, they got all confrontational and said I had a drinking problem. It was total bullshit, politics. Show me any hockey team, and I will show you twenty drunks. But it was too late. That was pretty much it for my career with the Devils."

I ask him where he went from there.

"I had nowhere to go. Everyone thought I was off my rocker, but I was fine. They just didn't like me. That's the politics of pro hockey. But I'm not saying I've never been off my rocker."

"When were you off your rocker?" I ask.

"Well, Vegas was definitely a low point. This was '96, I think. I was twenty-five and had just been dumped by Calgary. I thought my career was over, and I ended up in Vegas with an IHL team. I was really down on myself and getting shit from everyone. I was staying at the Luxor, on the Strip. The last thing I remember, I grabbed a razor and tried to slit my left wrist. Someone called the ambulance, and they came and took me to the hospital. They stitched me up, though."

I ask, "So you tried to kill yourself?"

"Sort of. Some of the guys on the team came to me and said, 'Sash, we know what you are going through.' My wife came down, and we saw a therapist to save our marriage and to see what the fuck was wrong with me. They tried to put me on pills, antidepressants and some shit. I tried those for a week, but they started to make me not feel like me. You know? I was slow, and I felt sort of dreamy all the time. I was too mellow, man. So I stopped taking the pills."

Sasha sees the shock on my face. "Don't worry, man," he adds. "It's not as bad as it sounds."

* * *

Fresno's Selland Arena is a rickety barn built in the Eisenhower era, and its puck-marked boards and glass appear to be about as old as the rink, which gets very loud and circuslike when they crank up rock music for the seven thousand rowdy fans who have come from across the Central California heartland on this Friday night to see their Falcons play their cross-valley rival, Bakersfield.

Sasha warned me this morning about his pregame ritual, and, as promised, just as the team is about to walk onto the ice, Sasha bends over a garbage can, sticks two fingers down his throat and empties his stomach. It's not clear exactly why he does this pregame purging, but it seems to fire him up. Maybe he's ridding himself of the demons . . . I hope.

Kells told the guys before the game that Willett is "sick" and back at home resting. I had noticed that he wasn't on the bus, but since it's only an hour and a half drive from Bakersfield, I thought he might drive himself. Kells tells us that Willie's absence "means everyone–to a man–has to pick it up a notch tonight." Then Kells delivered what is becoming his usual pregame pep talk–

"Keep 'er simple . . . A lot of emotion out there . . . Let's see what you're made of . . . We owe these bastards one for embarrassing us two weeks ago."

For the fifth straight game since the exhibition game I'll be in the stands in a sports coat watching and eating popcorn.

Though my goaltending skills are improving–I stop twice as many shots now than I could a month ago–it's hard spending so much time watching because I know how much better I could be. Plus, as my little brother reminded me, I don't have a lot of time.

Consequently, it's not exactly uplifting to see Looch, who was named this week's WCHL Goaltender of the Week for stopping 64 of 69 shots in last weekend's games, turn in yet another sterling performance against Fresno. For the third straight game, we are out-shot, this time 34–25, but Looch simply plays better than the other goalie. Sasha looks winded most of the game, but his presence alone is intimidating enough to keep the other team from taking cheap shots, lest they suffer the wrath of our resident kung fu master with an eye twitch. Even without Paul Willett, we win 4–3. Maybe Sasha is our savior, after all.

* * *

A few days after we get back to Bakersfield, we learn that our captain is sick—but the illness is far worse than we had thought. Turns out that Kells had tried to keep secret the real reason why Willett didn't make it to the Fresno game. Whatever it is, it's going to be reported tomorrow in the local newspaper. And from the look of things, it's going to be a public relations nightmare for the team.

I sensed something was wrong this morning when I saw the usually smart-alecky Willett riding the exercise bike with his head down, avoiding eye contact with anyone. Before practice, Kells calls a team meeting. Kells is pale as ice and his eyes are as red as a goal line. It looks like he hasn't slept in two days.

"I told you guys on Friday that Willie stayed home sick," he says. "The truth is that he had a problem at home and he was arrested. He spent the night in jail. I bailed him out and I told him to stay home, not because he was suspended, but because he had a family matter to deal with at home."

"Listen," he says, "No one's fucking perfect. I know Willie feels bad about what happened, but we're a family and we support him. I tried all day yesterday to keep this out of the press, but some news director thought otherwise. So it's gonna get out there. We gotta deal with it. I want you tell anyone who asks that this is a family matter that he's dealing with. Nothing else. It's no one's business. So we're going to move on from here, O.K.? Remember, Jonathan is big on community. You guys are a huge deal here. You are the only thing, the only celebrities.

That's the reason it's in the news. They got nothing else. So be careful, be smart. Stick together. When one guy gets hurt, we all do."

Willett is so ashamed of his arrest—for what exactly, none of us yet knows—that he can't bear to look any of us in the eye.

Kells continues, "We all come here as a bunch of hockey players. We're from different places, we got our own reasons for coming here. But over the course of the season, we become brothers, part of a family. And I've never met a perfect family. There's always a fuck-up in the bunch. I've never known of a family that didn't have the pot-head uncle or the loser brother. Never. Well, a member of our family has fucked up. So let's move on. Together. As a family."

Willett, near tears, breaks his silence. "I'm sorry, guys," he says. "I feel real bad about it. What can I say? I fucked up."

It's the most sincere apology I've ever heard, and I feel for him. But I can't help but think that a thirty-year-old father of two daughters shouldn't act this way. In hockey, the rules allow for outbursts of anger. A ref doesn't have to give you a penalty for throwing a punch at another player. It's a violent sport often played by violent men, many of whom take the violence home.

* * *

The day after Willie's apology everyone in Bakersfield, and anyone reading a hockey Web site, sees what runs in the *Bakersfield Californian*:

> Bakersfield Condors player Paul Willett was arrested for misdemeanor battery on his spouse, Bakersfield police confirmed Tuesday. Willett, the Condors' scoring leader last year and the league MVP the previous season, was booked into jail and then cited out on Friday, police reported. Investigative reports say Willett was arrested at 2 A.M. at his home in the 2500 block of Sutton Place where his wife, Lisa, 32, complained she was injured on her left foot and shoulder. She did not seek medical attention, the police said. The two argued, which escalated into Willett sweeping jars, utensils, and a cutting board off a kitchen counter, the reports say.
>
> She also reported he threw a wooden utensil holder at her arm and shoulder, but there was no visible injury, the reports say.

Police responded to the home based on a call from an adult third party who was not identified. Willett, who missed Friday's game, is scheduled to be arraigned November 19 in Kern County Superior Court.

Several days later, when the charges against him are dropped and his wife moves back in with him, it doesn't make it in the newspaper. When his name is announced during the first home game after the arrest, fans boo him. When we make our first road trip to Alaska in early January, a fan yells from the stands, "Wife beater!"

* * *

Kells, the director of what is looking like my swan song, lately doesn't even acknowledge my existence, let alone notice the drastic improvement in my game over the last two months—unless he's making fun of my brain tumor. Hard work is my only weapon in my war. Still, it's more fun being a frustrated third-stringer than a frustrated no-stringer.

Until I had The Dream, the only thing I had ever pursued so maniacally, so single-mindedly, was a date with Brooke. The problem was that she had a boyfriend, and I had a girlfriend. So I methodically took to the task of doing everything in my power to bring us together. I broke up with my girlfriend, wrote Brooke poems, sent her flowers, watched her play Frisbee in the park. I practically willed our coupling to happen.

But Brooke was not at all on the same courtship schedule. She was amused by my efforts, thought I was "cute" enough not to brush off too quickly, but she didn't *have* to have me the way I did her. The turning point in my romantic pursuit came the day when I, tired of her not being able to see the obvious—that I was the perfect guy in the world for her—informed her that she had been "excommunicated from Club Chachi." I told her to call me when she realized I was The One. That night, she phoned me at home. "I want to be let back in to Club Chachi," she said. "I miss you already."

A lesson I took from that experience is that I got what I wanted when I stopped trying and let whatever was meant to happen, happen. Yet in a Darwinian sports world populated by twenty-something pro hockey players, it's hard to be a thirty-one-year-old rookie not trying when no one—not the coach, not the players—is trying for me.

Inspire

Following our "family" crisis, we win two more games in a row, both against Anchorage. Maser has not yet lost a fight. Esselmont is getting more ice time. Cookie leads the team with eight goals. Ryan, whose shoulder has healed and who has beefed up a little by drinking protein shakes, finally scored a goal. The weather report in the locker room, gloomy with a 100 percent chance or rain two weeks ago, is now sunny and warm.

Our record has improved to five wins and two losses. A minor-league hockey Web site, InTheCrease.com, has ranked Bakersfield the fifteenth-best AA team in the nation. Yet most players are still out of shape and not working much harder in practice. Sasha, informing Kells that he's not going to play like a goon every night for a thousand bucks a week, isn't even pounding the opposition. Maser, making just over three hundred a week, has been doing that job. Plus, Kells, despite occasionally changing our fore-check from sending one man into their end to two men, has not greatly tweaked our basic game strategy: Win the battles ... go to the net ... stay positive ... clog the front ... hit their defensemen ... stay out of the box ... win.

The difference has been Looch, who almost single-handedly won the five straight games by playing like a AAA—not a AA-goalie.

But then, on November 9 in Long Beach, even Looch couldn't make up for our lack of offensive thrust, or our porous defense, which was allowing us to get out-shot virtually every game by not hitting guys, not tying up sticks, not back-checking, and by, well, just being lazy hockey players. Even Sasha, who finally did his part to throw Long Beach off their game, couldn't help: Six seconds into the game, he dropped his gloves and un-leashed a flurry of punches to the face of the 6' 7" Jeff Ewasko. Sasha, who's at least eight inches shorter, finished off the giant with a stiff right hook, bringing Ewasko to his knees. Sasha cocked his right arm back to throw another, but, seeing Ewasko's eyes rolled back into his head, Sasha showed mercy by tipping him over like a toy soldier.

Sasha's bare-knuckled diplomacy did nothing to inspire our pitiful offense. We went 0 for 11 on the power play and were out-shot 45–20. We should have lost 10–0, but the hockey gods were merciful, and Looch made several breakaway saves, so we only lost 4–1.

With Looch's winning streak over, Kells gave Scott Hay the start the following night against Long Beach. It's not good coaching to keep your backup on the bench for too long. If your starter goes down with an in-jury or falls into a slump, you need to have a goalie ready to step in and stop pucks. It's a role that Hay has not yet filled.

If I were living on a planet where the laws of hockey physics would have it that the worse a number-two goalie plays, the better the chance that a number-three goalie will get to play, I would have already played, because Hay, as he did in his first game, played like a human sieve. But hockey is not a science.

The game got off to a bad start for Hay. Just fifty seconds into the first period, a Long Beach player dumped the puck in around the boards. Hay skated behind the net to stop the puck. Instead of leaving it back there for our defenseman to pick it up, Hay let it bounce in front of the net, where their forward slapped it into the unguarded net. We ended up los-ing 5–3.

The following weekend we hosted San Diego, whom we had humil-iated in their home opener, on a Friday and Saturday night. Looch played the first game, letting in a couple of soft shots, and we lost that one 3–1. After winning five in a row, we now had lost three straight.

The next night, as I sat and studied the media notes in the training room before the game, Kells walked up to me and said, "We'll have to get you in one of these games." Before I could say anything, he walked out the back door to have a smoke.

Huh? He's going to get me in? I thought he had forgotten I even existed! Maybe he's starting to notice that, in practice, I am almost as sharp as Looch, and sharper than Hay. Maybe he's thinking the team will play better knowing a nervous rookie is in the net. Then again, maybe he's just trying to keep my spirits up. It's hard to say. Just be ready.

When Looch goes out and loses that night's game 4–0, I'm thinking I just might get my shot–very soon. It could come any day. Just like when I unexpectedly played in the exhibition game. Now, with Looch faltering and Hay winless in two games, I might get in there. Maybe I'm his secret weapon.

* * *

Per our owner's wishes, almost every day of the week a Condor, wearing a game jersey, visits a school or hospital or civic organization. Today, Josh Maser and I have been assigned to speak to a group of two-hundred kids at an elementary school in a low-income part of town. We're supposed to talk about the importance of staying in school, though Josh is an odd choice as an inspirational speaker, since he chose to play hockey rather than attend college. It doesn't matter. All the kids do is ask about hockey, anyway.

"Do you ever get hurt?"

"I've broken most of the fingers in my left hand."

"Why do you like playing goalie?"

"It's the most important position, plus the equipment is cool."

"Are you from Canada?"

"No, but Josh is. He grew up on a cattle ranch."

"Oooooh."

One of the teachers, a heavyset woman in her forties, shouts out, "What are you going to do when you're done playing hockey?"

Unlike the other questions, which I quickly answered, I have to stop and think. *What will I do?* Before I got to Bakersfield, I probably would have said I'd return to my job of writing about Hollywood celebrities. But a sense of dreadful boredom overcomes me at the mere thought of it. Even though I'm still the third-string goalie, I've had more fun in the last two months than I've had in the last ten years.

Feeling pressure to fill the silence, I say, "I'm not sure."

A few days later while on the bus to Fresno, I ask Quinn Fair, who graduated from Bowling Green State University in 1996, what he will do when he retires. He says he's considering going into sales or maybe joining the fire department. "I don't know what I want to do anymore," I say.

Quinn leans toward me and whispers, "At least you have options. Some of these guys, they have nothing else they can do."

* * *

I want to see just how much I have improved since I arrived here a little over a month ago. Not playing in games or getting any real practice time, it's hard to gauge my progress and a head-to-head contest might do the trick.

"Ten pucks, ten shots," I say to Looch.

I holler over to Ryan and instruct him to line up ten pucks ten feet in front of the net.

Looch goes into the net first, and Ryan starts firing away. As usual, Looch is a wall and stops nine out of ten. That's gonna be tough to beat.

Ryan lines up ten new pucks. "Ready?" he asks.

"Just shoot."

I stop the first nine. If I stop the last one, I will win.

Ryan winds up and slaps a high shot to my left. I drop to my knees and reach up with my glove, but the puck is already behind me and in the net.

Rather than stew over not beating me, Looch skates over and offers a tip. "When you go down, you're dropping your glove down to the ice," he says. "You're leaving the entire upper part of the net open. If you had kept your glove up by your shoulder, you might have caught that last one."

It's the first time either goalie has offered me advice.

* * *

Coming into Fresno on November 19 for the twelfth game of the season, we've lost four in a row and are in last place in the Southern Division. The statistics tell the story. We've scored fewer goals (thirty) than any other team. We don't have a single player among the league's top twenty scorers. Our power play is the worst in the WCHL, scoring just seven times out of sixty-seven man-advantage opportunities for a pathetic 10.44 percent success rate. Even more woeful, our penalty-killing is also last in the league: Our opponents score 24 percent of the time. Our goal-tending, though far from stellar since Looch ended his hot streak four games ago, is the least of our worries.

The situation is especially discouraging for Todd Esselmont, who, despite the lackluster performance of our "money" players, is lucky to get five shifts in a game while others get about thirty. Kells has even sat him out entirely for a couple of games. Granted, he doesn't have any goals or assists, but he's hardly getting more ice time than I am, and I'm sitting in the stands holding a pen.

"Why did he bring me here if he isn't going to play me?" he asks on the drive home from practice.

Esselmont has lost a lot of his preseason idealism. Then again, so have I. To survive, both of us have to block out reality. After all, when did thinking realistically ever make a dream come true? Idealism is what inspires greatness.

"I don't know how long I can do this, Bakes," he says. "After taxes, I'm making $268 a week. I could make $200 a night tending bar back in Vancouver. I'm sending almost all of it back home to my fiancée."

He confides that he has been arguing with his fiancée on the phone about the lack of money. She has two kids from her first marriage and, he adds, "bills up the wazoo." Things wouldn't be so stressful if he was playing, if he was scoring goals, and had a bright future. Instead, he's riding the pines, just turned thirty, and all he has to show for it is two cracked teeth, five stitches and two penalty minutes he earned by tripping a guy who skated past him as though he was standing still.

"What does your fiancée want you to do?" I ask.

"She says I need to stay down here and live my dream," he says. "But I know she wishes I would just come back home."

The same could probably be said of Brooke, who has driven down twice since the start of the season, and is already tiring from juggling all of her schoolwork and maintaining our long-distance marriage via the telephone.

The other night, after listening to me talk about how much happier I am playing hockey in Bakersfield than I am writing in Mill Valley, she got annoyed.

"What's so great about Bakersfield? I'm not there, Arthur's not there."

"Brooke, you just need to go out, have fun, get out of that crappy apartment."

She hung up on me, and we didn't talk for the next two days.

But the team's foibles are providing plenty of distraction from my personal life. Hay is getting the start tonight in Fresno, and Brearley is back from his knee injury. He has gained what looks like at least ten pounds, most of them in his gut, since his injury six weeks ago, and he will have to play with a knee brace for the first time in his career. He's not 100 percent. But we need him.

Luckily, Fresno is the only other WCHL team struggling as badly as we are. For the first time this year, Jason Firth displays the kind of talent that has given him over one hundred points each of the last six seasons. Firth shows Gretzky-esque play-making skills, sucking defenders to him with nifty puck-handling before dishing the puck off to an open man. He assists on four goals. Brearley, Cooke, and Willett score. Even Quinn Fair, our steadiest defenseman, scores two goals. And, unlike in other games, the third period is our strongest. Fresno manages just four shots on goal in the third, and though Hay strains his medial collateral knee ligament in the first period, he stays in and stops all 23 shots in the game and we crush them 6–0.

The next day in his column in the *Californian,* reporter Mike Griffith makes an astute observation: "The Condors, on paper, are a very talented team. Monday, on the ice, they looked like the team they are on paper."

It's safe to say that Hay's shutout doesn't exactly help my chances of finally dressing for a game. Another impressive outing five days later at home against the Colorado Gold Kings doesn't either. He makes twenty-seven saves, including several acrobatic ones, and leads our team to a 2–1 victory. The next night, Kells, convinced that Looch is still better than Hay but needs to get his confidence back, starts Looch. He didn't look very sharp in practice all week. Usually, Looch is the team's best practice player. Day in, day out, Looch works harder than any other player. He's not especially quick or reflexive, but he plays a thinking man's game: cutting down his angles and anticipating where and when a player will shoot. He leaves little to chance.

But ever since Hay's shutout against Fresno, Looch has been Austin Powers, *sans* mojo, as if Hay has gotten inside his head and made him question whether he is in fact the team's best goalie. But by starting Looch even though Hay won last night (usually a coach will go with the hot goalie), Kells is trying to boost Looch's confidence back up.

Attempting to break his string of bad luck, before the game Looch grabs one of my sticks from the rack. I use the Koho brand, not because I like them, but because they are made of cheaper wood, and Dickie won't let me practice with the expensive Sher-Woods. Nonetheless, Looch takes my Koho.

A minute and ten seconds into the game, Looch skates behind the net to play the puck, but he's beat there by a speedy Colorado forward, who steals the puck off Looch's stick, skates to the front of the net and stuffs it in.

1–0.

Three minutes later, Colorado forward R.J. Enga, wrists the puck to the right of Looch, who drops to his knees and kicks out his leg. The puck ricochets off his leg and into the net.

2–0.

Fans start booing.

Thirty seconds later, Looch lets a weak shot slip through his pads.

3–0.

It's as if he's trying *not* to stop the puck.

Kells has seen enough. He stomps down to the end of the bench and shouts at Hay, "Get in there!" Seeing Hay hustle onto the ice, Looch hangs his head and skates to the bench, steps off the ice, and heads straight into the locker room to hide. Immediately, the fans start chanting, "Hay! Hay! Hay! Hay!" Suddenly, the team's goalie-math equation has changed. Scott Hay is number one and Looch is number two and dropping.

Hay's presence jump-starts the team; we immediately go on the offensive, but their goalie, a long-legged fish-flopper named Kirk Daubenspeck, shuts us down. In the middle of the second, we fall behind 4–0. But Goldie answers with two quick goals, both assisted by nice passes from Ryan. Six minutes into the third, Firth feeds the puck to Cookie, who's standing unguarded in the slot. Most of the time players will stop the puck, then shoot it, but Cookie has been working on shooting the puck as it gets to him. It's called a "one-timer," and I've stayed after practice with him the last few weeks so that he could work on his. His hard work pays off. His one-timer sails straight into the upper corner, the place some hockey broadcasters call, "Where mom hides the cookies."

His goal, however, is not enough. We still lose 4–3.

In order to handle the new goalie-math equation, I consult with my goalie-math coach, Mitch Korn, via e-mail. After sending him a lengthy letter explaining the situation, Mitch replies: "Politically, it sounds like your chances of playing are worse now that Hay is number one. Because Looch, who was supposed to be number one, is probably being paid a lot more than Hay. The coach is not going to give you a shot over a guy he's paying premium."

I write back, "Thanks for depressing me."

"Sorry," Mitch replies. "That's pro hockey. But remember that pro hockey is also about change. Things change quickly. Stay positive."

* * *

With the team back on the winning track, and its being Thanksgiving time, Condors fans on the message boards can hardly contain their gratitude.

> **Betickchick22:** I'm thankful that we've got a great coach with a great bunch of guys playing for him. I'm thankful we've got our country to call home. Oh, well, I'm thankful for Canada, too, because that's where, what, seventy percent or more hockey players come from?

> **Ammearsgeron:** Things I'm grateful for: 1. My family and friends. 2. That I can watch the Condors. 3. Scott Hay and Looooch. Do I have to say more?

No, "Ammerasgeron." I think you've said enough.

* * *

A few days ago I gave Felix a drive home from practice. His wife took the car and went shopping with their two kids. Being thirty-seven, Felix thinks it gives him license to have an opinion–the right one–on just about everything.

After telling me that Maser needs to be "smarter at when and who and how he fights," Felix lays into Esselmont. "Seriously," Felix says. "C'mon, why is the guy here? Todd is thirty fucking years old and he is trying to start a hockey career? It's not realistic. The boat has passed, eh?"

"He's here for the same reason I am," I say. "He wants to live his dream. What's wrong with that?"

"That's fine, Kenny, and I respect what you're doing. But you have a life, a career to go back to. You're not hurting yourself. But Todd has a fiancée at home, and he's making less than three hundred bucks a week. What the fuck is that? I'd rather be at home with the wife working as a janitor for that kind of money. He's got good skills, but this is not the place for him. He should be home with his girl, building a life, not down here with us idiots. You have to know when the dream is over, you know what I mean?"

* * *

Brooke's parents have driven down from the northern part of the state to spend Thanksgiving weekend with us in Bakersfield. They got a room at a hotel on Rosedale Highway, the main east-west artery that runs through the middle of the fertile oil field on the east side of town. The last few days have been the closest thing to marital normalcy since I left Mill Valley. Brooke and I have been able to spend a few days like an actual married couple. We've seen movies, gone for walks, cooked dinner, sat around watching television, and we've even made love.

We meet Brooke's parents, Steve and Paula, at a restaurant on the edge of the oil field. I've gotten used to the gaseous stench from the nearby refineries, but Brooke's parents politely describe the odor as "sweet." I guess they don't want to offend me.

We've invited Ryan, who's fast becoming my adopted little brother, along to the feast. The dinnertime conversation soon turns to the subject of hockey, specifically the prospect of my playing. "Kenny's good enough, for sure," Ryan says. "But it's a tough situation."

Brooke's father doesn't know hockey very well, but he's trying to understand why I'm not playing if I am good enough. "It's all about paying your dues," I tell him. "I don't think the coach even took me seriously until that exhibition game. He probably thought I would quit by now."

"Even if you don't play it's still a great experience," Paula kindly offers.

I grind my knife into a slice of turkey. I've been thinking about what Felix said about knowing when the dream is over, and, well, I'm not ready to give up on it.

"Maybe," I say, "but if I don't play I'll feel like I failed."

Act

The pale-blue exterior of Long Beach Arena, with its giant mural of swimming whales, makes the rink look like an aquarium. Inside, the arena looks more like a zoo. Not an animal one, unless you count the Ice Dogs mascot, "Spike," who paces the stands in a giant dog costume. We're talking humans.

Minor league hockey doesn't attract the symphony crowd. Still, the majority of folks in the stands look normal enough. A father feeds his son cotton candy, a snuggling couple shares a beer, a group of flabby guys in ties ogle the Long Beach cheerleaders, the Ice Breakers, who could use a lesson or two from the Gulls Girls.

But every zoo has its mutated species. The most peculiar creatures tend to gather around the corner of the rink where the players come on and off. Most are female in gender, with plumes of hair-sprayed fur on the tops of their heads, and they aren't quite as attractive as other members of their gender. Yet their appearance does not prevent them from engaging in aggressive mating behavior. Perhaps to attract male attention, they wear colorful hockey jerseys, on which are scribbled autographs from their favorite players, about whom they know *everything*. Players refer to this species as "groupies."

As I observe these groupies, my esteemed colleague, Kells, sits down and joins my anthropological observation. Over the years, he has interacted with a geographically diverse group–from New Haven, to Muskegon, to Topeka, to Bakersfield. Kells played a few exhibition games for the Kings, but never made the team. He did spend enough time with them, though, to learn that the groupies in the minor leagues are genetically inferior to those in the big leagues, a fact that seems to upset him greatly. "This is my punishment for not making it to the NHL," he says. "I fucked up. So now I'm stuck here with retarded girls in four-hundred-dollar hockey jerseys with four teeth."

* * *

Going into tonight's game, we've won seven and lost seven, a fact that Kells points out in his pregame speech. "In my mind, tonight is the start of a new season," he tells everyone. "A fresh start."

Tonight is the first of a three-games-in-three-nights series. After tonight's game, we will drive two hours to San Diego. Then, on Sunday afternoon, we will head back home to play Long Beach again.

We'll be starting over fresh tonight, though without the services of Sasha, who is on injured reserve for two weeks due to a sore shoulder, and Todd Esselmont, whom Kells has sat out in order to play rookie defenseman David Milek. When Kells tells him he will be sitting out, Esselmont walks out of the building, only to turn up a few hours later in the stands.

Are you ready for some hockey at the Beach?

If the announcer were asking our tired team, the answer would be no. Long Beach's most dangerous forward is Kelly Askew, a thirty-year-old forward who, if he weren't 5' 9", might have made it to the NHL. He's currently the WCHL's leading goal scorer, with seventeen goals in seventeen games.

Hay has trouble all night with Askew's quick-release wrist shot, which nets him three goals. Hay isn't nearly as sharp as he was in his last three games, but, then again, neither is the team in front of him. It's a bad sign when the high point of the evening happens at intermission, when a few lucky fans don helmets and get shot by a bungee cord down the ice on a sled, smashing into inflatable Del Taco bowling pins.

We lose 6–4.

So much for a "fresh start."

The loss, however, is incidental to the postgame injury report:

- Ryan has ten stitches in his forehead from a high stick.
- Quinn popped out his left shoulder and is wearing a sling.
- Steve Zoryk tore his right bicep when he tried to fight Askew.

- Paul Rosebush is dizzy from a collision; he may have a concussion.
- John Vary tore a knee ligament and limped onto the bus.
- Most relevant to me: Hay and Looch are totally healthy.

* * *

The next morning, there's an optional pregame skate at the arena in San Diego. Only five guys show, while the rest sleep in at the Days Inn across the street. As the only goalie, I will get a great workout, facing hundreds more shots than I do in the typical Looch-Hay practice.

Afterward, not having to rest for tonight's game, I walk two miles to the Pacific Beach boardwalk and think about the first time I ever visited San Diego, back in the fall of 1996, a few months after I had moved from Virginia to L.A. to work at *People*. I drove down to San Diego to interview James Stockdale, the retired Navy admiral who was Ross Perot's vice-presidential running mate four years earlier. The article ran as a three-page story in the magazine, but my interview with Stockdale, who spent eight years in a Vietnamese POW camp, taught me a lasting life lesson that could help me now.

I was nervous about meeting the white-haired war veteran, a man who had survived unimaginable pain, torture, and isolation, a man who—unlike myself at the time—had faced his enemies and won. I was afraid he would see me for who I was: an out-of-shape ex-hockey player fraught with impotence and self-doubt, a ghostly shadow of the man whose life I was about to probe. While he had slain his demons, I had run away from mine. Alas, I didn't yet know a brain tumor was the demon dwelling inside my head.

Stockdale hobbled up to his library and returned a few minutes later carrying a stack of philosophy texts that he said contained "all the wisdom and insight on the human condition a person needs to grapple with the mental, spiritual, and physical challenges of modern life." His most influential teacher, he explained, was a Stoic philosopher named Epictetus, with whom Stockdale shares a numbingly similar life.

I have never been much of a philosophy fan. Maybe that's why I majored in geology. I have always preferred the black-and-white over the nebulous gray zones of life. Hockey is like that. There are winners and losers. Simple.

Stockdale was eager to introduce me to the story of Epictetus, a Roman slave who suffered a crippling leg injury at the hands of his master. Rather than cower or exact revenge, Epictetus was emboldened, and he used his physical and mental torture as inspiration for a school of philosophical thought that eventually became known as Stoicism. According to Epictetus, the way to find happiness is to concern ourselves with what is in our power and to be indifferent to things not in our power.

Stockdale had first read about Epictetus in graduate school at Stanford, years before his jet was shot down on a bombing raid over North Vietnam. "If it weren't for Epictetus," he said to me, "I might not have survived prison," the first three years of which he spent with his ankle chained to a wall. Stockdale walked over to my chair and opened a book he had written titled, *Thoughts of a Philosophical Fighter Pilot,* and he opened it up to page 215.

"Do you believe in God?" Stockdale asked me.

"Yeah," I replied.

"Okay," he said. "Epictetus calls God, 'The Author.'"

Stockdale pressed his stubby finger on a line containing one of his favorite Epictetus quotes and, adjusting his glasses, read it aloud: "Remember, you are an actor in a drama of such a sort as the Author chooses–if short, then in a short one; if long, then in a long one. If it be his pleasure that you should enact a poor man, or a cripple, or a ruler, see that you act it well. This is your business–to act well the given part, but to choose it belongs to Another."

Stockdale then spread out before me a dozen or so black-and-white photos. There was one of him in his flight suit from early in his career, one as a Stanford student, and a shot of him reuniting with his wife and kids on a tarmac after his release from prison. But it was his grimmest photo–one taken by his captors a year into his imprisonment–that he chose to hold up. "This is when I was at my best," he said of an image in which he looked pale and deathly skinny. "This is when I had to be strongest."

Later, on the drive back to Los Angeles, with the deep-blue sea extending to the horizon and the jagged mountain peaks poking the sky like tent poles, all I could think about was how much I missed the test that was playing hockey.

I realize that, more than ever, I now must "act well the given part." Yet, until I test my skills in a real game, I won't have the answer to the question that plagues me: Was it the tumor, or was I just not stoic enough?

Josh Maser certainly plays his role well, challenging San Diego's goon, Langdone, to a bare-knuckler halfway through the first period. The fight is a tie—with each guy getting in some good licks—but Maser retains his perfect record: He has not lost any of his five fights so far this year.

Going into the third period, it looks as though we might be able to pull out a win. Looch is playing with the kind of confidence he had last month, coming far out of his net to cut down the angle, controlling his rebounds. We're tied 2–2. In the locker room at intermission, Kells, who in a desperate attempt to try a new coaching psychology has not been as critical, says, "They're for the taking tonight, boys. This is the kind of game that if we don't win, we'll look back on it and say, 'We could've had that one.' So let's go out and get it!"

But, in what is our team's unfortunate pattern, we collapse in the third period, overwhelmed by San Diego's speed. To slow them down, and we certainly can't keep up with them, we take slashing and hooking penalties. It's a useless tactic. San Diego scores two power-play goals in a row, and, as the clock ticks down to a 4-to-2 loss, the eight thousand fans count the goals in unison while pointing at Looch: "One, Two, Three, Four. We want more! You suck!"

* * *

The bus rolls into our apartment complex at four o'clock on Sunday morning, thirteen hours before our next game, which will be our third game in three nights. The guys, bruised and exhausted, file zombielike off the bus and back to their beds. No one ever said minorleague hockey was glamorous, but it's at moments like this, when the guys—especially the tired, old ones like me—feel that life in the deep minors is at its most unglamorous.

Most guys wake up at two o'clock in the afternoon and drive over to the rink. They stretch, drink coffee, watch the NFL games on the tube in the training room, sit in the hot tub, sleep on the floor of the locker room. As the only player who didn't just endure two games back-to-back on the road, I got up around eleven and worked out at the gym. I have to be ready.

Unlike some of his recent tirades, in which he threatened to fire guys and called some players "fat," and "lazy," and "just bad hockey players," Kells preaches a surprisingly uplifting Sunday-afternoon sermon for a coach whose team just lost two straight and can't get over the .500 mark, no matter what he says or does. In fact, he's all smiles when he walks into the room and sees his frowning team. "I feel good about today," he says. "Slept in, laid the wife this morning, fixed the kids some breakfast. It's a great day, a new day. Let's not forget that this is a game–you get paid to play *a game*. Yeah, this is our third game in three nights. But, you know, sometimes the third feels the best because you have loose legs. I feel good about today."

Ralph leans over to me and says, "What the fuck is he smoking?"

In the first period, we skate like the pack of tired, old smokers that a lot of us are. We are out-shot 18–3, but Hay makes some acrobatic saves, and we pop one by Engren to lead 1–0 at the end of the period.

Kells is upbeat. "You guys got a chance to wake up, to get the blood pumping and, thanks to Haysie, we're winning. Now we have a forty-minute hockey game to win. Winning is 99 percent mental and 1 percent psychological."

But the physical toll on the players can be calculated in numbers:

4: Guys wearing knee braces.
25: Stitches on the faces of Ryan, Quinn, Ralph, and Todd.
4: Average hours guys slept last night.
5: Players receiving electrical stimulation treatment on injuries.
7: Players on pain killers or anti-inflammatory drugs.

But we play smarter to make up for our physical problems. Hay makes some big stops, looking nothing like the sieve he did at the start of the season, and we win the game 3–1.

As the other players enjoy the win with loud music and beer back in the locker room, I walk out feeling alone, an outsider. Watching is not fun. I'm given yet another reason to wallow in self pity when a sweet fifteen-year-old named Sandra, one of our team's biggest fans, approaches me outside the arena as I'm walking to my car.

"Will you sign my book?" she asks, clutching a copy of my memoir, *Man Made.*

As I take a pen and the book from her and start scribbling an autograph, Sandra says, "I'm sad for you."

"Why?" I ask.

Flashing her puppy-dog eyes, she answers, "Because you're not getting a chance to play, even though you deserve to. The same thing you wrote about happening in college is happening again. I feel bad for you."

I finish signing the book, hand it back to her and smile, pretending that for the last few weeks I haven't been thinking the same thing.

Love

You wake up in the morning and your mind is as foggy as the air was when the plane landed last night. It's dumping rain outside your chintzy motel room, and you're pretty sure you are in Tacoma today, but you're not even sure what day it is, or where the hell Tacoma is. You're thirty-one years old and married, but you are playing a kid's game and you haven't seen your wife in five weeks. The whole idea of this misadventure was to enjoy your newly healthy body, but ever since you arrived, your body has been bruised, battered and run down into a pale, skinny heap that can barely get out of bed and shuffle into the van that's waiting to carry you to morning practice. You want to believe that getting up will matter, that by stopping pucks the other two goalies don't feel like facing, that by playing your given role on the team, you will improve a little more and someday soon be rewarded; but your aching, phlegm-riddled body, seven pounds lighter than it was two months ago, is telling you it won't make any difference, to stay in bed because playing will all come down to luck anyway.

But your mind reminds you what your goalie guru in Buffalo had said—luck is preparation meeting opportunity—so you get up, go to practice and prepare yourself for the opportunity—an injury, a reward from your coach, an unforeseen emergency—the one thing that might call you into service. It could happen tonight against the Sabercats, but, then again, it might not ever happen. Guessing when you will play is starting to feel like predicting where a meteor will fall. *Fucking impossible.*

You go out and practice as hard as you can, but your body feels old and slow, cranky as an old Ford on a winter morning. Your nose won't stop running, and no matter how hard you cough, the gunk in your lungs refuses to come out.

You still have a piece of brain tumor in your head and so you fear you're getting sick again. The other day you read in the newspaper about the rise in cases of a rare disease afflicting local residents. It's called "Valley Fever," but doctors have a fancy name for it that you can't even pronounce. The article said it was a lung disease contracted after breathing in dust from local fields containing a deadly fungus called "Coccidioides immitis," another thing you can't pronounce. The article reports that last year there were 411 new cases of Valley Fever in the Bakersfield area; so far this year health officials have found 800 new cases. "It can lead to pneumonia, meningitis, and even death," the article said. Victims feel as if they have the flu, and they mistakenly think they will get better with some rest and aspirin, but then one day they fall asleep and never wake up.

The team trainer gives you some Sudafed, but that doesn't make any difference, and now you're afraid you've contracted this so-called Valley Fever. But you don't see a doctor because you don't want to know if you have the disease, because then the doctor might tell you to go home, he might prescribe bed rest for the next few months and, *voilà*, just like that, your dream of playing hockey is dead.

You'd rather die than see your dream die. And, being an as-yet-unpaid "pro" hockey player, your bank account couldn't handle the withdrawal. So you just skate hard enough to sweat out the demons, and then return to the motel near the freeway in Tacoma and sleep, but your roommate, the team's radio guy, keeps you up all afternoon. For the next two days, as your misery rises like your fever, your team wins two straight games against the Sabercats, and your team's goalies play like pros; one of them is the beefy one you had thought you could surpass with time, but he gets his second shutout of the year. For the fourth time in his last five games he is named the game's first star. You're thinking, Well, that sure is a shit sandwich.

But you saw him before the last game putting on a knee brace and icing the swollen knee after the game, then limping through practices, and your Darwinian instincts fill you with hope that he might need a rest, that you will then become the number-two goalie, play like a pro, never go back to being number three, become the comeback story of the year in pro hockey, get an NHL tryout next year and make that dream come more true than you ever wished for, that maybe you won't be a failure just like in college, the last time you chased the dream that became a nightmare.

Your flu symptoms start going away, but then you fly home in a turbulent puddle-jumper, landing back in the town where that rare lung disease is festering. Two days later you watch your team's injured goalie lose to the Anchorage Aces 3–0 and then wince in pain as he slides out of his knee brace, and, even though you're thinking you are a bad person for wishing someone harm, thus dooming you with some really bad karma, you pray for your chance.

But you don't get that chance. A few days later, after practicing harder and better than ever, you sit and watch San Diego come to town, and you see Sasha Lakovic attack the other team's goon, Ashlee Langdone, before the game even starts. And then when the game does start, Sasha pounds him again. Sasha gets sent to the penalty box, where he stands up on the bench and does the chicken dance, and the five-thousand fans cheer like he is The Rock, but your team still loses. And they lose again the next night, getting shut out 4–0, in fact, and it's not the goalies' fault, yet your team, a group that twenty-five games ago was supposed to bring Bakersfield its first championship banner, has lost as many games as it has won.

You practice hard–first guy on, last guy off–and you do all the drills in the Mitch Korn goalie bible (glove up, stick on the ice, pads flat, positive mental attitude), but you look around at the other guys and find little inspiration. The two other goalies ignore you, probably still hoping you'd just give it up and leave. Your coach is treating you well, not tooling on you so much, talking hockey with you in between periods and appreciating the input you give him, but, no matter how much you like your coach as a person, you also hate him as a coach for not making your dream come true.

Your friend and teammate, Todd Esselmont, the only other rookie in all of pro hockey who is over thirty, is on the verge of quitting. He is spending more and more games in the stands with you, the odd man out, the player the coach doesn't even think is good enough to take up space on the bench. "You're the best player in the league with no points," Kells told him yesterday, and that made Esselmont angry. "I don't feel like I'm part of this team," Esselmont says to you on a bus ride to Long Beach. "I sit and do nothing. It's embarrassing, eh? I'm thirty years old. I've gained ten pounds since I got here because I'm drinking again and not skating enough. It sucks, man. It's like it was in junior all over again. My coach was Ken Hitchcock. He didn't like me, wouldn't play me because he thought I was a pussy. Then one night he comes into the room before the game and goes, 'Todd Esselmont is going to get in a fight tonight. Pick someone and beat the shit out of him.' But I wasn't a fighter, man. I was a nineteen-year-old kid and wanted to play hockey more than anything else in my life. So I fought a guy. I broke my nose, got two black eyes and chipped a tooth. And what the fuck for? I didn't get any more ice time. So that's when I quit. I'm starting to feel the same way now."

So you tell your friend Todd that he could always go home to Vancouver, back to his girl, back to driving a truck for a living, and maybe life would be better now that he at least had tried to live his dream. But he says, "No way, I've come too far to quit now," and you are thinking the exact same thing about your sick, frustrated self.

You get to Long Beach and take your seat up in the mostly empty stands, where for the twenty-fourth time this season you watch your team. They lose yet another game, this one in a shootout in which Hay's sore knee is obviously bothering him. The season being a day-to-day roller-coaster ride of emotions, you play like a pro the next morning at practice in San Diego. Hay sits out the practice to rest his sore knee for the game tonight. But you play as though you are the best, showing the players and your coach that you can step in and do the job, even though you know deep down that not getting regular practice time like the other two goalies has hurt your progress. "Be ready," your team's captain tells you. "We might need ya." So you challenge the shooters by coming out extra far, reacting like the nineteen-year-old whiz you once were, diving to trap pucks with your glove, directing pucks into the corners, unafraid of the hardest slap shots they can whip your way. And, best of all, your wife is driving all the way down from San Francisco to see you tonight!

After practice, you find that your motel room has a leak in the ceiling and the room smells like mold. So you put on a Walkman and walk along the beach to enjoy San Diego's December sun. You listen to a call-in show on public radio. Listeners are asking an expert on the origin of certain words and phrases. One caller asks, "Where does the expression

'A watched pot never boils' come from?" And the expert says he doesn't know, but the proverbial light bulb goes off in your head and you think, "Hey, that's right! A watched pot does never boil!" Whenever you stare at a pot of water on the stove, and wait and wait and wait, it seemingly takes forever. But when you walk away . . . bam! Next thing you know, the water is bubbling over the edge. *What a perfect metaphor! So cliché, yet true.* You realize you need to chill out and not obsess so much about when, where, or if you will play. Just show up every day and hope for the best. *Act well the given part.*

You get to the rink and see your wife, whom you haven't seen in over a month, and she is wearing a sexy top and jeans. Suddenly, you don't care so much about your team—which you have watched play every single second of every single game this year, just in case you're needed to play. So you sit with your wife and drink a glass of wine, and then after the first period you decide to leave the rink. Who cares? you think. They don't need me. I'm never gonna play. I'm outta here for a while.

You and your wife run hand-in-hand over to the moldy motel room across the street and make mad, passionate love with half your clothes still on. No teammates, no roommates, no coach, no fans, no nobody. No hockey. Just you and the woman whose love and supportive voice over the phone has helped keep you sane.

And when you step back inside the San Diego arena with six minutes left in the second period, your cheeks red and your hair a sloppy mess, you learn that, while you weren't watching, the pot had finally boiled.

Play

The play seemed harmless enough. The shot came streaming straight at Looch, who, having been confidently playing his best game in over a month, easily stopped it with his right leg. But when he dropped to his knees to cover the puck, a San Diego player landed on top of Looch, who fell backward and twisted his right arm to brace his fall. With all two hundred pounds of the San Diego player leaning on him, Looch's arm could not bear the weight and his shoulder popped out of joint.

Oooooooooowwwww!

Larry came running out to treat him.

Oooooooooowwwww!

When Larry got to him, Looch was biting his bottom lip and screaming.

Unable to do anything but look down at the helpless heap of humanity, Larry and Jason shoulder-carried Looch off the ice, careful not to put him in any more pain. I ran down to the locker room, where I am now wondering if this brutal injury is my ticket to a dream come true.

A team of doctors stands in a circle around Looch as Larry cuts the jersey off his body and slides his chest and shoulder protection off. Lying flat on a padded training table, Looch is trying so hard not to lose it that he's frothing at the mouth. Unable to stomach it, I turn away.

"This is going to hurt," the doctor warns. Just then Larry grabs hold of Looch's hand. "Squeeze it," he says, as the doctor pulls Looch's arm out to the side like an airplane wing.

Oooooooooowwwww!

Once the arm is extended straight out at a right angle to his body, the doctor pulls it toward him and pops Looch's arm back into the shoulder socket.

Ooooooooowwwww!

God, I swear I'll never wish any harm toward anyone ever again! I feel like a fool. This doesn't feel right. In fact, it's nauseating. I haven't seen a guy so vulnerable since I last looked at the photos of my brain surgery, and I haven't heard someone scream in such agony since I was ten years old, when my father had a golf-ball-sized stone lodged in his right kidney and was rushed in an ambulance to the hospital, where a surgeon cut into his side and extracted the stone before it killed him.

A few minutes later, with San Diego out-shooting us 28–19 and up 3–1, the guys come back to the room for the second intermission, their heads hanging and sweat running down their defeated faces. I loiter outside the locker room in the hallway where the Gulls Girls are stretching for their between-periods dance routine, as I prepare for my regular season professional debut, hoping that a glass of wine and quickie sex hasn't sapped me of any energy I might need should Kells replace Hay with me. My heart is beating like a tom-tom when Kells walks out of the medical room and tells me, "Get dressed."

I do.

As the players drink water, treat their injuries, or just stare blankly ahead, I stand at a stall and perform the reverse of the undressing ritual that had marked the end of my career after my final college game on March 10, 1992.

I put on a jock, shorts, a T-shirt, and long socks. Then on goes the protective cup, socks, garter belt, pants, skates, pads, chest-and-shoulder protector. Then a black, red, and green Bakersfield Condors jersey. I wrap my hands in padded tape to reduce the sting from pucks.

When I put on my mask and gloves, and the team heads back onto the ice for the third period, I'm now the team's second-string goalie. Number two. I'm on the team. Part of the family.

I don't play, and we lose 5–1, but I am high on the feeling that just knowing that at any second I could end up in the net, and these twenty guys who have become my family will be relying on me, even though I am not sure I am ready for the task. Tomorrow, we play San Diego again, at home. As I am carrying my bag up the ramp to the bus outside, our towering defenseman Quinn Fair walks beside me. "Bakes," he says, "I had a dream last night that you played and were doing really well. Kind of weird eh?"

On the bus ride back to Bakersfield, Looch's arm is cocked in a sling. He winces with every bump in the freeway. I take a seat next to him and let him know this isn't how I wanted things to work out.

"I know, don't worry about it," Looch says, groggy from the pain-killers. "But you know what sucks, Bakes? I was playing so well. And then this happens."

* * *

"Baker," Kells says to me in his speech before my first game as the backup goalie. "You nervous, buddy?"

"No," I reply. "I'm fired up."

The guys respond approvingly with a chorus of "yeahs" and "all-rights." Jason Ralph, my neighbor, whispers, "Good answer."

Although I am the backup goalie, I'm not yet officially on the roster. Rather, my status is "emergency goalie," meaning I can only play if Hay is hurt or otherwise unable to compete due to an emergency. The league created this player status so that they can pay me $50 a game rather than the league minimum $325 a week. My goal is to make it on the roster and to play, but this is a nice start. It's only fifty bucks, but the money makes me a pro hockey player. Kells could sign me to a contract any day now. He is allowed to have twenty-one players on the roster, and ever since Steve Low returned to his wife in Quebec and Steve Zoryk left to play in the CHL a few weeks ago, we have had two open roster spots.

At the rink, Larry tells me that Looch will be out "four to six weeks," meaning he won't be in playing shape until the end of January. Even then, no one knows whether he will be able to play by then. He will need to rest the shoulder, then rehab it, strengthen the muscles and tendons that hold it in place, then see if he can play with a shoulder brace for the rest of the season. "That's a big 'if,'" Larry says. "This could be your big break, Bakes."

As soon as I step onto the ice for the warm-up, I am the focus of dozens of quasi-paparazzi: Brooke and her sister, Samara, capture images of me in uniform; fans bang on the glass and take pictures; the official team photographer snaps away. I didn't think anyone cared this much.

Even the shots in warm-ups are shockingly faster than in practice. And the guys skate much quicker, at a game pace.

When the game starts and I take a seat at the end of the bench, I'm all business, telling myself the entire time that I will play tonight. This must be the mindset of a backup goalie. At any point in the game I could be needed to go in, and—no matter how cold I am—I will have to be physically and mentally prepared to play. So every few minutes I stand and stretch, loosen my arms and legs, touch the toes, and take deep breaths to focus. I don't look in the stands up at Brooke, who is so proud and, perhaps for the first time, feeling as if our sacrifices over the last few months have been worth it.

* * *

San Diego has nineteen wins; we have twelve. But by the end of the game, as we wheeze and cough through another sloppy third period, it's amazing that we've won that many games. We're slower than other teams, don't check as hard or as often as other teams, our goaltending isn't as consistent as other teams, and half our team is injured.

Predictably, the Gulls finish off the two-game sweep with a 3–1 victory, even without the Gulls Girls around. Christmas is in just three days and our next game isn't until Wednesday, December 26. Kells has decided to give us the next three days off, the first time we have had more than one day off the entire season. But before he releases us for the holiday, before Brooke and I pack up and drive to her parents' house five hours away, Kells vents. "I want you to take three days to recharge your batteries," he says, his voice hoarse from shouting at the refs, the players, to no one in particular over the last three hours. "Maybe it's my fault, maybe I overestimated the maturity in talent in this room. Maybe I have been too soft. It's too much of a country club atmosphere around here, and that's my fault. We need to be more professional, be a team, work harder, stick together. There's a lot of things I see that I don't like. On and off the ice. I hear some of you think I favor the guys from Topeka. That's just bullshit. I might hang out with them more because I have known them longer, but I guarantee you that it doesn't matter when it comes to the ice. Everyone is on a level surface, no one is safe. Too many guys in this room think they have a role on the team. Well, in this league you need to do everything. Look at the guys on San Diego. They are some of the leading scorers in the league, but they are out there hitting every shift, killing penalties, back-checking hard. That is the kind of effort we need. And if I don't start seeing it after the break, there will be some changes. Because if you guys don't start playing better, you will be fucking with me. And if you are fucking with me, you are fucking with my family. I want a job next year, and I ain't gonna have a job if I let you guys fuck me this year. So if you fuck me, I will fuck back."

Listen

I've met far too many men over thirty who talk as if their lives ended the day they quit playing competitive sports. That, to me, is tragic. There's more to life than sports.

But hockey dominated my life ever since my first time on ice as a towheaded seven-year-old trying not to fall on my butt. I soon decided that I wanted nothing more in life—and that I would ask nothing else of my Catholic God—than to make a living as a professional hockey goalie.

"Dad?" I asked him one winter day in the car. "How do you become famous?"

Never short on steering-wheel wisdom, my nonfamous, but infinitely wise, father replied, "You find something you're good at and become the best at it."

Staring through the frosted windshield, I declared, "I want to be a famous hockey player."

Hockey was my escape from a childhood otherwise punctuated by my parents's divorce and older-sibling rivalry. My three older brothers—Kevin, Keith, and Kyle, all of whom by their teens had ditched sports for the Grateful Dead—called me KAK, standing for "Kiss Ass Kenny." They exacted their punishment in the form of pulling my undies into painful butt-wedgies, locking me in the hallway closet—just for yuks, even though I was claustrophobic—and punching me in the arm to see how ugly a bruise they could make. They didn't know it—and, frankly, neither did I—but their torture instilled in me a fighter's instinct, not to mention a high tolerance for pain, that would set me apart from most North American hockey players.

At fourteen, I earned a spot in the United States Olympic development program, having been identified by coaches as among the nation's top young goaltenders, one of the dozen or so goalies who the powers-that-be hoped would carry our country to Olympic gold, as goalie Jim Craig had done for the 1980 "Miracle on Ice" team that beat the Russians. That gold medal victory in Lake Placid had inspired my dreams.

Like tennis prodigies, prepubescent gymnasts, figure skaters, boy-band singers, and anyone else who rises to the top of a profession in their early- to mid-teens, I was obsessed with hockey to an almost dysfunctional degree. I spent my free time reading sports-psychology books, stretching, doing push-ups, watching hockey games. Safe to say, I wasn't your normal kid.

Rather than go to the movies, the mall, or–heaven forbid!–hang out with girls, I would beg my dad for ten bucks so I could buy a nosebleed seat at the Buffalo Sabres games at the Memorial Auditorium. Dad would drop me off an hour before the game so I could see warm-ups, and then in the first period after spying open seats in the "gold" section near the ice, I would sneak down into a seat behind the goalie, studying his every move. I would note how far he came out to cut down the angle on the shooter, where he positioned his hands, how deep he squatted in his stance, when he went to his knees, when he stood, how he caught the puck, how he controlled rebounds off his stick. When I observed the NHL goalies I was absorbing data with the goal of replication.

In between periods, I would stand outside their locker room and watch my heroes hustle onto the ice. Gilbert Pereault, Danny Gare, Larry Playfair. The Sabres had just drafted an eighteen-year-old goalie from Massachusetts named Tom Barrasso. He was only four years older than I was and, unlike the majority of pro goalies, was also an American. On the wall next to my bed I taped a photo of "Tommy B." that had appeared in *Sports Illustrated*. I figured that if he could make it, so could I.

From my perspective, hockey gave me all the satisfaction a boy could want, and in 1987 I experienced an athletic orgasm: I was chosen as the starting goalie on the United States's under-17 national team. We played in a world championship tournament in Chicago at Christmas time. In the championship game against a team of Canadian all-stars I stopped the most shots in a game I had ever stopped in my career. Thousands of fans chanted "USA, USA," as I out-dueled Stephan Fiset, Canada's highly touted goalie out of Quebec, and a future NHL star. After the win, our coach walked into the locker room and told us—a pack of hooting and hollering teen-agers—to pipe down for a few seconds because he had an announcement.

"I'd like to share an interesting fact with you guys," he said. "You are the first U.S. hockey team to win a world championship since the 1980 Olympic team. Congratulations, boys. You should all be proud of yourselves."

It turned out that I couldn't have picked a better night to play the best game of my life. Dozens of college coaches and NHL scouts were in the crowd that night. My performance put me on their radar screen as a bona-fide star in the making. People later called us the "dream team," because so many of my teammates—among them Jeremy Roenick, Mike Modano and Tony Amonte—would go on to win Olympic medals, not to mention to become NHL millionaires. My pro-hockey dream was fast becoming a reality.

I returned home from Chicago to a hero's welcome: My mother, who, unlike my narrowly focused father, had always warned me not to put all my "eggs in one basket," even started to believe that hockey stardom might be in my future. She proudly strung a paper banner across the front of our dilapidated brown duplex exclaiming, "Way to go, Kenny! Go USA!"

Throughout it all, my father, who was living in an apartment ten miles from where Kyle, Kris, and I lived with Mom since their divorce three years earlier, was my most loyal supporter and biggest motivator. Never too hard or too soft on me, he constantly reminded me of not only how good I was, but how good I could become with even more hard work and commitment to my goaltending craft.

Back then, I thought Dad was just being a regular dad. But nowadays, his dedication is awe-inspiring. He was the one who woke up at four o'clock on frigid January mornings to drive me to games, the one who racked up thousands of dollars in credit-card bills to pay for my equipment. Dad knew I would improve faster if I played against older kids. By age twelve, I was playing in the division two years ahead of me, because my age bracket wasn't challenging enough. Dad was right: It made me better.

An ugly side of youth hockey—back then, at least—was jealous parents. It wasn't unusual for a father to stand at the boards next to my goal and try to rattle me, shouting, "This goalie's got nothin'. Shoot high! That goalie is too small!" Dad never backed down from a fight. He would stand right next to the idiot and pump me up, yelling, *"Way to go, Kenny! Lookin' good, Kenny. Keep it up!"* This came from a guy so masculine, so emotionally contained that he never once said, "I love you." Sure, it would have been nice to hear it, but the truth is that he didn't have to. I knew he loved me. He didn't tell me, but he showed me, which, ultimately, I believe is more important.

Dad's childhood in the suburbs east of Washington, D.C., and his teenage years in western New York State, were poor, unfortunate ones. I grew up hearing how he couldn't play organized sports because he was so poor, and because his parents, by most accounts a couple of idiots who split before my dad was five, made him get a job when he turned twelve.

It doesn't take a genius to figure out why as a result he was so interested in seeing me achieve success in sports. So that is why my dream became our dream, a goal that we'd both fantasize about during long drives home from games I played from Chicago to Montreal. With Fifties stations supplying our soundtrack—our favorites being Buddy Holly, Roy Orbison, and Elvis—we'd talk about the day I would play for my hometown team, the Buffalo Sabres. "You won't forget me when you make it big, will you?" he'd ask, only half kidding.

To a lot of kids, this kind of intense fatherly involvement turns them off from playing because they are unable to meet their dad's expectations. This happened to all my brothers. Yet, for some reason, whether he had learned through trial and error not to be so overbearing or whether I was even more motivated than he was, my father inspired me.

By my junior year of high school, NHL scouts were flocking to see this boy from Buffalo who frustrated shooters with his quick arms and legs. A scout from the Buffalo Sabres even came to see me play. College coaches—from Colorado to Maine—wrote me letters inviting me to their campuses. Near the end of my senior year, I chose Colgate University, which, being just two hundred miles east of Buffalo, was the closest NCAA Division One college hockey program, besides Cornell, which didn't recruit me. The plan was working to perfection. Or so I thought.

* * *

It's hard to pinpoint exactly when my body began its insidious betrayal. Any elite athlete knows it's not productive to focus on the negative. He knows that one setback is only a setup for two future steps forward. An elite athlete knows that if you spend too much time focusing on what's wrong you will have a harder time doing what's right. In my case, that meant stopping the puck.

Staying positive and confident is especially important for a goaltender, unquestionably the single most important player on a team. With so much pressure weighing on him and pucks coming at him so quickly, a goalie can't afford to doubt his abilities. This might help explain why I missed the warning signs. After four years of struggling to be more than just a below-average collegiate netminder, not only did I no longer dream of playing pro hockey, I didn't even want to play the game.

Off the ice, things were equally distressing. Since I couldn't seem to weight-lift my way into a more muscular body (bad genes, I'd always thought, since my father and brothers were pudgy), I took constant ribbing in the locker room from the guys for my increasingly soft, pear-shaped physique. One especially cruel upperclassman nicknamed me "Pear," and I hated him for it.

Perhaps most troubling for a heterosexual college guy, I was afraid of girls. Not of what they might do to me, but of what I could not do to them. The first time I tried to have sex at age seventeen, I couldn't get it up. I was supposed to be in my sexual prime, but I had the penis of a disabled one-hundred-year-old man. I spent intimate moments with girls wondering if my pocket rocket would lift off; the countdown almost always ended in a main engine shutdown.

I did enjoy some moments of Big Man on Campus glory, like when I beat cross-state rival Cornell in its barn, and shut down the University of Vermont's attack, which was led by future NHL great John Leclair. Overall, I won more games than I lost, finishing with a collegiate record of fourteen wins, twelve losses and two ties. But just as often as I played well enough to win I would play as if I couldn't stop a beach ball. It was a far cry from my heady teen-age years when coaches compared me to Jim Craig.

I started having nightmares. One in particular repeated itself for years, like a bad sitcom. I dove to stop a puck that was flying at the net, but, every time, my face and body would stick to the ice as if my belly were lead and the ice were a magnet. I couldn't move. I was stuck. The symbolism was not lost on me.

Near the end of my college career, I began to suspect that something was slowing my reflexes and deflating my motivation, something had killed my career. It was maddening, in that Kafka-esque kind of way, yet it would take several even more maddening years before I would find an answer.

I groped to assess blame. Was it the fault of my college coach, who never seemed to have confidence in me? Or was it *I* who didn't have confidence in me? Was it my growing interest in academics and decreasing interest in dealing with pulled groins and bruises all over my body? Or was it my dad, a diabetic whose health problems had forced him to retire, disrupting my focus and plaguing me with sleepless nights? Had I just burned out? Had I simply lost my will to win? Had I peaked at age sixteen? Or did I just grow up–and out of–sports? I didn't know, and to avoid being depressed about it, I convinced myself that I didn't care.

What was clear was that I simply was not getting any better, no matter how hard I tried. In the 1990–1991 season (my junior year) I played in ten games and allowed an average of 3.97 goals a game, stopping 88 percent of the shots I faced. But in my senior year my goals-against average per game dropped to 4.55 and my save percentage fell to just 86 percent. And the team in front of me had improved. I couldn't blame anyone but myself for my downfall.

The inevitable result of my mental and physical deterioration came on March 3, 1992. The bulldogs of Yale University had just knocked my team, the Red Raiders, out of the play-offs. As I had done thousands of times in my career, I stood at my stall and began getting undressed. Only this time the ritual held profound significance.

I lifted off my goalie mask and jersey. I took off my upper-body padding, undid the leather straps on my leg pads and unlaced my skates. Glancing at the name on my stall's plastic nameplate–BAKER–I carefully hung my skates on the two metal hooks screwed into my locker, which, my being a senior, was near the front door. I had just ended what up until then had been the single greatest passion in my life. I had no other dream to pursue. Hockey had meant everything to me, and suddenly The Dream was dead. I was twenty-one years old.

That summer, I was asked to try out for a couple of East Coast Hockey League teams, but that didn't change my mind. I wanted out of the business of hurt and into a business of pleasure. I wanted a career that reminded me of what I could be, rather than what I used to be. Even so, Dad, who by now was so ill with emphysema that he couldn't walk from the car to the house without losing his breath, pushed me to try and play pro, if only so I could say I had tried. "You have to do it while you're young," Dad said. "And you're only young once."

Fight

Two years after retiring from hockey, I enrolled in a master's degree program in journalism at Columbia University, where in my free time I wrote freelance stories about the New York Rangers for a fan magazine. I hoped I would find as much joy writing about hockey as I did playing. I hoped.

I would sit in the Madison Square Garden press box, bored and frustrated, watching the Rangers goalie, Mike Richter, snag pucks. I'd stand in the press room between periods and listen to the cynical, overweight sportswriters babble on about a sport they knew only as spectators but that I felt in my bones. I didn't want to be one of them. Physically, being far from a svelte warrior, I might have been like them, but, mentally, I was still a player.

One night, the Dallas Stars came to town. Their top player was Mike Modano, my former teammate on the United States junior Olympic squad, who was now making millions as one of the NHL's leading scorers. The last time I had seen Modano he was a skinny teen with pimples, braces, and long, flowing blond hair he wore in the classic "mullet" style—short on top and long in the back. In the locker room after the game, a semicircle of microphone-toting reporters interviewed Modano. When the pack dispersed, I stepped up to a muscular, twenty-three-year-old hockey star with short hair and broad shoulders. Though he had transformed into a man, I looked just as juvenile as I had as a teen.

"Remember me?" I asked, standing before him clutching my tape recorder like a nerd. I shook his hand. "From the Olympic training program."

He squinted in confusion, obviously clueless as to who I was.

"Ken Baker," I said. "I played with you on the under-seventeen team. In Chicago. I was the goalie."

"Oh, Bakes!" he said. "Sorry. What are you doing here?"

I tried to tell him that I even though I played college hockey I had happily quit a year ago because I wanted to move on to journalism. I didn't believe a word I was saying.

"Good for you," Modano said, obviously not believing me either.

I wouldn't step foot inside a hockey locker room for another six years. It was too hard to be so close to the sport and not be playing it.

* * *

Now that I am playing again, and our team's ups and downs are chronicled in minute detail in the newspaper, I realize that, while I would rather play than write about hockey, media coverage off the ice can impact a team's performance on the ice.

After every home game, the *Californian*'s Griffith interviews Kells in his office. The postgame coach's interview is a pro-sports staple, a necessary evil in a business that relies on the public's interest, support and enthusiasm in the team. But while newspaper stories are mostly for the consumption of the fans, coaches know that players also read the stories, which might explain why Kells made some bold statements about the character of our team to Griffith after the loss to San Diego.

"Everybody has to do a little soul searching here," Kells reportedly said. "There's a lot of leaders in the room. They need to lead by example. We need to come together as a team."

Griffith, whom the guys call "Griff," added his own editorial opinion on the team's state of mediocrity: "On the ice, there is a growing mound of evidence that the Condors aren't playing as a team: bad passes, dumping the puck without chasing, and lines that often appear not to be on the same page with the same agenda. . . . Bottom line: The Condors will never rise very far above .500 if they do not figure out how to start scoring goals on the power play."

Griff closes his column with a quote from Kells: "Everybody has to realize we're at a point where the project is going to take a little longer than we anticipated or hoped for. Nothing in life is easy."

When Ryan and I read the column before tonight's game against

Fresno, Ryan says, "Kells is right. Life is hard. But what the hell does life have to do with having the worst power play and penalty killing in the history of man?"

We had three days off for Christmas, but it felt like a week. My body, especially my groin, is grateful that it wasn't abused for seventy-two straight hours on a vacation from Goalieville. Yet part of me wanted to stay in Bakersfield and take shots every day, to get in better game-playing shape now that I am the number-two goalie behind Hay.

Just as before, I prepare mentally and physically, as if I am the starting goalie. I don't talk to guys or read anything. I stretch, rub Atomic Balm on my groin, do some yoga poses on the locker room floor, and get dressed. Even though I'm only making fifty bucks a game, I'm still a pro; this is my job.

Two minutes into the game, a Fresno player lobs the puck over our defensemen's heads into our zone. Immediately, Hay decides to skate out and beat their forward to the puck, but, at the last second, he realizes he has to dive to poke the puck away before the speedy player gets to it. It's a tie, and when their sticks clash, the puck bounces over Hay and, as Fresno's Alex Todd flips the puck into the open net, our defenseman falls hard on Hay's upper back.

Hay doesn't get up. He's lying face-first on the ice as Larry scurries to his side to treat him. The fans quietly stare down at their starting goalie as if trying to telekinetically lift him off the ice so that the rookie writer-guy doesn't have to be pressed into service. I'm nervous–I haven't even had a solid practice since Looch was hurt–but also excited that I might get my shot to go in. Hay finally gets to his knees, and the fans cheer, as Larry puts his hands on Hay's right shoulder, which he apparently injured when our player fell on his back. My pulse has to be over a hundred, and I'm sweating. If that shoulder is separated, I am in.

The crowd starts chanting, "Hay! Hay! Hay!" and when Larry gets back to the bench I ask him what's wrong and he tells me that while Hay "tweaked" his shoulder, it doesn't appear to be separated.

When play continues, I closely watch Hay's every move, trying to detect any hint of seriousness to the injury. If it's hurting, he certainly isn't showing it. Hell, knowing the fans are probably afraid of the third-stringer playing first string, maybe he's just playing up the drama. But at the end of the first period, when he walks shirtless into the training room holding his right arm with his left hand–"Larry!"– and the team doctors look at his shoulder, it's clear the guy isn't faking it. Clenching his teeth in pain, Hay does what the doctor tells him and raises his arm out to the side and then moves it backward. Pop! The joint slides back into place.

"Is it separated?" Hay asks the doctor.

"Not anymore," he says. "I think it's just sprained. See how it feels. You should be able to play with it. If it were your glove hand, it would be harder to play."

When Hay walks back to the locker room, I quietly ask Dr. Hamilton if I should be ready. "I would," he says. "But it's hard to say. It depends on how much pain he can handle." They gave Hay some tablets of Vioxx, an anti-inflammatory pain medication, which should dull the pain. But I start stretching. Just in case.

The score is tied at 1 at the start of the second, and Hay, though careful not to unnecessarily move his right arm, makes stops a few shots from in close. What then happens is an example of the ugly side of hockey–that is, the side where an opposing team, whether instructed by their coach to or not, tries to further injure a player to take him out of the game. Brad Both, Fresno's 6' 2" goon, slashes Hay in the arm, sending Hay to the ice in pain, again. "Protect our fucking goalie!" Kells shouts to the guys on the bench as Larry runs out to check on Hay for the second time tonight. "We need him!" Needless to say, the fact that Kells is so vehement about not losing Hay doesn't say much about his confidence in me.

Hay's arm is sore, but his shoulder is unaffected by the slash, and Goldie puts in a power-play goal on a ping-pong-fast passing play from Willett and Firth. In addition to Cooke, Willett, Firth, and Goldie are our best offensive players. By the last few minutes of the third period, Hay's shoulder is clearly in pain, but he shows some serious toughness and plays as if it isn't killing him. The players notice his valiant effort. *Let's do it for Haysie! Let's show some sack like Haysie!* With the score tied 4–4, Kells puts Firth, Goldie, Cooke, and Willett onto the ice, along with our most offensive defenseman, John Vary, and best defender, Quinn Fair.

They pummel Fresno goalie Terry Friesen, a former San Jose Sharks prospect until Evgeni "Stop da Puck" Nabokov replaced him, with a flurry of shots, and with eleven seconds left in the game Goldie pops in a rebound past Friesen's sprawled-out body. For the first time since the first game of the season, as the clock ticks down and we hold on for the win, the fans send Mount Bakersfield into a major-league eruption. Before the cheers subside, Hay is already undressing in the locker room, icing his knee and shoulder. I ignore him and go ride the stationary bike.

* * *

The next morning, I get up early and head to the gym for a workout. When I climb atop the Stairmaster and start reading the sports section I have to step off the machine. The headline reads, "Goldie Locks Victory: Hay's shoulder injury puts damper on Bakersfield's thrilling 5–4 win as left winger scores late in the game." But it's Kells's quotes about the team's goaltending situation that send my blood pressure through the stratosphere. "He [Hay] sucked it up tonight like the warrior that he is. I'm sure he'll be ready to play, but I better go home and get some sleep because I have to be back here at 5 A.M. trying to find a goaltender."

A new goalie? Why does Kells think he needs a goaltender?

I haul ass back to my apartment and call Kells's office. I haven't once complained since I have been here. I have been a good soldier, put up with all the shit, sat on the sidelines waiting for my turn, worked hard day-in-day-out to improve and to earn the respect of him and my teammates. And now, before I even have a chance to prove myself, he's planning on replacing me with someone else? No way, I think. I'm not letting this happen without a fight. I went through three years of being ignored and disrespected by my college coach before I worked up the nerve to call him on it. But I don't have three years to wait this time around. In three years, I will be almost thirty-five. I will probably have a child by then, my groin will need surgery. If I'm still playing, I will be close to retiring. I'm calling him.

"Y'ello."

"Kells, this is Bakes."

"What can I do for ya?"

"I read what you said in the paper this morning, and I just want you to know that I'm ready. I've been working my ass off every day for this chance. I'm confident, focused and ready to win for this team. I will not let you down."

"Well," he says. "Be ready. The way it looks now you might just get in there."

"Good."

"Just do me a favor."

"What's that?" I ask.

"If you do get in, don't die on me."

"Don't worry," I say. "I'm done with that dying shit."

* * *

That afternoon, the team meets at the Bakersfield airport, a one-runway concrete strip in a field just north of the city, and we board one of those twenty-row puddle jumpers that bumps around the clouds throughout the entire three-hour flight to Colorado Springs. Guys, especially the ones who hate flying, get drunk on bloody marys and rum-and-Cokes and flirt with the skinny brunette flight attendant. Even Larry, our loveable butterball of a trainer, joins in on the fun, asking the friendly flight attendant, "Hey, what are you doing this summer?"

"Excuse me?" she replies.

"What are you doing this summer?" he repeats in a slushy jumble of words. "Ya think you might make it to Bakersfield?"

"It's December," she replies coldly. "How would I know what I'm doing this summer?"

Larry turns red.

Kells doesn't look at me or talk to me the entire flight, except for when we land and he hands me an envelope containing my thirty dollars a day in meal money, my first such luxury of the season. He pretty much ignores me over the next two days, even as I'm the only goalie out for practice for the next two pregame morning practices, even as we lose to the Gold Kings on consecutive nights (4–3 and a 4–1 loss in which we play in slow motion), even as Hay's arm is so sore he can barely hold onto his stick and is munching pain pills as if they're bar pretzels, even as the team might try harder with me in the net. Still, I don't play, and Kells doesn't talk to me. No more "What do you think, Bakes?" at practice, no more asking me to finish his crossword puzzle as we sit in the airport terminal. When we get back home, and I tell Ryan how annoyed I am that the coach won't talk to me, Ryan gives me a reality check. "You should be happy," he says. "He's treating you like he's your boss. He's finally treating you like a real player."

THIRD PERIOD

JANUARY 1, 2002

Play

I had begun playing hockey at eight years old because my pals Pat and Chris O'Connor did, and it was one of the only sports you could play in Buffalo from December to February. Plus, everything from putting on the gladiator-like equipment, to watching the Zamboni magically "make ice" on the rink was the coolest thing I'd ever seen. Plus, you can only make so many snowmen and igloos.

In college, it became work, a job that I wanted to quit before someone fired me, an option my disappointed college hockey coach must have given serious thought. Who could have blamed him? I was a failure, the hot-shot recruit who never panned out. Bruises were no longer totems of manly prowess; they just hurt.

Now, there are forty-two games left in this comeback season of mine, and it's looking like Looch will miss the next ten or so games. My window of opportunity to finally settle the score with my formerly insubordinate body might come down to the next month.

With Looch out, I get more of a workout—and more bruises—in one practice than I was getting in an entire week before I moved into the second-string job. I no longer come out to practice early because it takes all the energy I have just to finish our hour-and-a-half-long practices without getting exhausted. I am now risking the brain tumor growing back. I have gone from taking two anti-prolactin pills a week down to one pill because the side effects—dizziness, nausea, fatigue, parched mouth—are ten times more severe now that I am playing so hard every day. I think it's a gamble worth taking.

Even so, I often out-perform Hay in practice, partly because I try harder, but mostly because he floats through practice in order to baby his sore knee and shoulder. One morning I step on the scale in the locker room and I weigh 159 pounds, which is how much I weighed when I was wheeled out of the hospital after my brain surgery three-and-half years ago. The weight is just burning off me. I start drinking shakes with protein powder. I go to the gym with Ryan and do the bench-press, some squats, pull-ups, anything to keep mass on my thinning body. Fortunately, my right groin has strengthened so much that it no longer is sore. All the stress on my body has put me in the best shape of my life. I am ready.

The problem is that Hay is not ready to step aside, and it remains to be seen whether Kells has enough confidence to play me. If we were winning most games, my chances would look bleak. But our team, no matter how many threats and inspiring speeches Kells makes, no matter how hard Kells skates us in practice, no matter who he puts on the power play, no matter who starts in goal, can't put together more than two wins in a row. Our record is 15–15–2, and there is disgruntlement among fans, who thirty games ago were convinced that this was the year the Condors, perennial also-rans who always get knocked out of the first round of the play-offs, would finally break through. The rants on the Internet message boards, which a lot of the players read almost daily, have become increasingly negative.

Betikchick22: I don't want it to take another month or two to get things rolling. We need it now. We've made the play-offs, but we're kidding ourselves if we think the guys will be ready to face San Diego (or Long Beach) in the play-offs and win if they can't do it now.

Pucknuts: I have got to agree with you Betikchick22. John Vary at -16. He has given up about half as many points as the J-line [Jamie Cooke, Jeff Goldie, and Jason Firth] has scored. John has three goals out of 64 shots on goal. Only Willett, Firth, Cooke, and Goldie have higher SOG numbers. John needs to start playing as a defensive player on his line. Let the Js score the goals. If he cannot do that then move one of the more defensive players up to that line.

Debi: That's a problem I see with several of our D-men–pinching in, trying to jump up into the offensive play, and then what do you know? They're out of position and scored on. Maybe I don't know enough about hockey to understand why the coach doesn't see it, and do something about it. What I don't get is: new coach, overhauled team, same results. No defense, no one, other than Goldie, in front of the net, always waiting for the "perfect" shot (pass, pass, pass, lose possession) on the power play. I just wish they would get it together and play consistently.

Passer: I can't imagine why the coach isn't checking these boards for advice.

Pucknuts: Passer, I can't imagine why coach is so loyal to the Topeka players.

The issue of the "Topeka players"–that is, the eight guys whom Kells brought to Bakersfield from his CHL team who, except for Jeff Goldie, have had a disappointing season–is also a topic of discussion among the players. Some guys complain that Brearley, who has scored only one goal since coming back from his knee injury, would have been fired already were he not a Kells crony. Some guys wonder why Chris Felix, whose thirty-seven-year-old body shows its age in the form of a lack of speed and occasionally sloppy passes–is still even playing.

When a hockey team is winning, the biggest issue on a team usually is who will buy the round of beers after the game. But when a team is losing, a team's psychological dynamics grow complex. One of the first signs of team dysfunction is when the players stop hanging out together. What started off as one giant family in October has become a collection of warring tribes. Brearley and Edmundson, who are roommates, hang out almost exclusively with each other or other Topeka guys. Todd Esselmont, who used to regularly see movies and eat lunch with me and Ryan, now is solely buddies with Sasha. The two stay up alone late most nights drinking and smoking in Sasha's apartment. Last week in Colorado, a bunch of us went to drink at the hotel bar after the game, but Todd and Sasha stayed back in their room. They've become the team's pariahs, tucked naked under their respective covers, drinking beer and watching HBO, complaining about the team. "Honestly, I don't know what I'm doing here," Sasha recently told me. "I thought I would be in The Show by now. Man, I was making $600,000 with New Jersey a couple years ago. I need to feel like I am living. I am just taking up time and space here. And it bugs me."

Sasha is bugging everyone else but Todd. Some nights, after Sasha goes through his pregame kung fu routine in the stands, he will go out on the ice and ignore his teammates. When he gets the puck, he skates straight to the net and shoots, even if it is from a bad angle and one of his linemates is wide open. His excuse? "Why pass it?" he says. "Besides Cookie and Goldie, no one on this team can fuckin' score."

Sasha doesn't even want to fight. "It's not worth it anymore," he tells me. "Why should I get my head beat in, tear my shoulder, cut my hands in order to keep all these pussies from getting their faces beat in. Fuck them guys!"

But, to our fans, Sasha is Hulk Hogan. They love it when he drops his gloves and, without even having to throw a punch, frightens players into skating away. It keeps the cheap shots down. They love it when he mocks the opposition with the chicken dance. They love it when they see him performing kung fu chops and kicks in warm-ups. Our general manager, Matt Riley, needs to fill the seats. Jonathan wants to make money. Unable to market our team as winners, Riley sees an economic opportunity in our resident wild man by selling hundreds of red T-shirts picturing Sasha's kung fu grip on the chest reading "Lethal Weapons." Sasha is an entertainer. He is no longer playing for the team, or even for himself. He is a character in a one-man play. He is the mean, menacing muscle-head who can rile up fans in a single clench of the fist.

And so when we fly a turbulent five hours north to the dark January land of Anchorage, Alaska, where the sun shines for four hours a day, where moose walk freely through city streets, and where residents go to Aces hockey games just to get out of the cold, Sasha the Entertainer crafts a plan.

As grim as the season has been at times for the Condors, the Aces players have endured a spectacle that is known in pro hockey circles as a "gong show," a situation where everything that can go wrong does. With six games under .500, the Aces, whose nearest rival is Tacoma, about a thousand miles away, not only have the worst travel schedule, they have the worst defense in the league. Their coach, legendary New York Islanders player Butch Goring, was fired two weeks ago and replaced by Walt Podubny, who played for the Toronto Maple Leafs in the eighties but now lives in Anchorage and is better known as a regular at the Northern Lights bar. The Aces players, most of whom live in a run-down, cigarette-smoke-filled hotel with a broken elevator, and rooms with a hot plate for a kitchen, are getting paid in cash. According to the players, after games, the owner, after collecting money from the snack bars and beer stands, walks down to the locker room with a wad of cash and pays the guys because he has no other money with which to pay them. The fans are not only bored, but downright hostile. As Willett stepped onto the ice for the first game of the two-game series, a simian in a furry Eskimo jacket yelled down from the stands, "Wife beater!" We easily won the game 8–4, the only drawbacks of the night being that I once again did not play, and when Mears got checked into the boards by Chad Richard, he had to leave the game when he started coughing up blood due to what Larry diagnosed as "a bruised lung."

The next morning, I wake up early and walk past the glass-encased moose in the hotel lobby and slide on across the icy street to a diner to get a cup of coffee. I sit at the counter next to a couple of other players who are complaining about how awful the hotel is. Vary says his pillows are so hard they felt like "two rocky mountains" under his head. There's no hot water. And since there are only two channels on the TV, they talk about a case they saw yesterday on *Judge Judy.* They love their law-and-order in Alaska. On one of the channels the lineup is *Judge Judy* at 3 P.M., *Judge Joe Brown* at 3:30 P.M. and *Judge Judy* again at 4 P.M.

As the other guys chat and eat their eggs and bacon, I start reading a story in the local paper about how scientists have recently found out that the "Big Bang," which theoretically created the universe, may have happened millions of years more recently than previously thought. Before my mind gets too stuck in one of those brain-bending thoughts about the profound mystery of the universe and life and time and the meaning of life, I have to run out and catch the shuttle to the rink for morning practice, so I can get hit in the arms and legs and gut and head with frozen pucks.

At the end of practice Hay rushes off to ice his sore parts, and I stay out and take extra shots. When Kells and the guys start playing a game of sticks, I try a different method of puck-stopping. Rather than stare intensely at the puck, I look at their eyes, trying to anticipate where they will shoot by seeing where they are looking. It's a method that Mitch Korn, or any goalie coach worth a damn, would never teach a student. But when you are in Alaska in the middle of the winter, and you're not playing games, and it's not even noon, and the sun has already fallen to the horizon, and you're in no rush to go back to the hotel and watch syndicated judge shows, you have to try different things just to keep the game interesting.

It took a round of fifteen guys scoring twelve goals for me to abandon my innovative method. "The problem is that now that you're in better shape and a little faster, you're trying to outthink these guys," Kells said to me as I sat angrily on the bench afterward. "It backfired on you because, you have to remember, these guys don't know how to think."

As I sit at my stall and stare at the floor, thinking about nothing and everything at the same time, Dickie walks in and picks up the laundry bags from the floor and asks, "What's on your mind?"

"Life," I say.

"What about life?" he says gruffly.

"I was thinking about how silly this game is in the big scheme of things."

Dickie sits down next to me and says, "You can't do that. As soon as you start thinking about life, you're done. You can't do it. Just live life, my man."

* * *

That night, when we skate onto the ice for the second game, I witness a hockey-game first: a woman in the front row reading a newspaper with her shirt unbuttoned as she breast-feeds her baby. It's strange to see a woman doing something so intimate in front of forty hockey players, but I will soon witness something far more shocking.

As I walk down the hall to the locker room before the Saturday night contest, I see Sasha sitting in the stands talking to Chad Richard, the 6' 6", 235-pound goon for Anchorage. Chad Richard is Sasha Lakovic without the NHL speed or skills. Richard, 27, has been suspended more than any other WCHL player, including in 1996 when he was kicked out of the league for half the season for firing a puck at a referee. The Aces waived Richard the next season after he threw a chair that struck an usher after a game in Boise, Idaho. The guy, who is missing a front tooth, is what guys call a "piece of work." And in Sasha he must find a fraternity, what with the way they are laughing and joking and re-creating their recent fisticuffs. I should have known something was up when he comes back to the locker room to get dressed, and starts going on and on about how they should rename the WCHL the "XHL," and turn it into the pro hockey version of pro wrestling. "I'm telling ya, man, the fans would eat it up," he says. "We could stage fights, play off a script, make it more entertaining. The fans are sick of seeing the same old games every night. They want to see fights and shit." He's either a total fool or a genius.

Either way, the game, the second of our two-game series in Alaska, starts. I take my position at the end of the bench, hoping that maybe I will make my pro debut in Alaska, just south of the Arctic Circle on a sub-zero night in a barn-like arena under the bright northern stars. After the national anthem has been played, Sasha skates a series of laps around the rink, stretching his arms out and staring down Richard at the other end.

As the ref steps to center ice to drop the puck, Sasha and Richard line up next to each other for the opening face-off. They stare angrily in each other's eyes. They slash each other's shin pads. They elbow each other. They look like two pit bulls with only a leash keeping them from biting each other's heads off.

The referee finally drops the puck and the game starts. The two goons immediately drop their gloves and grab hold of each other's jerseys. It's an odd start to a fight for Sasha. I have never seen him begin by grabbing hold of a guy's sweater. Usually, he keeps his hands free and throws a flurry of jabs and upper cuts. Maybe, I think, he has met his match in Richard.

Richard frees his right hand from Sasha's jersey and throws a series of sloppy punches to Sasha's shoulder pads, chest and arms. Oddly, though none of the punches hits his face, the usually resilient Sasha crumples to the ice, covering his head like a nerd beaten down by the schoolyard bully. Thrilled that minor league hockey's most notorious goon has been pummeled by their hometown fighter, the fans stand and holler with malevolent joy. The mood on our bench, however, is anything but joyful. He fucking staged a fight.

Willett, who's sitting next to me on the bench, disgustedly shakes his head. "Now I've seen everything," he says.

Since no one wants to talk to Sasha, and most are afraid he will freak out if they tell him what a disgrace it was to the integrity of the team for him to turn the game into his own circus sideshow act, the guys ignore him in between periods, and try to pretend it never happened. Kells doesn't even look at him.

At the start of the second period, just as they did at the start of the game, the two stars of their own XHL line up against each other. This time, the fans are ready to see the fight between the warriors, to witness an attempt at revenge! The "fight" is even more absurd than the first one. Sasha unleashes a faux flurry of shots to Richard's shoulder area and wrestles the goon to the ice. Apparently, they had agreed that the home goon would win the first match and the visiting goon would win the second one. The fans have no idea. They cheer as if they really were fighting. The two players, meanwhile, do everything but squirt ketchup on each other's faces. What a fucking farce. The knucklehead theater depresses me. I have worked so hard to be a pro hockey player, sacrificed everything in order to get a taste of real pro hockey. This is my eighth game in a pro uniform and, until now, it was an achievement I was proud to have reached. Earlier tonight, Jason Ralph, our twenty-two-year-old rookie, scored his first professional goal. It was a moment of actual glory and accomplishment in a sport that is special, a sport made unique by its rawness. And Sasha has made a mockery of it.

Firth grumbles, "Why is he here? He's got no respect for the game or himself. He played in the NHL. Now look at him. What a fucking idiot."

As Sasha riles up the fans by blowing them kisses, I tell Willett, "You have to talk to him. He can't do this. It's bad for morale."

Willett calls a players-only meeting in the locker room during the second intermission. We're tied 1–1. We can still win this game, despite Sasha's theatrics.

Once everyone sits down, Willett closes the door, steps to the middle of the room and looks right at Sasha. "What the fuck are you doing out there? It's a disgrace. You can't fake a fight. That's just unbelievable. Just play the fucking game, Sasha."

The veins on the side of Sasha's shaved head look as if they are about to burst. The rest of us are silent.

"I *am* playing the game!" Sasha erupts.

"No," Willett says. "You're not."

"Oh yeah? I have been protecting you fucking pussies all year, and I'm sick of it. I'm just trying to find a way."

"Well, it's fucking wrong," Willett, now as angry as Sasha, replies.

"Yeah, well it's also wrong for me to fight for you guys when no one has my back. Who in this room would stick up for me? You all fucking hate me. I have to fight for you guys. I am sick of fighting."

"You don't have to fight," Willett says. "The other teams are already fucking scared of you. Maser can fight for us. Just play the game."

"Fuck it," Sasha says, and storms off to the training room, where he kicks a trash can, grumbling, "I don't need this shit."

He starts taking off his equipment.

"You don't have to quit, Sasha," Felix reasons with the unreasonable man in our midst. "Just play the game, buddy."

Sasha doesn't quit. Not because he doesn't want to. He can't. He needs the money. He has a son and an ex-wife to whom he sends a few hundred dollars every week in child support. Moreover, Sasha has few other job skills. He took some welding classes in Vancouver last summer, but he quit them to practice kung fu. Sasha might be sick of playing the goon, but it's the only game he can play.

Sasha suits back up and finishes the game. He doesn't fight and actually makes some good passing plays. Still, we lose 3–2 and end up losing six out of our next seven games, all of which Hay plays while I wait for Looch to come back and replace me when he is healthy. I am losing hope that Kells will believe in me. The team is losing its motivation to play for each other. But Sasha has lost something more important: his reputation.

Care

After ten seasons of pro hockey, John Vary is tired. Ten seasons of stitches, tears, strains, and body blows. The first five, John says, were for "my dream," and the last five have been for "them"–his wife, Robin, and their two kids, who have been living out of suitcases for six months every year for the last five years. "I stay in it for them," he says, "but this year it has started to hurt them. They miss home."

In the summers, John and his family stay in the city of Owen Sound, his hometown, a tiny mill town in western Ontario where John Vary is still a hockey legend for the string of records he set before he left home at sixteen and was drafted by the New York Rangers. He wasn't the biggest or the fastest or the niftiest defenseman, but he was smart, strong, and made very few mistakes. Steady. Solid. John Vary showed up to play.

But the Rangers had Brian Leetch and a band of other defenders who were bigger, and niftier, and just as smart and strong. The Rangers released him, but John didn't give up on his NHL dream. He embarked on a AAA minor league career that in five years bounced him from teams in Binghamton, to Erie, to Wichita, to the swamps of Louisiana. But in 1996, with not a single AAA team offering a contract, John was offered a AA job with the Fury of Muskegon, Michigan, in what is now the United Hockey League. The NHL dream was over. Once you go down to AA, there's no going back up. He was turning twenty-five. It seemed like time to quit and move on. He could head back to Owen Sound, get a real job before he got so old no one would let him get a foot in the door. He didn't want to be one of those old guys who plays minor league hockey because he has no other options.

But then Paul Kelly, the new coach of the Muskegon Fury, who had just retired as a player, convinced him to come play for the Michigan-based team. Paul Kelly told John if he didn't like it he could pack up and leave, no questions asked. But once he got there, John Vary had fun playing hockey for the first time in five years. No longer burdened with the pressure of living his "dream," John played just to play. He was a veteran, a leader, wise beyond his years, a step ahead of almost everyone else at that level. He was an all-star, scored game-winning goals, won a championship against the Quad City Mallards with a slap shot from the point. Sure, he wasn't going to play in the NHL. Sure, he was making half the money. But John Vary was a legend all over again.

He had two little girls, Jamie and Nicole, the cutest little things a dad could ever dream of having. The plan now was to play until he was thirty and then go work for the city of Owen Sound, cut the grass at the parks and plow the streets in the winter. A good job would be waiting for him. He could retire with a full pension at forty-nine. Not too bad, he thought. Even though the pay caps out at twenty-one bucks an hour, that's pretty good in a small town.

A few years later, when Paul Kelly took over the Topeka Scarecrows, John Vary followed his guru, and they had fun there too. Fun! Hockey should be all about fun, he thought. *When it stops being fun, that's when I'll quit.*

Now he is in Bakersfield, and the fans are booing him every other night, and his body aches, and the team is losing, and his little girls just want to go home. It's not fun.

He recently told his eighty-two-year-old grandmother about all the injuries he has suffered this year, to which she replied, "Johnny, you don't want to do something now that in the future will make you unable to walk straight." And John thought about what she said for the next week.

Then, the other night, as John is wondering why he keeps doing this damage to his body, his older daughter starts crying soon after going to bed. "What's wrong, Jamie?" John asked her. "I miss Grandma and Grandpa," she cried. "I want to go home."

And so does John. But he can't. He makes good money, as much as any player at this level, over a grand a week, which is double what he would make back mowing lawns back in Owen Sound. He needs to make the most money he can before his body quits on him. His family needs him. He has to play.

And that's exactly what he's thinking on this Saturday night in Boise. An Idaho player accidentally slashes John in the face, shredding his upper lip and spattering so much blood onto his jersey and the ice that even some of the hardened mountain-bred hockey fans fall sick to their stomach. John skates off the ice, runs past me and into the locker room, pressing a towel against his face.

It finally stops bleeding, at least enough to take the towel off so the doc can get a look at it. The doctor has him lie down on a table so he can sew him up and get him back on the ice. The score is 2–2. We're playing the first-place team in the league, and we could win. We need John. "This might hurt a little," the doctor warns him. "The needle is a little dull."

John's eyes grow as wide as saucers. "What the fuck does that mean?" John asks the doctor. "What is *dull*?"

The doctor explains that the only clean sewing needle he has is the one he uses on arms and legs and less sensitive skin than the face. The needle is like twice the width of the facial needle. Instead of waiting a half hour for another needle, John tells the doctor to go ahead, he needs to get back out there.

A few days later, John would recall to me what happened next: "He said it would hurt, and it did. I had nothing numbing it. Nothing. I just held Larry's hand and stared at the ceiling. While I'm lying there, and this butcher is cutting into my face, and I'm bleeding so badly they've run out of gauze, I am thinking, 'Why am I here? I don't need to do this anymore.' But then I start thinking of three people: my family. That's all that matters is those three people. They are all I care about and I can't think about anything else. This is my job."

After the Boise game, after our fifth loss in the last six games, the guys are beyond disappointed. A sense of despair and desperation has overtaken the locker room. Kells kicks the garbage can over and looks as if he would punch the locker room wall if it weren't concrete. "We need some passion in this room," he says. "Some fucking passion!" Now he is shouting. "The truth is that we need some new blood, because God knows I've tried everything to get you guys to play better. We need some guys to stir it up. Every week, I get on the phone and Jonathan, my boss, is telling me to do something, to turn it around. The other day he told me to get rid of fucking all of you and start over with a whole new team. But you know what? I believed in the players in this room. Now you're making me look like an asshole. Well, this is the last time you will make me look bad. There are a lot of quality players out there, and I am looking. And no one in this fucking room is safe. Nobody."

We have to catch a 6 A.M. flight back to Bakersfield. That's eight hours away, just enough time for a handful of the guys to hit the downtown Boise bars and the strip joint where the girls will do things the strippers in Bakersfield won't. In the morning, when our plane takes off in a blizzard, Jason Firth and Paul Willett are nowhere to be found. But in the back of the cabin sits John Vary with two black eyes and a matching black zipper of stitches across his lip.

In three weeks, John will turn thirty. When he wakes up in the morning everything hurts. His right knee, his left shoulder, his ankle, his back, and now the ten stitches in his mouth ache. He doesn't just feel old; he feels as though he's dying.

* * *

Dressing as the second-stringer for the last fourteen games has been fun, a thrill, a step closer to realizing The Dream that sent me on this journey in the first place. It's Monday, the day after we get back from Idaho (our MIA's, Willett and Firth, hopped a late flight back after a long night of partying who-knows-where), and when I get to the rink for the morning skate before playing Anchorage at home for the last time this season, it could be another last game—mine.

Looch is already out on the ice taking shots. It's his first practice in a month. Larry expects Looch to get back into the lineup this weekend, as long as his shoulder, which he healed with two weeks of rest and then two weeks of rehab, holds up. On the ice, Looch looks sluggish, a split-second behind every shot. He's babying his shoulder, too. He won't dive or fall backward, which is how he injured it. In the locker room afterward I see why he looked so stiff. He's wearing a shoulder harness that limits his range of motion so the shoulder doesn't pop out again.

"The doctors say I have to wear it the rest of the season," he tells me.

"How does it feel?" I ask.

"Sore," he says. "Real sore. But I'll be ready to back up this Friday."

I've hitched a ride with Looch back to the apartments. The hum of wheels on the road fills the silence. I don't want to let him know how much it disappoints me that his return could mean the end of my playing season. Plus, I have a lot of respect for Looch and think he deserves to come back. He's certainly a better goalie than Hay. The goalie math equation needs to be balanced. Looch should be number one again.

Looch breaks the silence, saying, "You're probably disappointed. You deserve to play. This could be your last chance."

"That's nice of you to say, but it's fine," I tell him, not wanting to show him how much it bothers me. "I've learned a lot, had fun. It's fine, really."

I ask him how much longer he wants to play pro hockey. He has a math degree from Michigan Tech and wants to be a high school math teacher. He is twenty-seven. "I didn't think much about retiring until this year," he admits. "It's been a hard year, and with the injury, it makes you think. I've pretty much given up on the dream."

I haven't.

* * *

I arrive at the rink for the Anchorage game a half hour early. If Looch returns in five days, then this could be my last game in uniform, and I want to talk to Kells. I don't want to complain. The fact is that we're not winning games because we're not scoring, not because the goaltending hasn't been good enough. I just want him to know that I think I might be a catalyst for the team, a secret weapon. By starting my first game in ten years, I might inspire the guys, give them that little extra spark. Plus, I've improved so much in the last fifteen games that I think I am just plain ready to get the job done.

"What can I do for you, Bakes?"

Kells is sitting at his desk. His eyes are bloodshot with dark circles under them. The team's record is 17–20–2 and the pressure to win is clearly getting to him. I feel guilty for what I want to say. The poor guy already has enough to worry about.

"Bakes, what are we doing wrong? What do you see?"

"I see a lot of guys who don't appreciate how lucky they are to get paid to play this game. I mean, you know how badly I want to play."

"I know you want to play, Bakes. And I want to get you in there before the end of the year. The fact is that the team is struggling right now, and it ain't because Haysie isn't getting the job done. If he wasn't, you might have played already. But I do want to get you in there."

Kells sips from coffee mug, and we walk down the hall and out to the loading dock so he can have a pregame Marlboro Light. Kells has lost the summer tan he had back in September. He no longer drinks with the guys, hasn't sung on the bus since October. He's gained at least ten pounds.

"You're right, though," he says. "The guys don't appreciate anything. There are too many players who think the game owes them something. It doesn't. You get out of it what you put into it, and a lot of these guys just don't put in enough. Listen, we're all here for a reason. Everyone needs to see that they can be better, and they have to want to be better. I can draw up every play in the book, but, at the end of the day, if players don't want it–if they don't have the heart–we're not going to win. We're all not in the NHL for a reason, you know what I mean? We all can be better. None of us is perfect. If we were, we sure as hell wouldn't be here."

He's right. You can go right down our roster and find at least one flaw that is keeping each player from The Show. Willett is too small. Cookie is too slow. Brearley doesn't like to check. Sasha is mental. Felix is too old. Looch is too small. Hay is too slow. And I've got a brain tumor. We're all wounded ducks in the pro-hockey flock. "At this level," Kells says, "where we all have about the same amount of skill and talent, the difference between winning and losing often comes down to who wants it more."

We go out against Anchorage and out-shoot them 39–24 and Sasha plays, rather than acts, like a hockey player, assisting on a goal by Vary. But when we still lose 3–2, and Hay plays with a fraction of the desire burning inside me, Kells's pregame speech doesn't make my not playing any more tolerable. And when Kells walks in after the game and in-structs every player to embarrass himself by heading back out onto the ice to do sprints as the fans file out of the arena, the whole gong show just feels tired.

* * *

Throughout my term as the second-stringer, I have focused more on the control Kells has over me than the control I have over myself. I've worried that he would replace me with a more experienced goalie (he didn't, but he did call Tacoma about signing their third-string goalie, who wasn't available). I've worried that Kells will rain on the party that was supposed to be my comeback season. All this worrying has made me unhappy.

Remembering that the key to happiness is to worry about those things I can control, I focus on my goaltending. Whether I play or not, at least I can say I am the best goalie I can be. I can take pride in that. This is my comeback season and no one else's. I will make this what I want.

As a result, for the first time in over a month I open Mitch Korn's goalie bible and go back to goalie school.

"Always give yourself a chance to make the save . . . . Stay off your butt . . . . Always close holes . . . . Be able to do everything equally well to your right and your left . . . . Never give up on a puck . . . . You cannot play mad . . . . There is no substitute for hard work . . . . Have patience."

* * *

Fresno comes to town on Friday, and Looch dresses for the first time in thirty-four days. Depressed about it, I take my seat up in the press box for the first time in thirty-four days, and before the game Kells calmly explains that, despite what he might have said last week, he is not giving up on the guys in this room. "Someone asked me the other day if I was stressed out and I said no. Why? Because I am involved with *a game.* Yeah, it is my livelihood, and it is a business, and this is our job, and sometimes things get to you and you blow up, but we are still playing *a game.* There are a lot more important things happening out in the real world, more things at stake, but this is our jobs and it is *a game.* You can't lose that perspective. I worked yas hard this week, and we tried some new things, new drills, we skated a lot. I am trying to find a way. Tonight we will do a 2–1–2 fore-check–really aggressive. We have to start creating our own chances because they aren't happening on their own. Now that's all you have to do. One last thing, guys. I have never seen a team that was perfect and where everyone got along. I have been on teams where everyone hated each other and we had a great record; and I've been on teams where everyone loved each other but on the ice we sucked. A ship in calm seas doesn't look like it's moving. Our seas are a little rough, and you know it might be the best thing for us. I know I said last week that you guys lacked passion. I don't think that really. I know you all do or you wouldn't be here. What I am asking is for more. Find a way to win. These next three games are a good test. Fresno tonight and Long Beach tomorrow, then up at Fresno Sunday. I believe that things happen for a reason. It's not what happens that matters, it is what you do with what happens to you."

The guys are fired up, loose, ready to play and start over again. He believes in us. Then five minutes into the game Sasha, frustrated, throws his stick in the air like a boomerang and gets a ten-minute misconduct penalty. His freakout reminds everyone of Anchorage, and all the momentum we had fades and for the rest of the game we are totally out-skated, out-hustled and out-shot (41–26). We lose 5–3 to a weak Fresno team that has won only 12 games all year. I sit in the press box, away from the increasingly hopeless fans, and can't help but think that I might have made a difference.

Write

As a child, David Aebischer took a fast liking to goaltending. He was always a big kid, and by the time he was in his late teens he had sprouted to a muscular 6'1". He was good enough to turn pro at eighteen and play for the professional team in his Swiss hometown. He was also good enough that the Colorado Avalanche believed he could someday play for them and so selected him in the sixth round of the 1997 NHL draft.

Two years later, he left Switzerland in an effort to work his way up to the NHL. Colorado assigned him to the Chesapeake Icebreakers of the East Coast Hockey League, where he put in a below-average record (5–7–2) and an equally unimpressive goals-against average (3.35). The following year, and a year before "Looch" Caravaggio would play for the same team, Aebischer played ten games for the Wheeling Nailers of the ECHL, and his 85.8 percent save percentage was among the worst in the league. But the following season, in 1998, Aebischer matured into the kind of goalie that Colorado's scouts had hoped he would become. He made Colorado's AAA farm team in Hershey, Pennsylvania, playing in thirty-eight games with a goals-against-average of 2.45, posting a 92 percent save percentage. After another solid season with Hershey, Aebischer was promoted last season to the big team, and given the role of understudy to future Hall of Famer and Colorado starter Patrick Roy. So far this season, Aebischer has proved himself to be one of the best young goalies in the NHL. And although David Aebischer has never been to Bakersfield and has no idea who Ken Baker is, he is about to give me an early thirty-second birthday present.

* * *

It's Monday, February 4. There are twenty-seven games and eight weeks remaining in my comeback season on the rink.

Tick, tick, tick. That's all I've been hearing since Looch came back five games ago. If my comeback season were divided into three periods, then I'd be well into the final period. It's becoming more difficult to be Zen Ken, simply to act well the given part, to not try too hard. My team has eighteen wins, twenty-four losses and two ties. We've won only two of our last twelve games. We are mediocre.

Looch is half the goalie he was before the shoulder injury, and I am twice the goalie. Yet when we were in Idaho losing 8–1 and clearly not going to win, Kells didn't even put me in. I was the team's "emergency goaltender" for thirty-four days, but Kells never put me on the official team roster. Yes, the goaltending wasn't that bad. Yes, Kells has to deal with more vexing problems. Yes, except for one period in the exhibition game, I am unproven. But, yes, I deserve to play. "Honestly, Kenny," Cookie told me the other day. "I was amazed that Kells never put you in." Ryan told me the other day, "You deserve to play more than any of us." Even Looch concedes that I should have played at least one minute. When it comes to the part of the season out of my control, I have been hosed. As in life, pro hockey isn't always logical.

I sat on the couch a couple of nights ago and came up with some revised goalie math:

    127 days=0 game time
    115 practices=0 game time
    15 games as backup=0 game time
    $50 a game=0 game time

At practice this morning, as I watched Hay go through the motions, and Looch struggle to stop shots I was easily stopping two weeks ago, I sit on the bench and mentally craft bad, self-pitying poetry just to ease the pain of the boredom and frustration.

    Here I sit
    A piece of shit . . .
    I would stop pucks
    If it weren't for these two fucks . . .

An old goalie who misses his wife
Is an old goalie who needs a life

As I said, it's bad poetry.

After practice, Kells calls a mandatory meeting. He says that Matt Riley, who has not addressed the team since the first game of the season, wants to talk to the players. None of us knows why Riley has come down. But when he walks in, he starts handing out sheets of paper to all the players. I look at mine and it reads:

Players calling season ticket holders

Hi, may I speak with _____. This is _____ with the Condors hockey team. I just wanted to say how much we appreciate your support and your sticking with us. We haven't had too many bounces go our way lately, but we're really working hard and we have confidence we will turn things around. I want to assure you that the effort is there.

As we read the script, Riley, his usual all-business tone, explains how he feels the organization has reached "a point of desperation."

"Friday night really hurt us," he says. "To lose like that, to blow a three-goal lead in the last five minutes, in front of the biggest crowd of the year, is a real big blow. A lot of those seven thousand or so fans come just once a year; now we don't know if they'll return." Riley is a businessman who knows that if his hockey team doesn't stop stinking, the fans will stop coming.

Chris Peace, the team's arena announcer, stands up in his cowboy boots and gives us the bottom line. "Look," he says in a lazy Bakersfield drawl, "people in this town have a chip on their shoulder. This is a great place to live, but when you look up 'second rate' in the dictionary, it says, 'see Bakersfield.' On the flip side, the people here will do anything to be associated with a winner. You guys have the power to make them feel like winners."

Riley adds, "We all have worked too hard over the last few years to bring fans into this building, and an effort like Friday's can erase all that hard work. So I want you all to take twenty names off the season ticket holder's list and call them. I know it might seem goofy to read this script, and some of you might think you are above doing this. But look at it like it is your job. I am asking you to do your job. We do ours, and we want the fans to hear from you that you are doing yours."

Firth, who has played for seven different minor league franchises in eleven seasons, has never heard of anything so *ridiculous* as having players do the job that front-office guys get paid to do. Plus, he is shy. "I don't want to call people I don't know," Firth abruptly announces to everyone. "I don't know these people."

"But they know you," Riley says.

Firth laughs. "Yeah, they're yelling at me and saying I suck."

Willett doesn't want to make the calls either. "This is fucking embarrassing," he says. "We are working hard, we are doing our best. You think we're not going out there every night, putting it all on the line, so we can lose?"

"I know you guys are working hard," Riley says. "I don't question that. We're just asking for some help."

Kells has been sitting silently in the corner of the locker room the entire time. Finally, he stands up and lets out a therapeutic exhale. "I feel like I've tried everything," Kells says.

"I disagree," Willett counters. "You haven't tried everything. You haven't made any trades, haven't brought in any new players. I think I speak for every guy in this room in saying that if you think getting rid of one of us will make the team better, we would take a trade. I'd take a trade if it would make the team better."

Willett is doing what a captain is supposed to do: represent the players. Lately, most of the players have been wondering why Kells hasn't traded or cut anyone, brought in some fresh blood. He had been threatening to do that all year, since the second game of the season! But after months of lackluster losses and bad efforts, his threats were deemed hollow. Guys stopped listening. He lost credibility. We're seven games below .500 and in last place. We have twenty-seven games left to turn things around.

As Willett speaks, Kells's pale face turns red with anger, and he interrupts, "Well, it's not like I haven't tried to trade some of you, because I have. Nobody wants you. You're either too expensive or they look at your stats and decide you ain't worth it. But that's my job to worry about. It's your guys' job to play and find a way to win."

Willett replies, "But it's hard to win when we're not all on the same page. I mean, Sasha will skip practices, tell you to fuck off, disrespect all of us, and you won't do a thing about it. That shit hurts a team."

Sasha shoots bullets at Willett with his eyes.

"Listen," Kells answers, "our owner likes him and the fans like him." He conspicuously doesn't say that *he* likes him.

"Fuck the fans," Looch blurts out from his stall. "You can't play this game for the fans. You have to play for yourself and your teammates. Last year in Topeka, whenever I got scored on the fans would start chanting, 'Hay! Hay!' I almost had a nervous breakdown. If I were playing for the fans I would have killed myself."

After the meeting, a few guys head to Woody's, a bar out by the oil fields, and cynically make the team calls from their cell phones. Others crumple up the script and toss it in the garbage. Ryan, though, heads back to the apartment and pleasantly makes his calls.

I refuse to call anyone. I have nothing to be sorry for; I don't owe anyone an apology or an excuse, except, possibly, my wife. I have given my all every time I have stepped on the ice. I have come ready to play, acted like a professional. So if the team's brass don't have the balls to play me, that's their problem, not mine. There are only eight weeks left in the season, and they're really sticking it to me. Screw them. If I were their property, I would ask for a trade. If I felt any other team wanted a thirty-one-year-old backup goalie with twenty minutes of pro hockey (exhibition) under his belt, then I would contact teams. Realistically, I am stuck here, like it or not.

As Ryan makes his calls on the couch, I log onto my laptop computer at the dining room table, a machine on which I have been writing my diary nearly every day since I arrived. I'm not writing today. I'm too burned out. I don't want to think about my fear of becoming a far less talented version of Johnny Unitas, Willie Mays, Muhammad Ali or Michael Jordan—old jocks who came out of retirement for one last sniff of glory, but only made fools of themselves. And I especially don't want to think about the Bakersfield Condors. The fans are spreading rumors about players getting traded, about Kells getting fired or "resigning," which, in pro sports, is a nice spin on being asked by the owner to leave. I don't want to think about pucks, about my lack of playing time. Instead, I'm going to surf the Internet, read some news about those Hollywood celebrities whose lives seem so much more interesting than mine right now, check my e-mail for signs of life out in the real world.

There's a message from Brooke, a note from my mom, several unsolicited pornographic spams and ads for penis enlargement. There's also a message from Howard Cornfield, the owner and general manager of the Quad City Mallards, the team that, in retrospect, I probably should have joined in the first place. I haven't heard from Howard since October, when he sent me an e-mail tauntingly asking when I was going to play "for a real team in a real league." This time, Howard, with whom I share a similar sense of humor, writes, "I don't know if I will ever be able to get over the fact that I was dumped for a Condor. How can you make it up to me?"

I immediately type back, "I assumed you had blown me off. I'm still waiting for the invitation to come play for you. Are you trying to tell me you haven't at least needed an emergency goalie this year?!?!?!?"

Later that day, Howard replies, "Strangely enough, I need a backup goalie for next weekend and maybe the following week. We're sending our goalie to Hershey. You want to come out for a while? We would need you to suit up this Saturday and Sunday, maybe longer."

Instantly, I phone Howard at his home outside of Davenport, Iowa, where he has been running the most successful AA hockey franchise for the last five years.

"Are you serious?" I ask

"We're sending our goalie Brant Nicklin up to the AHL in Hershey. I'll need you for next weekend."

I ask him why Nicklin is getting a call-up

"Hershey is the farm team for the Avalanche," he says. "And they just lost David Aebischer to the Swiss Olympic team."

So long, suckers!

Test

"Welcome to the Quad Cities," the flight attendant announces as you look out the window at the leafless trees and the patches of ice on the runway and, still being just a boy from Buffalo, you already feel at home in this four-city community straddling the Mississippi River a couple of hundred miles west of Chicago. Waiting for the team's media guy to pick you up at the terminal, you sit on your equipment bag and read in the local paper that Howard, the man who brought you here, doesn't plan on playing you. "I'd never say never, but we're trying to win a championship," Howard told the *Quad City Times.* "He has been considered an emergency goaltender at Bakersfield and probably would be considered an emergency goaltender with us. He is capable of playing, though."

But his less-than-glowing comments don't bother you, because you are here, and not back there. Your team in California is in last place with a record of 18–25–2. And, still, they don't play you. The Mallards are in first place in the league with 36–10–2 and are paying you for your services. They are winners, and an average of six-thousand fans flock all winter long to see their local heroes dominate the league with an all-star team of young NHL prospects and rugged old-timers with faces only a mother could love, like Gary Gulash.

Ken Jacoby drives you down to The Mark of the Quad Cities, a modern concrete box of a building located across the street from the John Deere tractor museum, the cornbelt area's other claim to fame. At the rink, Howard and the head coach, former NHL'er Paul MacLean, greet you with firm handshakes, and you put your equipment at a stall in the locker room with a BAKER nameplate already glued on it. And you feel even more at home. Coach MacLean, whom you grew up watching on *Hockey Night in Canada* when he played for the Winnipeg Jets, asks you to go out on the ice and take some shots to "get your legs." But you know he really just wants to see what you got.

So you suit up and step onto the ice in the empty arena and feel different, not just like the extra guy, the annoying writer who just won't go away, the third-string goalie on a last place team in California. You feel like a winner, and when the assistant coach fires pucks at you and you deflect them like a superhero and Howard and coach MacLean smile, you feel like a real pro.

The Mallards play the Flint Generals tonight, but you won't need to dress tonight. Brant Nicklin doesn't fly to Hershey, Pennsylvania, until tomorrow. But you will be needed to dress when the Mallards play the Muskegon up in Michigan tomorrow night, and then you'll dress again on Sunday when they play the Port Huron Border Cats back at home. Howard is not sure how long he will need your services, though you secretly hope it is forever as long as you are feeling as comfortable and *wanted* here.

You shower and head up to Howard's suite and watch the game. The fans, all seven thousand of them, cheer with the kind of raw rah-rah one usually sees at college basketball games. In California, the fans just don't let it all hang out as much. *You're in the Midwest, baby.* But the Mallards uncharacteristically lose in a blowout. The shock of the fans, the helpless anger of Howard in the owner's suite, and the funereal silence in the locker room afterward lets you know this is a team of champions. Unlike in Bakersfield, these guys expect to win, not to lose.

After the game, you take a seat on the team bus, a Boy Scout tent on wheels with a satellite dish perched atop it and a big-screen TV built into the back wall. You're uncomfortable, ill-at-ease in your role as the New Guy, so you keep to yourself and eat your pasta dinner from the aluminum tin they gave you and just, well, try to fit in. "Where should I sit?" you ask Nick Ganga, a tall kid with a friendly smile who answers, "Anywhere on the bottom." Rookies on the bottom; veterans on top.

Bolted on each side wall of the bus like triple bunk beds are three rows of cots stacked morguelike on top of one another. If this bus slides into a ditch, you think to yourself, you'll die in a heap of bodies on the floor.

It's a five-hour drive east to Chicago and then north up the Lake Michigan coast to the tiny city of Muskegon, the same place where Paul Kelly lured John Vary out of retirement. It's a small hockey world. One Mallards player is from London, Ontario, where he grew up with Mark Edmundson, and he asks how he's doing. Most of the players know Firth and Vary, who played several seasons in the UHL, and were always all-stars.

The first thing that hockey guys ask you is "Where you *from?*" And they don't want to hear "Bakersfield" or "Mill Valley." Rather, they want to know where you are *from*–that is, where you learned to play the game. For it is in your answer–be it Toronto, Boston, Minnesota, Vancouver, Detroit, Montreal, or Sweden–that a player can instantly understand a thousand things about you as a player and a person. For example, if you're from Toronto, they'll think you are the real deal, a tough kid who knows the game and plays with some sack. If you're from Boston, you might have some good skills, but that doesn't necessarily mean you are tough or blue-collar like the rest. So when you say "Buffalo," and they nod approvingly, you know you have earned their respect because Buffalo guys have hockey in their blood, ice in their veins.

The players are tired. The guy across from you suffered a charley horse from a slap shot to the thigh and is moaning. "Keep moving it," Ganga instructs the poor bastard. "Or you won't be able to in the morning."

Coach MacLean turns off the cabin lights, and so you lie face up in your casket and try to fall asleep. But you can't. The bunk above you is like six inches from your face, and you feel as if you're in that MRI tube that detected your brain tumor three and a half years ago. Now, fortunately, the only health scare you have is the possibility that the restless two-hundred-pound defenseman above you will collapse onto your face.

It's one in the morning when you finally fall asleep along with the twenty other snoring, farting, injured, tired band of brothers. Kells had told you recently that he missed the long bus trips, which the WCHL lacks, because, he believes, they bring guys closer together, and now you see what he meant.

You wake up a few hours later and look out, and the bus has stopped outside the Holiday Inn in Muskegon. Your watch says it's 5 A.M. You want to sleep forever, but you grab your shoulder bag and stumble into the lobby, where Howard hands you a key to a room where you and your roommate, the team's goon Kerry Toporowski, crash on your respective queens until noon, at which time you're rousted out of bed by the coach, who wants everyone in the downstairs banquet room for a pregame meal and pep talk.

The Mallards have lost three straight games—the first time they have lost more than two in a row all season—and MacLean, a burly man with a mustache as wide as a harmonica, is none too happy about the recent skid. When he stands, every player stops eating and devotes his full attention to the coach. He isn't a jokester, he isn't Paul "Kells" Kelly. Paul "Mac" MacLean is the general, this is his war, and these are his soldiers to fight it. "No guy in this room should be happy right now," he says. "Except for Mr. Baker, who, if you don't all know it, is backing Joe up tonight. Last night was embarrassing, guys. Totally embarrassing. We've got twenty-five games left in the season and they're all for me. You will do as I say or you won't play. You will compete. You will score, hit, have fun. You will win. I believe with all my heart we will win the championship, but winning is hard. If it wasn't, everyone would win. So tonight, be ready to play how I say to play, and to win. That's all."

The players do everything but salute their general.

After the meal, you head to the hotel gym and run on the rickety treadmill for twenty minutes, an effort to keep your conditioning up in case Joe Dimaline, the Mallards' veteran goalie, cannot, and you need to play. You will be nervous enough; you don't also need to be out of shape when your time comes.

When you get back to the hotel room, Toporowski tells you Howard wants you to see him in his room on the third floor. So you shower and walk down to his room, and when you enter, Howard is sitting on his bed talking on the phone to other teams' general managers. He's trying to recruit a star player for the final stretch of the season. You're not sure why Howard has called you in, but you hope it is a good thing. Hey, maybe you're starting tonight!

As he finishes his call, you sit down on the chair and look out at the snow flurries dancing in the slate-gray winter sky and wonder what plan God has in store for you next, what part he wants you to act. Then Howard hangs up the phone and hands you an official-looking sheet of paper and says that, if you sign it, you will no longer be an "emergency goalie" getting paid game by game. Rather, you will now earn $250 a week as an official contract player on the Quad City Mallards. Your dream will have come true. You will then be a pro hockey player.

It's two-thirty on Saturday, February 9. You grab a pen, sign your name on the line at the bottom, and, just like that, you have signed your first professional hockey contract. No one is there to witness it. No fans cheering, no crying wife in the stands. But it's a moment as glorious as it is quiet. And you smile.

* * *

In Howard's hotel room, after I sign my contract, I tell Howard something I haven't had the guts to tell anyone in Bakersfield.

"I don't want this season to be my last one," I say. "I'm not ready to retire. About halfway through this season, I realized that, if I really am serious about playing, I will do it next year. What do you think?"

"I think it would be the fulfillment of a dream," Howard says.

"Yeah, but do you think a team would hire me?"

"It will be tough," he says. "Ten minor league teams might fold after this season, and that will mean fewer jobs. Only the strong will survive."

"Yeah, but do you think I'm being realistic?"

"Well, I'd hate to tell you no. It's your dream, and after what you've been through maybe you need to do it to be O.K. If you can get yourself into a camp, do well, then maybe someone will pick you up. You'd be cheap as a rookie. Yeah, you could do it. What about Brooke?"

"She'd have to come."

"That's good, because if you are really serious about coming back, you'll have to go where the job is. You could end up in Macon, Georgia, or you could end up in Anchorage, Alaska. Are you willing to do that?"

"I think so," I say. "But I don't know if Brooke is."

"Well," Howard says, "the first thing you have to do is try to get at least some playing time in this year. You'll need some statistics to get a tryout next year."

"Any advice?" I ask.

"Yeah," Howard says. "Just be ready."

* * *

Knowing I'm a legitimate contract player changes my entire self-image. I'm a pro now. I am valued. I am on the team. I didn't realize it at the time, but I have been held back psychologically in Bakersfield as an "emergency goalie." I call Ryan on his cell phone to tell him the good news and check in on the team. They played two games in Tacoma this week, and I purposely didn't pay attention, didn't check the scores on the Internet. I am on a playing vacation.

Ryan's news is not good. Sounding groggy, Ryan tells me the team just got back to Bakersfield from a two-game set in Tacoma. They lost 6–5 on Wednesday and won 2–1 last night, he says, adding, "But I am pretty messed up, buddy."

I ask him what happened, and he says he doesn't remember anything, but everyone said it was one of the scariest things they'd ever seen in pro hockey. Early in the second period, Ryan lined up for a face-off in our end. Our center won the draw and the puck trickled back to the boards. Ryan skated toward the puck with his head down, and as he scooped it with his stick, a Tacoma checked him hard against the glass. Ryan was immediately knocked unconscious, and his helmet popped off. The momentum of the blow knocked him backward, and the back of his head slammed violently against the ice. He lay face up and knocked out on the ice for over minute. Looch, afraid that Ryan wasn't breathing, knelt next to him and shouted at him to wake up. Larry leapt onto the ice and the first thing he did was put his head near his nose to check for breathing. He was. "The first thing I remember is sitting up in the locker room and not knowing where I was," Ryan says. "I recognized Larry and, being that I was sweaty and in hockey gear, I put two and two together, that I had been hurt in a game, but, Kenny, it was a very, very scary feeling. I remember looking at the Condors jersey and thinking it should be a Topeka Scarecrows' jersey. It was as if all my memories for the past year were gone and I was scared as hell. I remember repeatedly asking Larry, 'Why am I wearing this jersey and where am I?'"

"So how are you doing?" I ask.

"Oh, I'm all right," he says. "I have a really bad headache, and I'm a little dizzy, I guess. Larry said it was one of the worst concussions he'd ever seen."

"When will you be ready to play?"

Ryan doesn't answer right away, and the pause is an answer in itself. After a few moments, he says, "They don't know yet."

* * *

My welcome to the UHL comes from a rather rude Muskegon fan. As I stretch during pregame warm-ups, a drunk guy in a Muskegon jersey pounds on the glass and yells down at me, "Go back to Bakersfield!" I'm not the only focus of their love. They're yelling, "You suck, Toporowski! . . . Gulash, you fat fuck! . . . Hey, Hugo, go back to France!" (Even though Hugo Proulx is from Quebec. Boisterous they are; smart they are not.) Muskegon is in second place, just two points behind the Mallards, and they are going to be gunning for us. And they do. The game is a see-saw battle, with great goaltending on both ends, and several fights. Toporowski savagely pounds a guy's head into the ice. Some of the fans dump beer onto him in the penalty box. It's a real barn burner. But while the guys skate hard, make great plays and do what Mac tells them to do, they lose, and I don't play. So it's on the bus right after the game and back to Quad City, where we arrive at three o'clock in the morning. The players are greeted by several loyal wives and girlfriends in their cars, and a fifteen-degree wind chill. I'm greeted by a sore throat, achy body, and a runny nose. I need some sleep.

* * *

When I walk into the locker room and read what Coach MacLean has scrawled on the chalkboard–"The Heart of a Champion is Tested Through Adversity"–I tell my heart to get ready for a test, because from the moment I woke up this morning I barely felt strong enough to walk to the bathroom, let alone don my equipment and play a hockey game. The fever, the sweats, the dizziness, the sore muscles, the sick stomach, the coughing. The flu.

Luckily, as Howard had told the newspaper a few days ago, the Mallards are too busy trying to win a championship (Muskegon is now just two points behind them) to put in an untested goalie. Joe Dimaline, age twenty-nine, a six-year veteran who played for Kells in Muskegon in the 1997 season, will get the start in goal again tonight.

To the other players, the adversity referred to in MacLean's chalkboard saying has to do with their having lost four games in a row, and now having to play fifteen hours after they arrived last night from Muskegon. To me, adversity has to do with my body. An hour before game time, I feel so cold I am shaking. I sit at my locker in sweat pants, three T-shirts, and my hockey jersey to stay warm. Normally, I hate playing with even aspirin in my system. I like to be fresh and natural.

But it's obvious that if I don't take some medication, I may faint. I walk over to the training room and tell the trainer, Lou Bustos, how I feel. He checks my temperature: 102 degrees. "Doesn't that mean I'm close to dying?" I ask. "No," Lou says, "you've got a few more degrees before you need to worry about that."

Lou hands me two Dayquil tablets, a few Sudafeds (nondrowsy formula) and, after rubbing some Flex-all on my stiff back, tells me to go out in the warm-ups and sweat it out, which I try to do, but from the second I step on the ice and start skating laps, my body refuses to sweat. I'm wearing three undershirts (I usually wear one), and I can't sweat! I want to throw up, undress, go back to Howard's house, and sleep for the next two days. But I can't. I am the number-two goalie. This is my job. I need to get better. This is my adversity.

To say my head is spinning as if I'm drunk as Mac gives his pregame pep talk would be a gross understatement; it feels more like I'm wasted and approaching an alcohol-induced coma. Of course, I think to myself, with my luck the game in which I feel like death will be the game in which I make my pro debut. Call it Baker's Law.

There's no better team for the Mallards to end their losing skid against than the Port Huron, Michigan, Border Cats, which have a record as bad as Bakersfield's, and which, due to a recent rash of injuries, will dress only thirteen skaters for tonight's game, compared to our healthy sixteen. And the Border Cats will have only four defensemen, meaning they should be pretty tired by the third period. "Too bad for them, good for us," Mac says in the locker room before we head out. "Let's go out and get the first goal, the second goal, the third goal, and never look back. Let's play like champions."

And we do. By the end of the second period, we're up 6–1, out-shooting them 30–13, and my fever has broken. I'm praying to the altar of Lou the trainer and his magical medicine cabinet. Inside the locker room before the start of the third, Howard tells me that Brant Nicklin will return from Hershey tomorrow, so I won't be needed after tonight. "Thanks for coming out," he says. That means I'll leave for Bakersfield tomorrow morning. But, first, I have twenty more minutes to enjoy belonging to a championship team, albeit from the vantage point of a seat in the penalty box next to the team bench because there's not enough room for me on the bench.

The penalty box attendant must have read the newspaper article about my arrival here, because in the middle of play he leans over and asks me what it's like playing back in Bakersfield.

"It would be nice if I played," I say.

"Paul Kelly's the coach, isn't he?" the man asks.

"Yeah," I say flatly.

"I always liked Paul Kelly," he says. "He's a good guy."

Yeah, I think, *especially if he would play me.*

Nick Ganga takes a penalty and joins me in the box. I ask him what the story is behind Port Huron's number ten, a nifty forward who's clearly the team's best player, but who's wearing an awkward-looking helmet with a metal face mask. "That's David Beauregard," Ganga says. "He's the league's leading scorer."

"So what's with the face mask?" I ask.

"He's blind in one eye. A few years ago, when he was a rookie with San Jose, he went in on a breakaway and took a stick to the eye. He ended up losing his eye, but he finished off the play and actually scored. He was on his way to The Show, but being blind in one eye ended his hopes for an NHL career. Still, he's a damn good player."

With about five minutes left in the game, we're up 7–1 and many of the five thousand fans, certain their team has won, start heading for the exits. And as the game winds down and the players start going through the motions, it occurs to me that I should be ready to replace Dimaline, since we have such a commanding lead. Sure, it might be wishful thinking, but the job of a goaltender, especially one flown in from a team in another league, is to be ready to do your job; plus, I wouldn't be surprised if Coach MacLean, a competitive-but-classy guy, puts me in, if not for any other reason but as a kind gesture toward minor league hockey's oldest rookie and the only player in uniform tonight with zero professional minutes played, zero saves made, a zero goals-against average and a zero-point-zero percent save percentage. I look up thirty rows behind the Port Huron goal and see Howard smiling in the owner's box.

With just under four minutes remaining, John Doolan, the Mallards' equipment guy, leans over the glass partition separating the penalty box from the team bench, hands me a stick and says, "Start stretching."

I put on my mask, stand up, twist my torso, touch my toes, and do some deep-knee bends to get my flu-ridden blood pumping after sitting on my butt for the last two hours, not exactly the ideal preparation for my pro debut. The play continues and I wait for the call, which could happen at the next whistle.

With two-and-a-half minutes left, a Port Huron player comes in on a breakaway against Dimaline, who gets a piece of it with his glove, deflecting it to the corner. That could have been me in there. I'm not so sure I could have stopped that.

A few seconds later, there's a stoppage in play, and I look over at MacLean, waiting for him to give me the nod. But he doesn't even look at me. Rather, he looks up at the clock and out onto the ice. *Don't tell me he's not going to . . . . Is he afraid I will give up seven goals in the next two minutes?*

Then, with a minute and nineteen seconds left in the game, a Port Huron player takes a tripping penalty. Being up by six goals, and now on the power play, MacLean must have enough confidence to put me in there. He can't think I'm going to screw up their first win in five games.

I glance at MacLean, who turns his head toward me and barks, "Get in there, Bakes!"

I hop over the boards and onto the ice and, smiling wide, stare MacLean in the eyes and skate toward the net. Dimaline taps my pads with his stick and says, "Go got 'em."

"Now in goal for your Quad City Mallards," the rink announcer says. "Number thirty, Ken Baker!"

The remaining fans rise to their feet and cheer as I drop to my knees and loosen my legs with some last-minute stretching, sensing several thousand pairs of eyes staring down on me. I'm not nervous; we've won the game and we're on the power play. However, I want to face at least one shot, maybe a few, so that I can leave Quad City tomorrow with some statistics, which, as Howard told me yesterday, I will need if I am to come back for another season.

We control the play in their end and take a couple of point shots on the Port Huron goalie, Kevin St. Pierre, a giant of a man at 6' 3". When I left the game ten years ago, I was an average-sized goalie; ten years later, I'm a shrimp.

With forty seconds left, Port Huron gains control of the puck and a player dumps it around the boards into our end. I skate back behind my net and set the puck for my defenseman, and the moment I touch the puck the crowd erupts wildly. I'm not talking about polite clapping. I'm not talking about enthusiastic applause. They're cheering and banging the glass and stomping their feet as if it's game seven of the Stanley Cup finals. Why are they so behind me? Unbeknownst to me, tonight's program featured a profile of me that told the story of my Olympic prospect past, of my forced retirement in 1992 due to an undiagnosed brain tumor, of how the tumor was removed three and a half years ago, of how I came out of retirement this season in an attempt to live a lifelong dream of playing professional hockey. Their high-decibel support gives me chills—and not the kind I had earlier from the flu. I am honored.

We take the Port Huron zone and set up the power play. Toporowski is at the point. When he gets the puck with about twenty seconds left, he tries to force a pass down low to a winger, but it's too soft, and Port Huron's speedy David-Alexandre Beauregard, the leading scorer in the United Hockey League, steals the puck and skates in on me. One on one. Me versus him. Nothing between us but ten years of retirement and my throbbing heart the size of Iowa. If I stop this breakaway, I will have perfect statistics: a 0.00 goals-against average and a 100 percent save percentage, and they will be the best statistics in all of North American professional hockey. But if Beauregard scores—and any betting man watching this impending David versus Goliath duel would certainly put his money on Beauregard—then I will have the worst statistics in all of professional hockey: a 0 percent save percentage and a pitiful goals-against average of 46.15.

Fifteen seconds.

I push off with my right skate and come out five feet in front of the crease to cut down the angle.

Ten seconds.

Beauregard crosses the blue line at full speed, just left of center ice. He will have dozens of options at his disposal. He could shoot it—high, low, between my legs, between my arm and my body, over my shoulder, wherever he sees net. Or he could fake a shot, and hope I take the bait and drop to my knees, then wheel around me and pop it into the open net. Or he could head-fake me, shoulder-fake me, flinch-fake me and then during my split-second body freeze change his angle enough to score.

My only option, however, is to stop the puck no matter what he does. I am out far, challenging him, reducing his chances of scoring on a shot because he can't see much net. He will have to stick-handle the puck around me if he wants to score.

If there's anything positive about my lack of regular practice time all season long in Bakersfield it's that when I stay out after practice and take shots the players usually just want to do breakaways because they are fun. As a result, I have had more practice at breakaways than any other game situation. Maybe Admiral Stockdale is right. This could be the role that The Author has been preparing me for.

Beauregard is a left-handed shot, and as he streaks toward me I make sure I am lined up with the puck on his blade, not his body, as I slowly back in to guard my flanks. I've done this thousands of times this year, but this is the one that matters.

Six seconds.

Beauregard cocks his shoulder slightly as if he will shoot, but I don't take the fake. It's unconvincing. Instead, I remain firm in my stance—knees bent, chest up, glove up and open, stick flat on the ice, ready to do what I have been dreaming of doing ever since I was a kid, and especially since I had The Dream two years ago: stop a shot as a professional hockey goalie. Seeing little net behind me, Beauregard has no choice but to maneuver around me.

With Toporowski nipping at his heels, Beauregard must make his move quickly. As he skates across to my right, I dig the toe of my left skate into the ice and slide like into home plate, forming a wall of padding with my legs.

Three seconds.

With the bottom half of the net taken away, Beauregard tries to lift the puck over my top leg. I raise my top leg and . . . the puck bounces off my toe and flips end over end. All I can do is watch the puck as it rises and falls back down to the ice in front of me. I stopped him.

The crowd roars, the buzzer sounds, and I hop to my feet. Immediately, my teammates are enveloping me in a giant group hug as I raise my arms up over my head like a champion.

* * *

I lie in bed two hours after my first pro save and replay the save over and over again in my mind—the players congratulating me, the fans, many crying, standing and cheering loudly, Howard frantically running down the aisle to the arena entrance and hugging me with all his might.

Though it was a beautiful, dream-like moment, and I'm touched that so many people were moved by it, I feel empty thinking about those who did not share the moment. There was no Brooke, no Bakersfield fans, no teammates who over the last six months have become my family. There was also no Ryan, my roommate who sits back in Bakersfield with a serious concussion that threatens to end his pro hockey career just as mine is starting. My eyes are still sore from tears of relief that flooded my cheeks as I called Brooke and told her, "I did it!"

My team in Bakersfield might be teetering on the edge of implosion, Kells might not see my potential, and I might be running out of time to heal the wounds that have festered since the disaster that was my college hockey career. But, still, that hapless Bakersfield team is *my* team. I love them, and I hate them. By definition, that means they are my family, and that means it's time to head home.

Learn

$\mathbf{W}$ hen I pull into the parking lot of the Bakersfield apartment complex there's no welcoming parade, no congratulatory banners strung across the entrance. Inside the apartment, Ryan is on the couch watching TV with three of our neighbors, Cassie, Michelle, and Stephanie, students at Bakersfield State who live across the courtyard. A benefit of Ryan's grade-three concussion (about as close as you can get to vegetable status) is that now he gets three cute college girls taking care of him.

"Oh, Ryan, do you need an Advil?"

"Can I get you something from the store, Hartsy?"

"You want to go to the hot tub with us?"

Things definitely could be worse, but Ryan isn't allowed to do any exercise until he is "symptom-free," which means until the headaches and dizziness go away. If the symptoms don't end in the next month, the doctor says, Ryan's season–and career–may be over.

As for my health, the fever that broke during last night's magical game in Quad City came back today somewhere over Colorado, and I sure could use some nurses myself. But I'm married, so I head to my room and sleep for about ten hours. It's Monday night; tomorrow we play Fresno at home. While I was in Quad City, we won two games in a row–the first time since January 4 that we won more than one game in a row–and Ryan reports that the guys look as though they might finally be coming together. "It took everyone being afraid of losing their job," he says.

The next day, it feels good to get back on the ice with the guys, even though it means back to being number three, back to sitting on the bench watching Hay and Looch take all the shots during practice. A few of the guys congratulate me on my save in Quad City. "You should have made your debut here," Cookie says. "That's not your fault, though."

But just when it looks as if Kells has inspired his men, they disappoint him for the twenty-sixth time this season and Fresno kicks our asses 7–3. Something clearly is missing from the team, and, sadly, it is not good goaltending. Hay is looking sharp, and even though Looch is not yet back to his pre-injury shape, he's not to blame for the losses. A goalie can do only so much. We are too old, too slow, and our offense is as impotent as it gets: too many shots taken from the outside perimeter and a power play that is last in the league.

We end up losing four more in a row, and I start wondering if Kells just might throw me in there, if for no other reason than desperation. I know that *I'm* starting to feel desperate. The glory of my 1:19 in Quad City two weeks ago is already starting to fade, and the skills I built up as the second-stringer over January and the confidence I gained in Quad City are deteriorating.

A hockey season is nothing if not an emotional roller coaster. My growth has come in a predictable cycle: the more I practice, the better I get; the less I practice, the worse I get, and the more miserable I get. It's about as predictable as our team running out of gas in the third period. You can take it to the bank.

In Fresno on February 19, just when John Vary thought his season couldn't get any worse, Fresno forward Brad Both throws the hardest body check I've seen all year, instantly knocking John out and sending him falling backward. He's lucky that, unlike Ryan, his helmet stays on– the back of John's head slams so hard against the ice that it bounces three or four times.

Larry runs out on the ice and when he gets there, John is out cold, so much that he is snoring. I run down from the stands and stand at the glass praying that he will wake up. All Larry can do is wait, along with the rest of us, as I think about his wife Robin and daughters, Nicole and Jamie–the family back in Bakersfield that I hope is not listening to the game on the radio.

After two minutes of waiting for him to wake, the Fresno team doctor runs onto the ice and two paramedics wheel out a stretcher. Finally, John comes to . . . to where exactly, he has no idea. Whenever you see a player get knocked out from a bang to the head, the first thing you look and hope for is that he will move his arms and legs, eliminating the possibility that he has been paralyzed.

Move your legs, John. Move!

When I see John's right knee flex, I breathe a sigh of relief.

The medics and a couple of players lift his inert body onto the stretcher, and wheel him into a medical room under the stands. I follow the stretcher back and help the medics take off his skates and shin pads. John's brown eyes stare blankly at the ceiling, and I wonder if he will ever be the same again.

The doctor asks John if he knows where he is. He doesn't.

The doctor asks John what month it is. He doesn't know.

The doctor asks John if he remembers how he got hurt. He doesn't.

The doctor asks him if he has a wife. "Yeah," he mumbles. "Robin."

As Larry and the medics discuss whether to take him to the hospital, I walk outside the arena and call Robin from my cell phone. As I feared, she's been listening to the game on the radio.

"He's O.K.," I tell her, thinking to myself, *they always say he's O.K.*

"What happened?" she asks urgently.

"He got knocked out, but he's fine now," I lie. "They're just making sure everything is O.K."

"Please have him call us as soon as he can," she says.

I tell her I will, and head back to the medical room. John asks me what happened, and I tell him that Quinn Fair, his defensive partner, passed him the puck and he lost it in his feet, and while he was looking for it with his head down, the Fresno guy–smack!–knocked him flat on his back.

Back in the room a few minutes later, John asks me the same question, and I explain again what happened. He obviously has no short-term memory. After the fifth time he asks what just happened, I patiently tell him that he keeps asking me the same question over and over. "Sorry," he says. "It's just scary is all."

The fact that the game being played out in the arena is yet another gong show featuring Willett throwing a water bottle at the referee as the clock winds down, and our losing 2–1, is irrelevant. Who cares about winning? This sport is not only starting to hurt me, but my friends, too. It's taking more than it is giving. I never want to put Brooke through what Robin just endured. This was never part of The Dream.

On the bus ride back to Bakersfield, no one starts singing Bob Seger tunes. With twenty-one games still left, we're all too tired. It's a moonless night, and I stare out the window at the blur of highway paint. I call Brooke. "This is no way to make a living," I say.

* * *

The next day, Mike Griffith pens his most critical newspaper column of the season, writing that "Kelly has stuck with his players since day one but it is agonizingly apparent that the current mixture–no matter how impressive past resumes are, no matter how much 'potential' this group may have–is not getting the job done."

Griffith doesn't know it, but Kells has made a bold decision, one that required the swallowing of a lot of ego, as well as admitting that he needed help. It was a decision that not only will revive the team, but it's a decision that saves his job: Kells has hired an assistant coach, Marty Raymond.

Raymond is no stranger to the WCHL. Two seasons ago, Marty won the league championship as head coach of the Phoenix Mustangs, which folded just a few months later due to financial problems. Marty, a native of Quebec, whose English is still spoken with a thick French accent, decided that summer to leave hockey and make the transition into a more stable career, so he studied to be a police officer for the city of Phoenix. He has a son with his ex-wife in Las Vegas, where he had also coached a AA team before it ceased operations.

But Marty, age thirty-seven, had earned a reputation in minor league hockey as a winner, a hard-working, smart coach who uses his master's degree in sports psychology to get the best out of his players. God knows, our team could use some therapy. Marty is also known as a an x's and o's kind of coach who likes to use the dry-erase board to diagram plays, something I haven't seen Kells do since he chalked out a few drills back in October.

When Kells, at the suggestion of Matt Riley, phoned Marty a few weeks ago and asked for help in turning the team around–only asking Marty to stay for the rest of the season, no questions asked–Marty couldn't resist. He was working a civilian job for the Phoenix police, getting the homeless off the streets and the junkies into rehab. Once hockey came knocking, he couldn't ignore the call. Like all of us who are here because the real world isn't as attractive, he loves the game too much to say no. And so he came. Now that he's here, the players wonder if it's the nail in Kells's coffin. "Fleisig probably didn't have the balls to fire Kells," one player quips. "So now we have two head coaches. What a fucking gong show." Another player suspects that Kells is only still around because he signed a two-year contract. "They probably think they might as well make him work if they have to pay him," he says.

I don't know what to think—except that maybe Raymond will see my potential, and suggest that Kells play me.

According to Kells, Marty's assignment is twofold: to inject some new game strategy and motivation into the players, while helping Kells recruit five or six new players from Europe for the stretch-run to the play-offs. Stacking your team at the end of the season with guys from the European pro leagues, whose seasons end in early March, while ours run through the end of April, is a common practice in the WCHL. Marty, who coached in Sweden and France before returning to North America in the late nineties, knows where to find the good ones. But the league rules state that players can't be on a team's play-off roster unless they have dressed for at least eight regular season games. That means, whatever players Marty brings in will have to arrive before March 20. Today is February 21. It's safe to say that the guys who either haven't been playing well or who aren't getting a lot of ice time are vulnerable to getting replaced, tops among them Sasha, Todd, Maser and, of course, Ryan, who still can't climb the stairs to our apartment without getting a headache, and is scheduled for a CAT scan to see if he has any brain swelling.

Understandably, when Marty addresses the team for the first time, everyone is rapt with attention, including Kells. "I'm not going to bull-shit you guys," Marty says. "Kells has brought me in to turn things around. And I have all the confidence that we will. But there will have to be some changes. Most of you guys have been around long enough to know that means some of you will be let go. But I'm here to tell you that you can control your own destiny. You're all here now, and you'll all have an honest chance to prove that you can help this team win. All we're going to ask for is effort."

Marty has a buzz-cut and a muscled body second only to Sasha's. Obviously, he's a fitness nut, so it comes as no surprise when he gets to the next part. "It starts with conditioning. I understand about half you guys smoke. That's just fucking brutal. This isn't fucking *Slap Shot,* boys. I'm thirty-seven years old and I'm in the best shape of my life, so there's no excuse why all of you, even the older guys, aren't in better shape. I also understand there are a few boozers on this team. Listen, I'm not going to tell you how to live your life, but I will tell you that how you live your life affects how you play this game. And if you're not playing this game well, you're of no use to anyone."

It's about time someone gave these guys a reality check.

Kells sits on a chair in the corner of the room with a look of relief and respect at the wisdom spewing forth from our guru. Kells no longer looks helpless. Kells stands beside Marty and adds, "I will be honest with you guys: I had a dart and coffee for breakfast this morning. I know I need to get better. It's gotten to the point where I was out playing hockey in the driveway with my kids, with a dart hanging in my mouth, the other day and thinking, 'What the fuck am I doing?' I want to be better. I don't know that I can quit right now, but I need to do something today to be better tomorrow. And that's what each of you has to do. We're all in this together."

Marty, a nonsmoker, continues, "No matter how bad things are going for the team, you guys have to remember that it's nothing compared to real life. Sports, more than anything, is a great school of life. You can go to college, take all the classes you want, read a million books, but I'm telling you that, if you pay attention, you will learn everything you ever need to know about life by playing hockey."

Amen.

The very next night, we lose 3–1 to San Diego. It's not due to a lack of effort, or a lack of desire. San Diego is just better. As Chris Felix, whose age (thirty-seven) has been showing more and more lately in the form of late-game fatigue, walks off the ice, a burly male Bakersfield fan cups his hands around his mouth and yells, "You're ruining hockey, Felix!"

Felix snaps back, "Why don't you come down here and say that?"

The fan stands up and yells, "Because you're not worth it!"

Pray

*I*t's yet another business-as-unusual Bad News Condors game. Hay is in the net letting in weak goals through his legs, our defensemen are about as effective as turnstiles at stopping guys from passing by them, I am sitting on my ass in the stands, and, of course, we are losing.

But then Pam, our team's massage therapist and resident Christian, walks up to me and says, "Your dad is coming tonight."

My dad? He has been dead for seven years. How would Dad even get here? Why's he coming here now? I'm glad he's here, but he only will be upset that he came all this way to see me play, only to find out that my hockey career is just as disappointing as it was when I retired ten years ago. Why didn't he call? Dad's not going to be happy about my not even dressing in uniform.

I make my way through a mob of fans gathered down by the locker room, not thinking about how bizarre it is that my dead father has come to visit me. Being a third-string nobody, I am invisible to the fans, whom I look at closely, hoping one of them will be my father. I just hope he won't be disappointed that I'm not playing.

The last time I saw Dad was in Buffalo in December 1994, when I had come home for the holidays from Virginia, where I was working my first job as a newspaper reporter. Dad's doctors had diagnosed him with lung cancer ten months earlier, at which time they gave him a year to live. He had recently been spending most of his time asleep on the couch, drugged out on prescription narcotics for pain, an oxygen mask clasped over his face. The nurse had urged me and my brothers to put him in a hospice for his final few months of life, but Dad refused. He wanted to die at home on *the couch, with Rush Limbaugh on the kitchen radio, CNN playing on the tube, and Elvis and Roy Orbison wailing from the stereo speakers.*

When he'd wake to go to the bathroom or to get a drink of water–or, as horrible as it sounds, to have a cigarette–I would talk to him just like old times, as if nothing were wrong, as if he weren't going to die in a few months. We no longer talked about hockey; it was a sore subject between us ever since I quit against his wishes. A part of Dad died when I quit; I didn't want to upset him by bringing up hockey.

Before leaving for home, I walked over to the couch and gently nudged awake the drugged pile of bones that was now my once superhero-like father. He was only fifty-one years old, but his saggy skin and sloppy head of gray hair made him look one hundred years old. "Dad, I have to go now," I told him.

He opened his eyes and struggled to his feet. He adjusted his black cotton sweatpants and shuffled over to the back door, where I had placed my suitcase. Being December in Buffalo, it was very cold, in the low twenties. Still, Dad walked outside with me to say goodbye. He wasn't about to let terminal lung cancer stop him. He always waved goodbye.

He shook my hand (he never liked hugging), and I told him I would call him when I got back to my house in Virginia. As I backed the car down the driveway and looked out the windshield at the old man lazily waving his right hand, I cried. I should have said, "I love you." But I didn't.

Now, seven years later, Dad is here to see me. I stand outside the locker room, scanning the crowd, trying to find the man whose dedication and sacrifice and encouragement enabled me to have the hockey career I did.

Finally, I spot my father standing in the back of the assembled crowd. He's wearing a suit and tie. He looks fit and healthy. His skin is tan, not the grayish color of his final days before death. I run to him through the crowd, and I give him a hearty hug and tell him I love him, which I never did when he was alive. I tell him I'm sorry that I'm not playing, considering that he came all the way from heaven.

As we hug, the crowd erupts in cheers, and we look out onto the ice and see that Hay has let in a goal. Strangely, rain has started to pour down from the ceiling onto the ice.

I turn to Dad and ask, "What do you think are the chances that I'll play tonight?"

Dad just smiles and gives me a carefree shrug of his shoulders. He doesn't say a word. He doesn't have to. His loving smile tells me what he's thinking: It doesn't matter whether or not I play.

* * *

I'm awake in my bed in Bakersfield. It's dark outside. The digital clock next to my bed reads 4:45 A.M. I must have been dreaming.

But to call what I just experienced a dream isn't accurate. It was a visitation.

I'm a spiritual person, but not very religious or mystical, and I certainly don't believe in ghosts. But I do believe that my father just came to me in my sleep. I want him back. We need to talk.

When I realize he's gone, that I'm alone in my nondescript bedroom with nothing on the walls and a suitcase-full of clothes in my closet, away from my wife and family and all the things that really matter, I cry. Like a baby.

The team bus is scheduled to leave for San Diego at 7 A.M. from the apartments. Rather than pack my bag and travel with the team for another game in which I will not play or even dress, I decide to get in my car and do something I haven't done since I arrived here five months ago: go home.

I don't need to be here. I don't have to practice and suffer bruise after bruise every day to chase a dream. I don't have anything to prove. I don't have to play.

Ever since I got here I have known what I want to do: Play. But I haven't understood why. Now I do. Even though I have tried to convince myself that my comeback was about me, now that Dad, with a simple smile and a shrug of the shoulders, has liberated me from caring so much I realize it was more about pleasing him than pleasing myself. So I am leaving town. I don't know if I will even come back.

I pack a suitcase with as many clothes as I can fit in, write a note to Ryan telling him I'm going back to San Francisco, get in my car, and start driving north. And as I'm speeding through the flat farmland's morning fog, I can't stop thinking that none of this hockey-playing stuff matters. When he was alive, Dad used to care more about hockey than I did. He wanted me to play pro hockey, and I disappointed him when I did not.

But, now that he is in heaven, Dad apparently doesn't care. Perhaps he now realizes what's important in life: love and family. Judging by his indifference, I can only conclude that they don't play hockey in heaven. Why would they play hockey in heaven anyway?

Hockey is one of the most unbiblical of sports. In hockey, you're not encouraged to turn the other cheek. In fact, you usually crack the other guy in the cheek before he cracks you. In hockey, it's all about what thou shalt do to win, not what thou shalt do to glorify God. Football and baseball are Christian havens, where end-zone genuflections and on-the-field prayer-huddles and pregame prayers led by ministers are commonplace. You never see that in hockey.

Since arriving in Bakersfield, I've seen rookie Jason Ralph get seventeen stitches sewn into his forehead. I've seen men cry from the kind of pain usually only seen on the military battlefield. I've seen men suffer dislocated shoulders, hip pointers, concussions, chipped teeth, bruised lungs, knee strains, broken jaws, broken fingers, and lacerated faces. I've seen a man cross-check another man face-first into the boards.

Of course, they don't play hockey in heaven! It's a devilish sport, a gritty, dirty, naughty, earthly pleasure. And that's why it is so much fun to play, and why I love the game. But, clearly, they don't play hockey in heaven.

* * *

I get home five hours after hurriedly leaving my Bakersfield apartment and I hug Brooke harder than I ever have before, and I tell her I love her with passion I have never had before, and I apologize for leaving her alone for the last six months, and I tell her that I don't want to go back to Bakersfield.

But Brooke disagrees. She wants me to go back and finish what I began, because she doesn't want me to regret anything. It's March 1 and there are only five weeks left in the season. But I want to be here, not there. What else is there left for me to do? The season has been, as Marty Raymond so eloquently stated last week, "a great school of life." I have learned life lessons I never would have learned sitting in my writing chair, and almost all of the lessons came when I wasn't playing. I don't have to play to find happiness; I don't need to prove myself. I certainly don't have to do it for Dad.

Not playing has taught me so much: Comfort isn't contentment, mirrors don't lie, keep it simple, it's right when you smile, everyone needs a team, regret will eat you alive, boring can be beautiful, luck is preparation meeting opportunity, trust thyself, be patient, hit or be hit, believe in miracles, never flinch, live in the moment, dancers dance, failure precedes success, turn the page, don't try too hard, idealism inspires greatness, act well the given part, a watched pot never boils, play with love, nothing in life is easy, play the game, heart beats talent, focus on family, write bad poetry, adversity makes a champion, sports is a great school of life. And it took me two years of toil on the comeback trail to conclude that, since Dad doesn't even care if I play, they don't play hockey in heaven. Now I can retire in peace.

But Brooke refuses to listen to my quitting crap.

"Maybe there's more for you to learn," she says. "And if you walk away now, you might always wonder what would have happened."

I consider her point, but I am not sold on why I should make a return. I change my mind the next day when I read a newspaper article about Mario Lemieux's comeback in the NHL this season. At thirty-six, he has a rough year. A swollen hip threatens to force him to sit out the rest of the season. "I'm willing to play and try to help the team any way I can," Lemieux said. "If that means playing with some young guys and teaching them how to play the game . . . as long as I'm going to have fun playing the game, I'm going to play. If I'm not having fun, I'm going to step aside."

Hockey is about fun. Even when I am sitting in the stands desperately wanting to play, it is fun. Even when we have lost six straight and my closest friends on the team are leaving, it is fun. Even when I only get a chance to face shots before and after practice, it is fun. And because it is fun, and because Brooke is right that I may have even more to learn, I can't leave after coming this far. The next day, when I wake up in the same bed in which I had The Dream in December 1999, I also realize that I still have not lived that dream. The next day, I drive back to Bakersfield.

* * *

No longer placing so much pressure on myself to play, I have fun at practice like never before. And while the chances are slim that I will return for a second season, my mind tells me I want to play pro hockey forever. But my body—the upper-back spasms that won't go away, the constantly sore groin, the dizziness whenever I take my anti-tumor medication—tells me this is my swan song. I have accepted the forces of nature. I have to let it go.

So when Kells comes up to me before practice on March 6 and says, "I have some good news to tell you," and I think he is going to start me soon, but he instead tells me, "Idaho wants to borrow you to back up for a few games this week," I am not bummed out. Rather, I'm thrilled that another team even knows I exist and I vow to have fun playing the role for another team, which I do with the Idaho Steelheads on their five-game California swing, backing up Blair Allison, one of the premier goalies at the AA level. (Their rookie number-two goalie, Jason Cugnet, has a strained knee ligament.) And when Blair tells me on the bus ride to San Diego that in the ten years he has been pro he's learned more about himself by losing than by winning, I'm glad I came back as Brooke suggested because I have just learned another valuable life lesson.

It's even fun when, a week later, Kells finally makes the roster changes everyone was expecting. He releases Maser, who has been getting three shifts a game, not even enough ice time for him to pick a fight. He trades Sasha to Anchorage, who hasn't staged any fights lately but has managed to alienate everyone else (except for Todd Esselmont) with his antics. Kells waives David Milek, our rookie defenseman who improved greatly, but not enough over the season. He was playing paired with Glen Mears, who also was let go after five seasons in a Bakersfield uniform. It's a total housecleaning, a wholesale retooling of the team that is completed after Todd Esselmont earns a ticket back home to Vancouver when he shows up at the rink in Long Beach moping, not talking to anyone, because Sasha, his best friend and drinking buddy, is now gone. Esselmont, the thirty-year-old rookie who was driving a truck a year ago, the family man who had come back to live a dream, has lost his heart. And when he goes out for the first period and is listing around the ice as if he's at a Saturday afternoon public skate, Kells walks into the locker room at intermission and delivers the final nail in Esselmont's pro-hockey coffin: "Don't forget who gave you a job in hockey this season after no one else would. Take your gear off. You're done."

Although Esselmont leaves the team in a state of bitterness and frustration, David Milek, age twenty-six and college educated, leaves with no regrets. "At least I can say that I tried," he tells me after Kells gives him the phone call. "I can say that I put on the helmet without the visor and got paid to play pro hockey. I wasn't a superstar, but I did my best."

By releasing five players, Kells has instantly deleted one-fifth of the team, which allows room for just enough guys to make an impact. With Marty Raymond's expert recruiting help, Kells immediately signs defensemen Josh MacNevin and Patrick Aronsson, and forwards Ryan Foster and Aaron Brand, all of them hot shots from the European leagues. The next thing you know we have won three games straight and we look nothing like the lackluster, plodding, diseased-lung team of games past. And it helps not having Sasha distracting everyone with his puck-hogging, fight-faking, trash-talking antics.

We are 6–1–1 in the last eight games and there are only three games remaining in the season. "It's fun again," Felix says in the locker room after we beat San Diego for the first time in three months. "No matter where you play, no matter what level or age, it's all about winning. Winning is contagious. Once you start, your confidence keeps growing."

I may not be playing, but the newfound winning feeling helps me keep it fun. So does the feeling that Dad is looking down on me approvingly.

But Ryan won't be able to enjoy our final stretch run to the play-offs. The headaches persist; he grows dizzy when he rides the stationary bike. "And I feel a little dumber," he says after yet another aborted attempt to skate symptom-free. He has no choice but to inform Kells that he will not be able to play for the rest of the season. And since Josh MacNevin has been living in the Holiday Inn for the past week because there's no available apartment space for players, Kells tells Ryan he is placing him on season-ending injured reserve and politely asks Ryan to leave town. Ryan hopes the injury is not career-ending. As he's packing up his car the following morning, he says, "I would like to play another season. It would be hard to stop playing. Hockey is like just six months of blood, sweat, and tears and a bunch of guys working together. It's blood and guts. There's nothing like it."

I wave goodbye to Ryan as he drives away, wondering if I will ever see him again. I walk back to the apartment and see that he has left on the kitchen table his room key and a piece of paper, on which he has scribbled a note. "I don't know if I could have made it through this season without you," it reads. "I'll miss you."

And I feel the same way. I may have just lost a teammate and a roommate, but I have gained a friend for life.

* * *

We play Tacoma tonight, and it's the second-to-last game of the regular season. We are now 10–1–1 in the last twelve games, which makes us the hottest team in all of pro hockey after months of being Bakersfield's Bad News Bears. After hitting a season-low statistical point of 23–34–4 on March 15, we've clawed our way back in the last two weeks to a respectable 30–35–5 record.

The timing of our resurgence couldn't be any better. Tomorrow night we play Idaho, the best team in the league, in the final regular season game. Then, next Friday, we will start the play-offs, though we don't yet know whom we will play. There are four teams in our division. The first-place team, our arch-nemesis San Diego, will play the fourth-place team, which currently is us. The second-place team, which is Long Beach, will play the third-place team, which currently is Fresno. But since Fresno is only two points ahead of us, there's still a chance that we could knock Fresno out of third place. Fresno has one game left–tonight against Idaho. If Fresno wins, it clinches the third-place slot against Long Beach, which is half the team that San Diego is. But if Fresno loses tonight, and we win tonight and tomorrow, we will take third place.

It's a Friday night. Brooke has come down for this weekend, the final two home games of the season. I haven't yet decided for sure whether I will retire once the season ends, but, aware that this likely will be the end of the road, we're suddenly nostalgic about my time in Bakersfield: the cute kids who ask for my autograph, the supportive fans who have always hoped I would play, the teammates who have grown to become my family, and the coach whose ability to laugh through his worst season of pro hockey has made my personal struggle that much more tolerable.

I go through my usual pregame ritual when I am not dressing: I leave the apartment at five o'clock and drive to Centennial Garden. I park my car at the Holiday Inn and walk around the back of the arena to the security entrance next to the loading dock. As usual, Kells is standing alone in the early-evening darkness, wearing a dark suit, his hair slicked back, nervously puffing on a Marlboro. I wave to him as I open the door. Just as I am stepping into the arena, Kells says, "Hey, Bakes."

"What's up?" I say, walking over to his smoking spot.

Kells blows a tobacco exhale strong enough to push a sailboat. "If we lose tonight, or if Fresno wins, you're gonna start tomorrow," he says. "So be ready."

"What if Fresno loses and we win?" I ask.

"Then you won't play," he says.

Kells hasn't exactly showered me with praise or empathy this season. In fact, at times he has been downright nasty. Still, I can tell from his downward-turned lips and crinkled skin around his eyes that it pains Kells to tell me that after all the commitment and effort I have made for the team all season that I still might not play.

"I know I probably should have played you before now," he says. "But it just didn't work out that way. I'm sorry about that."

"Don't worry, Kells," I say. "You know I want to play, but you've had more important things to worry about than my little situation."

Kells says to come see him after tonight's game, no matter what happens in our game and the Fresno-Idaho game. Warm-ups are about to begin, and I walk straight up to Brooke's seat behind our bench to tell her the (possibly) good news. But I decide to watch the game from the press box; that way, I can keep tabs on the score of the Fresno game. It's selfish of me, but I do hope that Fresno wins tonight. I want us to win too, but I want Fresno to win more.

It's 1–1 at the end of the first period. A hundred miles up the freeway in Fresno, the Falcons are already up 3–0 over Idaho. I walk over to the off-ice official's table every few minutes to check the score coming in on the Internet. By the start of the third period, as Fresno pulls ahead to 5–1, and it's looking as though I will play, my stomach clenches as tight as my hand on my stick. Am I ready? Will I be able to do it? What if I embarrass myself?

Although we cruise to 4–2 victory and extend our winning streak to five games, we will not take third place: Fresno has won the game. Down in the locker room, Kells makes an announcement to all the players. "Listen up, guys," he says. "We've all been through a helluva lot this year, and there's been a lot of ups and downs. There's someone who has been with us through the entire ride, a guy who has put his heart into every practice, every game, a guy who has taken a lot of shit— a lot of it from me." Kells points to me and says, "That guy is sitting right over there. And tomorrow night's for him."

OVERTIME

APRIL 6, 2002

Survive

I've received a hug and a kiss from Brooke at the apartment before I left for the game, signed the league-minimum $325-a-week contract, fasted for the last six hours so I won't vomit, broken a muscle-loosening sweat in warm-ups, darted onto the ice under a spotlight as they announced "from Buffalo, New York . . . number thirty, Ken Baaaaaaker." I've taken several deep breaths during the national anthem and dropped to my knees for some last-minute stretching. Now the referee stands at center ice, the players take their positions at the face-off circle, and the more than six thousand fans—urged by the arena announcer to "make some noise in here"—clap and stomp with electric anticipation. After ten years of tumor-induced toil, after a season of paying my dues, it's show time.

My heart races as the ref drops the drops. I breathe—in through the nose and out the mouth, to focus on my task: stopping the puck. I'm not up in the press box taking notes like a nerd as another goalie back-stops the team. I'm not even sitting on the bench watching someone else play the team's single most important position. I stand here alone, guarding a four-by-six-foot rectangle of a net. I am the starting goalie. This is my game.

Idaho wins the draw and a defenseman dumps the puck into our end. I stay in my crease; I would hate to get stuck out of the net and make an ass of myself in the first ten seconds. I let the puck slide around the boards behind me. Kevin Smyth, a natural goal scorer and former NHL prospect, races down the left wing and gets a pass from the corner from Idaho's Bobby Stewart, the WCHL's leading scorer. When Smyth gets the puck on his stick, he switches to his backhand and shoots low to my right. I drop to my knees, kick out my right toe and make that ever-important first save of the game. Most things in life are easier when you get off to a good start, and, thankfully, I have done that tonight.

My team gains possession of the puck and rushes down toward the long-legged Idaho goalie, Jason Cugnet. Firth tips a point shot from Vary, and Cugnet gets a leg on it. Now we're all over Idaho, controlling the puck in their end as though we're the Harlem Globetrotters and they're the Washington Generals. Unable to wrest the puck from us, and tiring from the chase, an Idaho forward trips our Quinn Fair as he passes him along the boards. We take several shots on Cugnet, but the bulky netminder, who is a good five inches taller and thirty pounds heavier than I am, is perfect. Idaho kills the penalty.

Idaho's—and perhaps the league's—top offensive line of Greg Bullock, Bobby Stewart, and Kevin Smyth rushes back onto the ice and takes control. Bullock digs the puck from the low corner to my right. He sees Stewart standing alone in front of the net and quickly feeds him the puck. Stewart will have half the net to score on, if I don't slide across fast enough. This will be my first real test of the night. Am I good enough to play pro, or will I forever be regarded as an old practice goalie who worked hard but just didn't have that extra bit of speed a pro goalie needs? The puck zips left-to-right across the net toward Stewart. Just as the puck reaches Stewart's stick, I slide feet-first across the crease onto my left hip and stack my pads wall-like just in time to block Stewart's rapid release. The crowd roars with approval as I jump to my feet. *I can still play this game.*

I'm filled with confidence as the crowd chants my name. I try not to think about how the crowd was chanting my name in The Dream, because now I must focus on the here and how. This is not a dream. It's reality.

A few minutes later, Cookie gets caught out of position and allows Idaho's speedy Derek Paget to come in on a breakaway. I've gotten good at breakaways; they're all the guys want to do after practice. But Paget, who has twenty goals this year, is a sniper. I come out to the top of my crease and get set. Paget races in and, not even faking a deke, snaps the puck into the lower-right corner of the net. He beats me clean.

Idaho 1, Bakersfield 0.

O.K., now that we got that out of the way, now that I don't have to worry about being perfect, I can really relax, and just play as if this is the last game of my career, which, in all likelihood, it will be.

Idaho smells blood. They win the face-off after their goal and charge down toward me. If I were their coach I would have instructed the players to shoot anything on the rookie goalie. He'll be nervous, I'd tell them. Shoot from anywhere. And Idaho does. But I stop all of them, challenging the shooters by coming out extra far and controlling the rebounds so they don't get a second shot for free. Ten minutes into the game, I have faced five shots and enough sweat has already poured off my body to fill a bucket. This could be a long night.

We go back on the offensive, which is good: I need to catch my breath and recharge. Fatigue can be a goalie's biggest enemy. First the arms get heavy, then the legs get weak and slow, and then the concentration goes. Once the concentration goes, so do your puck-stopping abilities.

With four minutes left, Idaho takes a penalty and we slip a rebound over a sprawling Cugnet to tie it up 1–1. But Idaho didn't win first place in the league this year by sitting back after letting in a goal.

Idaho likes to set up offensive plays from behind the net, the way the Kings used to do when they had Gretzky. Idaho has Bobby Stewart and Kevin Smyth, the Gretzkys of the WCHL, and they're enough to make a goalie paranoid. My primary goal was to make my first save; my secondary goal was to have a good first period. And with two minutes left, and having only let in one goal on nine shots, I'm starting to think about how nice it will feel to go back to the locker room and rest for fifteen minutes. But then an Idaho forward steals the puck from our forward near center ice and skates around my defenseman and scores from a bad angle to my right. I should have had that one. I would have had it, but I lost my concentration. Now we're down by two goals. I will have two more periods to find my groove, to make my dream come true.

My debut is going well. I stop four shots in the first minute and a half of the second period. I'm more relaxed than in the first period. And it's a good thing Kells has let me stay in the game. After the first period, Marty Raymond suggested to Kells that he pull me out of the game because Marty felt I was lucky to get away with only allowing two goals. "The guy's nervous," Marty told Kells. "We want to win heading into the play-offs. Just put Looch in" Kells turned and walked away. He believed in me.

Now that Idaho is swirling around us in a hockey hurricane of two-on-ones, breakaways, and screened point shots, I am trying extra hard to prove Kells right. Idaho is shooting everything at me–their coach must have reminded them about the old guy who is in the net for Bakersfield. But I pretend that there aren't five thousand fans watching my every move, that there isn't an assistant coach who thinks I should get yanked, that this game could be the only mark I get to leave on my pro hockey career. When I make a save on a shot from the blue line, and I'm standing five feet in front of the crease, the TV color commentator tells the folks watching at home, "This is Baker's first game in nine seasons? Give me a break! Look at him way out there, he's playing with confidence." That, I am. Not because I know that I am good enough to do this, but because I know that I won't be good enough if I don't at least pretend I am good enough.

Idaho's full-ice press forces one of our forwards to take a holding penalty when an Idaho player races in to slap a rebound off my pads. But that's what ends up happening a minute into the power play when a point shot pops off my pads and onto the stick of Smyth, who, being a goal scorer, is standing in just the right place and the right time to put the puck into the net to stretch the lead to 3–1.

But the fans are behind me. They know it's not all my fault we are down. They know this is my first game in ten years. They start chanting my name–*Baker, Baker, Baker*–and, though I'm trying to focus on nothing but the puck, their cheers help me forget about the three shots that have gotten past me.

Idaho doesn't let up. The halfway mark of the second period also is the halfway mark of the game. This being a hockey game with ten men slamming into each other as a black disc slides from stick to stick, perhaps the most chaotic of sports, with nine minutes left in the period I then suffer from what hockey pundits call a "bad bounce."

Two Idaho forwards race down on a two-on-one against my defender, who backs up, staying between the two opponents. I square up with the right winger bearing down to my left. My job is to play the puck; the defender's job is to play the pass, meaning he is to prevent a pass from connecting with the second forward. As the puck-carrier nears the net, he passes it across to his winger. Rather than making it to the winger's stick blade, the puck hits my defenseman's skate blade and deflects upward over my shoulder and into the net. I could make a hundred excuses why that goal wasn't my fault, but I am the goalie, and it's my job to stop any puck coming at me, even if it's off my own player's skate.

The "bad bounce" goal making it 4–1 lights a fire under our team's ass, and we pummel Cugnet with shot after shot, finally getting one past him. But we have been outplayed the entire period. Idaho has peppered me with twenty shots. I made eighteen saves, which is more than some goalies have to make in an entire game, but it's the two shots I didn't stop that make me fear that Kells, with his team losing 4–2 and needing to end the season on a win, will succumb to the pressure from Marty and replace me with Looch in the third period.

Kells has legitimate reasons to pull me out of the game after the second period. We are down 4–2; Marty, the assistant coach who over the last six weeks has helped jump-start our team, keeps insisting that Kells get me out of the net. "We can't win with him," Marty said.

I can't totally blame Marty for his lack of faith. One look at my sweat-soaked body makes it quite clear that I'm exhausted. Plus, Looch, my backup tonight, is a veteran who has led his team to a comeback dozens of times. But as I start stretching in the locker room before the start of the third period, I pray that Kells will do what he has done the entire season: not make the obvious decision.

Kells walks into the locker room to read the starting lineup for the third. I go put on my mask and slide on my gloves, thinking, they'll have to *drag me out of the net.* Kells looks down at his lineup card and barks out the names, "Foster, Brand, and Brearley. Aronsson and MacNevin on D." He looks up from his card and before striding out of the room forcefully adds, "All right, Kenny. Let's go!"

As if knowing this could be my last twenty minutes of pro hockey isn't enough motivation, as if knowing that the woman who talked me out of quitting is sitting fifteen rows up cheering me on isn't enough motivation, now I have another reason to shine: Kells.

The third period is the final and most important period of a hockey game. It's when a game is won or lost, when the character players are separated from the fair-weather players, when a goalie's true mettle is tested. The greatest goalies in the history of the sport have played their best when the game was on the line. Dominik Hasek, Jacques

Plante, Tony Esposito, Patrick Roy, Ken Dryden—they all rose to the occasion.

Mitch Korn, who coached Hasek in his Buffalo Sabres heyday, tells his students that "it's not how many saves you make, but when you make them." I've let in four goals on thirty shots so far tonight, but a solid third period will make or break my professional debut. I have improved every period, feeling more comfortable playing in front of a crowd of over six thousand people, gradually adjusting to the fast game pace. It helps that I practiced with Idaho for a week when I was the backup for five games last month. I know I can stop all of them because I did just that in every practice, including Smyth and Stewart. And having been on their side demystifies their stardom.

But four minutes into the period, Petr Suchanek, a 6' 3" rookie from the Czech Republic, who was my roommate during my Idaho stint, fires a shot from the point. I easily stop it, but, its being my first shot of the period, I let the rebound dribble out to the front of the net, and an Idaho forward flicks the puck over my outstretched left leg and into the net.

The fifth goal of the net silences the crowd. Their team has won five in a row and nine out of the last ten games, but tonight—the regular season finale—just might mark the end of our winning streak.

Believe in miracles.

The difference between a team that's used to winning and a team that's used to losing is that a losing team (say, our team two months ago) would fold after falling down 5–2 in the third, but a winning team (say, our team for the last month) will battle back until time runs out. Winning teams hate losing.

That fifth goal works as a wake-up call to my players, many of whom have been coasting through the seventy-second game of the season, a game that means nothing in the standings.

Everyone needs a team.

The first shift after the fifth Idaho goal, our forwards buzz around the Idaho end as though they're the eighties-era Edmonton Oilers, throwing shot after shot at the net. Sensing a goal, the fans come alive. Brearley breaks down the right wing at full speed as Jeff Goldie races down center ice. Just as Goldie reaches the mouth of the goal crease, Brearley feeds a pass through a maze of skates and sticks over to Goldie, who tips the puck between Cugnet's legs.

Failure precedes success.

Earlier in the season, before Kells cleaned house and brought in our European ringers, our team would score another goal, but be unable to keep the momentum. We just didn't have the depth.

But the very next shift, Willett steals the puck from an Idaho player and wrists it high at Cugnet, who blocks it with his shoulder and falls to the ice. Quinn Fair, normally a stay-at-home defenseman who rarely ventures deep into the offensive zone, sees the puck sitting free in the slot and bolts toward it. As Cugnet struggles back to his feet, Fair sneaks the puck beneath the goalie's knee to cut the Idaho lead to 5–4.

Fair skates down to the net and taps me on the pads. Over the roar of the crowd, Fair shouts to me, "We're gonna win this one for you, Bakes!"

Idaho isn't going to lie down and play dead just yet.

Heart beats talent.

Idaho coach John Olver puts out his top guns—Smyth and Stewart up front, and Jeremy Mylymok on defense—not only to protect their one-goal lead, but to extend it. Idaho has the number-one offense in the league; they're not about to go into a defensive shell with eleven minutes left.

Idaho wins the draw and carries the puck into our end. Stewart sets up his partner with a pass, but I focus on nothing but executing the save and I expertly kick out the shot with my left toe.

Keep it simple.

The crowd is back on my side. *Baker! Baker! Baker!*

Our two toughest grinders, Jason Ralph and Paul Rosebush, throw several vicious body checks, as if warning Idaho that they can't expect to come into our barn and spoil our goalie's big game.

Hit or be hit.

Aaron Brand, our forward who has netted eleven points in the eight games since he joined us from the Austrian pro league, owns the puck. Idaho players, who usually play a solid positional defensive game, are chasing wildly after Brand in their end. And with just under nine minutes left in the game, Brand fires the puck at the net and the rebound bounces onto the stick of Aronsson, another late-season Austrian league addition, who fires it over Cugnet's diving body. In just four minutes and twenty-eight seconds, we have tied the game at 5–5. If I don't let in another goal, we will at least tie.

Play in the moment.

Rather than think about how great it would be to win, how awful it would be to lose, how dramatic it would be to hold off Idaho, I remind myself to focus on each shot as it comes.

By now, everyone in the crowd is standing, and every time I touch the puck, even when it's to stop it along the boards, the crowd repeatedly chants my name. Just like in The Dream.

I keep telling myself not to look at the clock, to focus on the moment. *A watched pot never boils.*

My teammates play with an intensity I have never seen in the seventy-one games before this one. Idaho is flustered, barely able to get the puck out of their end, let alone manage to get a shot on me.

But with two minutes left, an Idaho forward slips past our relentless fore-check and skates in on me untouched, and as he winds up for a slap shot–this better not be a fake–I skate out to cut down the angle. He whacks the puck and I kick out my right leg and send the puck to the right corner.

Baker! Baker! Baker!

And as the clock ticks down toward zero, and my teammates are able to keep even Smyth and Stewart from maneuvering into scoring position, I breathe with relief knowing that the game is going to be decided by my ability to do the one thing that this season I have most practiced doing: stop breakaways in a shootout.

There's a two-minute break between the end of regulation time and the start of the shootout, and so I skate to the bench, take off my helmet and gloves and drop to my knees to drink some water. Though I know Brooke is standing just behind our bench, I don't look at her. One look at her, and I will cry. This journey started two years ago on a frosty December morning when I hadn't even stepped inside a rink in almost eight years. I have changed a lot since waking from The Dream, learned life lessons that will guide me long after the time comes to retire from this sport forever. And Brooke has supported me every step of the way. I stare in the eyes of my teammates, the twenty men who have become my family in every sense of the word. We have drunk together, lost together, won together, fought together, hated each other together, loved each other together. Then I glance over at Kells, who, as is his usual superstitious practice, doesn't look or talk to his goalies during a game. Instead, he stares at his pacing feet. Kells believes in me. But, more important, for the first time this season I believe in myself.

In goal for your Condors, number thirty, Ken Baaaker!!!!

Each team will get five shots in the shootout. The ref will drop a puck at center ice and the player, each team alternating (the visiting team shoots first), will skate toward the net and have one chance to score. The team with the most goals after five, wins the game.

The Idaho coach sends out Bobby Stewart, a former All-American at the University of Maine and currently the WCHL's leading scorer with thirty-nine goals, to shoot on me first. Stewart, a left-handed shot, has an intimidating arsenal at his disposal. I recall from practices that he likes to back the goalie into the net and then shoot the puck, usually high.

The fans are banging their hands against the glass and shouting as if it's a rock-concert as Stewart skates to the puck and races toward me. My strategy is to come out extra far so that if he shoots he will have to thread the needle, and, if he tries to deke around me, he will have to make a quick, nifty, lateral move.

Stewart comes straight in, but he sees no net to score on. He cocks his shoulder as though he will snap a shot, but, rather than shoot, he switches to his backhand. Luckily, I haven't taken his fake and I'm able to move to my left and drop to my knees in one motion as Stewart quickly tries to slip the puck between my legs. I squeeze my knees together and fall back behind the goal line. I can't see directly in front of me and only realize that I have stopped him when the crowd erupts.

Baker! Baker! Baker!

Kells sends Aronsson out to take our first shot. The agile Swede skates quickly in at Cugnet and does the same move as Stewart: fakes a shot and tries to tuck a backhand into the net. Unlike Stewart, Aronsson scores.

1–0.

Next up for Idaho is Kevin Smyth. I spent a half hour after practice one day last month doing breakaways against Smyth, so I know just how good he is at them. There's no predicting what he may do. All I can do is bear down, stay in position and react.

Smyth pulls off a fake worthy of a CIA double agent when he winds up for a shot and in a blink of an eye turns to his backhand and slips the puck beneath my sliding body and scores.

Our second shooter is Gable Gross, a slight, twenty-one-year-old rookie who joined us eight games ago and has more talent than size and experience. But the kid has ice in his veins, skating straight in on Cugnet and firing a wrist shot over the tall goalie's right arm.

2–1.

Idaho has no shortage of snipers, and they send out a a nifty stick-handler named Greg Bullock, whose reach has to be the longest in the league. Monsters like Bullock are tough to stop because they can change their angles by three feet merely by shifting the puck to one side of their bodies. Bullock launches a rocket that sails over my left shoulder, dings off the crossbar and lands in the net.

Then Jeff Goldie, our team's leading scorer with thirty-two goals, hops the boards and carries the puck in on Cugnet. Rather than try to fake out the goalie, Goldie opts to try and beat him clean on a snap shot from in close. But it doesn't work. Cugnet reads it all the way.

2–2.

Each team has two shooters remaining, but I'm so caught up in the moment, so locked into the zone, that I don't know how many are left. All that matters is the next shot.

My fourth shooter will be Jeremy Mylymok, a tough defenseman who has only scored eight goals in fifty-one games this year. Mylymok skates in at me slowly, and I come out far. Since the slower a guy is moving, the harder it is for him to stick-handle around the goalie, I know that if I just come out far and cut down his angle I have a good chance of stopping him. And, as expected, by the time he gets ten feet in front of me he sees very little net and hurriedly takes a shot to the lower left corner of the net. I remain standing and slide my foot out sideways and kick the puck to the corner.

The fans then go wild as Ryan Foster hustles in on Cugnet and beats him with a blast to the lower left corner.

3–2.

If I stop this last shot, we will win; we won't even have to take our fifth and final shot. I will be the hero. Just like in The Dream.

The Idaho coach takes his time selecting the player to take this important shot, finally tapping center Matt Oates, who has twenty-one goals in fifty-nine games. But he has none tonight. I can stop him.

Oates practically sprints toward me, almost double the speed at which the four other shooters approached me. Like the other shots, I have come out far, but it's not until Oates is at the top of the slot area that I realize I have to back up faster or risk giving him too much room to go around me. So I move backwards faster, anticipating a deke to my right or left, but Oates surprises me: He snaps a hard shot to my lower left. Instantly, I am on my knees and kicking out. But he sneaks it a fraction of an inch over my right leg.

3–3.

Kells sends Aaron Brand out to take our last shot. If Brand scores, he will be the hero. If he doesn't, the shootout will turn into a shot-by-shot sudden death shootout. Brand has been our team's best player since arriving from Austria. He's a natural choice to take this potentially game-winning shot.

Exhausted, I squat and rest my elbows on my knees, worrying more about stopping my next shot than thinking about how wonderful it would be to win my first professional start in a shootout.

Brand is short, but he has the quick wrists and bull-strong legs one sees in the NHL, which is where he played with the Toronto Maple Leafs earlier in his career. But now he is a minor-leaguer, a hired gun brought in at the end of the season to give our team a chance at glory, and, I hope, to make my dream come true.

Brand barrels down the ice at Cugnet. He's a left-handed shot and is carrying the puck straight on his forehand. When a shooter carries the puck in the middle of his body, he can shoot or deke. But when a shooter carries the puck to his side, he almost always will shoot. But rather than wait for Brand to make the first move, Cugnet slides his stick out to poke the puck away from Brand. Brand sees the resulting hole left between Cugnet's legs and flicks the puck between the goalie's toes and scores and, just like that, we win.

The crowd erupts. I drop to my knees. My teammates hop the boards and skate in a swarm around me. Quinn Fair is the first to reach me. "You did it, Bakes! You did it!"

In just two weeks, San Diego will knock us out of the play-offs, ending my comeback season. I'll see some of my teammates again, others, not. But we will always share the memory of this special night that almost never happened.

Amid the struggle of daily life, there occur few moments when everything makes sense, when you can escape your body and travel to a place few people will ever go, a place where hard work pays off and where good things come to those who wait, a place where dreams come true. Until I dropped to the ice in Bakersfield, I didn't know whether such a place existed.

The Buddhists know it as nirvana; the Christians call it heaven. If I know anything as my teammates rub my head, the fans scream with joy, my wife cries a river, and my father smiles down on me, it's that playing hockey is heavenly.

Afterword

Following the 2001–2002 season, I planned to return to the Bay Area, where I was to heal my sore groin and, most importantly, reconnect with my wife and dog. I figured I'd settle into my laid-back Northern California lifestyle, where I would live amid the redwoods, feed deer apples in my backyard, hike in the woods and spend a few months writing this book. But my hockey season of life lessons should have taught me better than to expect the expected.

Less than a week after returning home I received a phone call that erased my idyllic plans. The call was from Bonnie Fuller, who had become *Us Weekly*'s new editor while I was off playing hockey. Fuller was recruiting a new West Coast bureau chief and asked whether I wanted to move back to L.A. Of course, I was available (and deeply in debt too!), but I wasn't so sure I wanted to return to Hollywood, the town where I once wrote about other people's dreams so that I could ignore my own.

Even so, I agreed to try out the job for a month and then decide whether the gig would be long-term or just a way for me to make some quick cash. Immediately, I went from the world of slap shots and bench brawls to one of Britney Spears and box-office grosses. As bureau chief, I served as the coach of a young reporting team, which every week competed against other magazines for scoops. Being the magazine's Hollywood boss was as fast-paced, testosterone-charged, and competitive as being a pro athlete. I loved it. Two years–and dozens of exclusive stories–later, I am still in Hollywood, and I now believe that being a pro hockey goalie is what made me tough enough to succeed here.

* * *

On the second anniversary of my win, Condors General Manager Matt Riley invited me back to Bakersfield to sign hardcover copies of this book. A lot had changed around Condorstown since I had left. Only a few players remained from my season. Jamie Cooke had quit halfway through the season after getting into a fight with Kells after a loss in Las Vegas. My roommate, Ryan Hartung, now worked as a dental pharmaceuticals salesman in Minnesota. My fellow goalies, Luciano Caravaggio and Scott Hay, were playing in New Mexico and Scotland respectively. Sasha Lakovic was working as a part-time actor (he played the menacing captain of the Soviet Olympic hockey team in the film *Miracle*). Chris Felix, a one-time member of the Canadian Olympic team, was working on the production line at a steel mill in Sault Ste. Marie, Ontario. Todd Esselmont was tending bar in Vancouver. Most of the other players had either retired or moved on to other AA leagues.

As for Kells, after directing my losing comeback season (32–35–5), the next season he led the Condors to their winningest season ever (41–22–9) and was named the WCHL's "Coach of the Year."

Unfortunately, throughout the 2003–2004 season the team struggled well below .500, forcing team owner Jonathan Fleisig to make the difficult decision to fire Kells and replace him with associate coach Marty Raymond. When I learned of his dismissal, I phoned Kells, with whom I had stayed in regular contact over the phone.

"Sorry to hear the news," I said.

"Hey," Kells replied. "Everything happens for a reason."

I couldn't have agreed more.

On my second-anniversary visit to Bakersfield, I watched the game from a seat, appropriately, behind the net. My thirteen-month-old son Jackson sat in my lap. It was his first hockey game, and his big blue eyes popped wide open as the crowd cheered, booed, clapped, and stomped its feet. All his senses were stimulated like never before. Indeed, there's nothing like the world's fastest sport to make one feel so alive.

I rarely play hockey anymore. My equipment sits in a dusty pile in our back shed, waiting for the moment when I might find time in my hectic work schedule to suit up for a pickup game. Sitting in the stands that night, I realized Jackson might never see me don that equipment and play the sport of my dreams. It didn't matter, though. I felt content knowing that if Jackson ever wants to chase a similar dream, he will know where to find my equipment. And, like it was for me, his dad will be his biggest fan.

Acknowledgments

Brooke Baker, you are my goal posts, guiding me into the right position and, when I'm not, always being there to save me. Jackson Lawrence Baker, the world is yours. Kristofer Baker, it's time for you to live your dream.

I wouldn't have had the courage were it not for the love of Marcia and Norm Seiflein; Steve, Samara, and Paula Ricketts; Jack Brennan and Judith Brant,; and all my family members. Dad, I wish you'd visit more often.

The events of this book also never would have happened were it not for the members of Team Baker: Jonathan Fleisig, Paul Kelly, Matt Riley, the front-office staff and all of the fans and, especially, the players of the Bakersfield Condors; Howard Cornfield and Paul MacLean of the Quad City Mallards; John Olver and the entire Idaho Steelheads organization; my goalie gurus, Chris Economou and Mitch Korn; my all-star literary agency team, Jane Dystel and Miriam Goderich; Drs. Joshua Trabulus, Glenn Braunstein and especially the *uber*-talented Los Angeles-based surgeon Hrayr Shahinian; and the gracious citizens of Bakersfield who always made me feel at home in "the hockey capital of the West."

Special thanks also to Ann Treistman, my editor at The Lyons Press; Joyce Maynard for her early encouragement; Kris Hicks and Chuck Giambra for always being there; Ryan Hartung for his friendship; Kevin Bartl for the laughs; Josh Brewster, Craig Cooper, Joe Dominey, Mike Griffith, Ken Jacoby, and the kind folks at *The Hockey News* and *InThe-Crease.com* for getting the word out; the Quackheads for their support; John Friberg, John Marrin, and Glenn Gaslin for their humor, intelligence, and friendship (not necessarily in that order); Admiral James T. Stockdale for his stoicism; Becky Koh for her vision; Michael Duffy, Pam and Susan Sears for their photography; the editors of *Us Weekly* for the time away, and the magazine's talented reporting team for inspiring me with their dedication; Heidi Strom-Moon for her Internet genius; Blair Allison, Jason Cugnet, and Joe Dimaline for their brotherhood; David-Alexandre Beauregard for not scoring on me; the Oakland Thirsty Bears for reminding me how fun hockey is; and for the wise woman who reminded me that the future belongs to those who believe in the beauty of their dreams. Thanks, God.

I apologize if I have forgotten anyone, but I will use the usual excuse for my absent-mindedness: too many pucks to the head.